WOMEN IN FILM NOIR

WOMEN IN FILM NOIR

New Edition

Edited by
E. Ann Kaplan

This revised and expanded edition
first published 1998
by the British Film Institute
21 Stephen Street, London W1P 1PL

Reprinted 2000, 2001, 2003, 2005, 2007

The British Film Institute is the UK national agency with responsibility for encouraging the
arts of film and television and conserving them in the national interest.

First edition 1978
Revised edition 1980
Reprinted 1981, 1984, 1987, 1989, 1992, 1994, 1996

British Library Cataloguing-in-Publication Data
A catalogue record for this book is available from the British Library

ISBN 978–0–85170–666–5

Cover design: Swerlybird Art & Design

Set by Fakenham Photosetting Limited, Fakenham, Norfolk
Printed in Great Britain by St Edmundsbury Press Limited, Bury St Edmunds, Suffolk

Contents

Acknowledgments

I want first to thank Ed Buscombe, then Editor of Publications at The British Film Institute, for inviting me to expand the 1978 edition of *Women in Film Noir*. Ed hoped to see the volume to press, but it turned out to be impossible.

It has been a stimulating and rewarding experience working on the new volume. I regret that not all of the people invited to contribute to the revised edition were able to do so, but I am delighted with those who could and whose essays are now included here.

Let me express my gratitude to Robert White, Editor of Publications, for his help and support with this project. I appreciated his close reading of my own new contributions, and his patience was unwavering as the new authors and myself struggled to complete our essays within an ever-expanding time schedule.

Laura Mulvey has been a constant source of support and stimulation during the length of this project. My intellectual debts to her here and always are, and have been, enormous.

Finally, thanks to all those old and new authors contributing to this volume for submitting to my email pressures. Transcontinental editing has its pitfalls but also its deep pleasures.

I hope that students will find this expanded volume a useful stimulus to their own research.

E. Ann Kaplan
August 1998

Notes on Contributors

Pam Cook is Professor of European Film and Media at the University of Southampton. She is editor of *The Cinema Book* and co-editor of *Women and Film: A Sight and Sound Reader*. Her recent publications include *Fashioning the Nation: Costume and Identity in British Cinema* (1996) and *Gainsborough Pictures* (1997). She is currently working on a study of Powell and Pressburger's *I Know where I'm Going!* for the BFI Film Classics series, as well as a collection of her own writings.

Richard Dyer teaches Film Studies at the University of Warwick. He has published widely on topics in film and cultural studies. Among his many publications are his books *Stars*, *Heavenly Bodies*, *The Matter of Images*, *Now You See It* and, most recently, *White*.

Christine Gledhill is Reader in Media and Cultural Studies at Staffordshire University. She has written widely on feminist film theory, melodrama and more recently on early British Cinema. She is editor of several anthologies, including *Home is Where the Heart Is: Studies in Melodrama and the Woman's Film* and *Stardom: Industry of Desire*. She is currently at work on a study of British films of the 1920s, *Reframing British Cinema: 1918–1928*.

Sylvia Harvey teaches film and media at Sheffield Hallam University where she is Reader in Broadcasting Policy. She is the author of *May '68 and Film Culture* (1978) and co-editor of *The Regions, the Nations and the BBC* (1993) and *Television Times* (1996). She has also written about Bazin, independent cinema, Channel Four and broadcasting regulation. She is a board Member of the International Documentary Festival.

Claire Johnston was born in 1940. She co-organised the first ever Women's Film Festival in Edinburgh in 1972 and was a prominent and intellectually visionary activist. She was involved in organising the independent film sector in Britain and, together with Laura Mulvey, she laid the foundations of feminist film theory, notably through her influential work on Arzner and counter-cinema. Her *Notes on Women's Cinema*, the first publication to address the politics of a feminist film theory, continues to be a standard reference. Her work on film noir opened up new avenues of research at the intersection of psychoanalysis, feminism and film theory. She committed suicide in 1987.

E. Ann Kaplan is Professor of English at the State University of New York, Stony Brook, where she also founded and directs The Humanities Institute. She has published widely on women in film, feminist film and literary theory, postmodernism, psychoanalysis and cultural studies. Her many authored and edited books include *Women in Film: Both Sides of the Camera, Motherhood and Representation:The Mother in Film and Popular Culture, Postmodernism and Its Discontents* and *Psychoanalysis and Cinema.* Her most recent books include *Looking for the Other: Feminism, Film and the Imperial Gaze* and *Generations: Academic Women in Dialogue,* co-edited with Devoney Loser. She is currently researching a book on trauma, aging and beauty culture.

Angela Martin was a Commissioning Editor of Publications at the BFI (including the first edition of *Women in Film Noir*) before becoming a film and video editor on numerous films and television programmes, several for Channel Four. She edited *African Films: The Context of Production* (1982), contributed to the *Women's Companion to International Cinema* (1990) and has written on Chantal Akerman, African film-makers and Arab cinema. She currently teaches film theory and practice at Sheffield Hallam University and is preparing a collection of texts on *The Art of Women Filmmakers.*

Janey Place was a lecturer in semiology and communication theory at the University of California, Santa Cruz. She is Executive Vice President of NationsBank Strategic Technology Group. She is responsible for advanced technology R&D, information technology architecture, and strategic planning using information technology to advance NationsBank business strategy. Prior to joining Nations-Bank in 1994, Ms. Place was Senior Vice President in charge of Direct Banking Strategy at Wells Fargo Bank in California. She was also Information Technology Manager at Hughes Aircraft Company, Los Angeles. She is a business technology futurist with extensive hands-on experience managing technology and developing technology-enabled business strategies.

Kate Stables is Research Liaison Officer at the BFI. She has written on the media for *Intermedia, Campaign* and *TV Week* and is the author of *The Marx Brothers* (1992).

Chris Straayer is Associate Professor in the Department of Cinema Studies at New York University and author of *Deviant Eyes, Deviant Bodies: Sexual Re-Orientations in Film and Video.*

Patricia White is Assistant Professor of Film Studies and English Literature at Swarthmore College, Pennsylvania. Her essay is drawn from her forthcoming book on lesbian representability and classical Hollywood cinema.

Introduction to New Edition
E. Ann Kaplan

It is not, I think, accidental that as I write, noirness seems to be back in style in both the movies and American culture more generally. Indeed, the very phenomenon of 'noirness' or 'retro-noir', in its repeating nostalgically of a cultural mode from another era, signals the 90s as a postmodern moment.[1] This contrasts with the still largely modernist moment nearly twenty years ago, in 1978, when the first edition of *Women in Film Noir* was published. The introduction of an Internet website, *NoirNet*, and the space devoted in *The New York Times'* 'City' section under the headline 'Noir York' (11 May 1997), are only two examples of 90s nostalgic, postmodern noir,[2] in which noir becomes generic, beyond film. In the 40s, noir expressed itself mainly through the many 'B' films that were made. In the 50s the genre was fading, and it all but disappeared between the 1960s and the 1980s. Its filmic and generic return in the 90s, is, then, interesting. In both the above examples of retro-noir, but in different ways, the term itself, i.e. noir, has been broadened beyond the generic connotations (broad as these already are) of film studies' film noir.

In the first instance, noir has been broadened out to apply to films by black film-makers about their 'dark' condition in white America; in the second, while retro-noir is evident in the sense of characters standing on an abyss, and the gloomy paranoid atmosphere, the specifically *crime* narrative has been replaced by variations of the thriller which mix film noir with the serial killer genre. The proliferation of serial killer noir films (often called neo-noirs) perhaps attests to the issues of catastrophic sickness (most obviously AIDS), or of a drastic fall from wealth into poverty which marks our era. Despite the different form of social crisis in the 90s, what links the 40s to the 90s is the political and social sense of something amiss in American culture – a sense of drift, of pointlessness, political helplessness, and of inaccessible and hidden power creating generalised angst. US culture's renewed interest in noir participates in a nostalgic return to what can seem from a 90s perspective a far simpler 40s paranoia, cynicism, greed and resulting violence. But there is also a genuine sense of connection to the dark, incomprehensible, fragmented universe of 40s films. Perhaps above all, the obvious gender trouble (and less obvious racial trouble) and their interconnection, haunt the imaginary of both the 40s and the 90s in especially accute ways.[3] Gender and racial destabilisations add to the experiences of alienation, fragmentation and inconsistency that characterise both film noir and neo-noir.[4]

Since I allude, albeit schematically, to the 90s context for this revised version of *Women in Film Noir*, it is perhaps important to say something about the original

1978 context. What was the specific intellectual and political conjuncture in which the volume is implicitly embedded? I say 'implicitly' because rereading the book in 1997, and in quite a different intellectual, political and institutional conjuncture, one finds little self-consciousness within the volume about its moment in time. The authorial voice in the Introduction clearly has a specific intellectual and feminist agenda, but it assumes no need to identify that agenda explicitly. For in that moment, we the contributors (largely emerging academics in London) saw ourselves as a small group of film scholars, stimulated by feminist and other political liberation movements, who sought to move beyond the kind of film scholarship that dominated film publishing at that time – namely, historical, archival and biographical criticism – so as to bring our political agendas into our scholarship.

We were greatly supported in this task by Paddy Whannel, the inspired director of education at the British Film Institute in the 60s and 70s. It was Whannel's vision for a different kind of film pedagogy and scholarship, linked to issues of politics and culture, that initiated what was to develop into a new intellectual and scholarly field – institutionalised as cinema studies or film studies. The result was that in the 80s, undergraduate and graduate majors were developed in many universities worldwide, and film publications mushroomed.

At the time we could not have known what was to happen to our little volume, published almost as if we were talking just to ourselves. We could not have predicted that it would be used in numerous courses worldwide; that it would be translated and taught in Japan; or that it would go through several reprints. We could not have known how many students would be assigned the book, and how influential its theoretical positions and methodologies would become for the emerging area of feminist film theory. What now seems like the book's understated address can be explained only by knowing something about the 70s and film studies in Britain and the USA.

There was very little organised film studies even in the late 70s. In Britain, where universities are often slow to introduce new academic subjects, film studies was being developed via a non-academic institution, the British Film Institute, which at the start focussed on introducing film studies into further education and teacher education colleges; and then on setting up courses in schools where students were not going on to sit exams for university entrance. Only gradually did schools accept film studies as a discipline worthy of the university entrance exams. Meanwhile, in the US, mainly one found specific professors in a wide range of academic fields and institutions teaching an isolated film course when a disciplinary department was willing to experiment. We did not, therefore, have in mind as we wrote anything like the current established academic film studies context.

But what about the theoretical and methodological aspects of the 1978 volume? What accounts for these perspectives?. The confluence in London of several young Oxford scholars, trained in literature and linguistics, their turning to film, and their interest in 60s and 70s French and German intellectual developments, produced the intellectual conjuncture behind *Women in Film Noir*. As a result, the theoretical assumptions of the book include such influences as Louis Althusser, Julia Kristeva, Jacques Lacan, Roland Barthes, and, to an extent, Michel Foucault as well as Freud and Marx, Adorno and Benjamin, and sociological theories. Working on the assumption that we were speaking largely to ourselves, we did not see a need to make such underlying theoretical concerns explicit: readers will have noticed how relatively infrequent are citations to any of the above French theorists despite the reliance on them being quite obvious in many places.

Explicit in the Introduction is our staking out a claim to a specific kind of *feminist* methodology similar to that which Claire Johnston and Pam Cook had initiated in Johnston's little-known 1973 volume, *Notes on Women's Cinema*. A main, overriding intention behind the book was to introduce a specific feminist perspective into some already developing film theories around the journal *Screen*, which was at the time partly sponsored by the British Film Institute. The contributors to the volume adapted the concept of the 'classic realist text' to the specificity of gender – something male critics had hitherto largely ignored. Film noir, precisely because of its potential for subversion of dominant American values and gender-myths, provided an ideal group of films through which to make feminist uses of classic-text arguments. Many of the essays build on prior *Screen* film theories in their (then) innovative critique of classical Hollywood 'realism' as always implicitly colluding with the patriarchal status quo that positions women as subordinate in a (Lacanian) male Symbolic Order. Applying Foucault's concept of a hierarchy of discourses in any culture, the authors showed how the female discourse within film narratives is subordinated to overarching heterosexual male discourses. As Christine Gledhill put it so persuasively in her essay on *Klute* which opened the original edition of this book:

> The problem for feminist analysis of the impulse of traditional criticism to locate meaning in character is first that it leads the critic into moralistic assessment of the heroine and her subjectivity in terms of its truth to the actual condition of women, or to supposed female aspiration, or to a feminist perspective on either. The problem with this is that ideological myths about women are as much a part of the real world as any other construct.

Not all the authors argue from this feminist position (Janey Place, for example). Richard Dyer also takes up different concerns in his pioneering of gay perspectives. I always saw the theoretical heterogeneity of the volume as a reason for its continued usefulness to scholars, but a dominant aim was to introduce a focus on how meaning about woman is produced through the work of a film (in contrast to the then prevailing feminist concern with what kinds of female characters were portrayed in film). It seems to me that this point about how meaning is produced is now well taken, so much so that it no longer needs arguing. The pieces that are added in this revised edition betray a very different historical, political and intellectual moment. The influence of three new main concerns in film studies – that is, postmodern theory, gay/lesbian issues, and postcolonialism/racial foci – may be seen in the new essays. Since these influences do not arise from the specificity of focus on film noir in the intervening years, I will say something about film noir research in general before turning to the new concerns in this expanded volume, and to what they show about the 90s and about what I call 'noirness'.

3

Noir research

While general scholarly interest in the noir film has continued, it has been in a muted, quiet fashion. There has been a steady stream of publications, but (with the exceptions noted below) these have been mainly by male scholars continuing traditional kinds of studies apparently only casually influenced by our volume. In the period since *Women in Film Noir* appeared, William Marling has continued to explore literary backgrounds of film noir and also, briefly, to link noir styles with design features of other consumer goods in the 40s (Marling, 1995). Alain Silver and Elizabeth Ward published the useful book *Film Noir: An Encyclopedic Reference to the American Style* (1987); and Silver has gathered together new essays along with reprinting 'classic' noir ones in his collection edited with James Ursini (1996). Far from developing new perspectives on film noir, this collection deliberately looks back to past noir scholarship. Revisited are debates as to whether or not noir is a *European* or *American* style;[5] and on the degree to which noir is confined to its particular historical moment, and thus only 'readable' within that frame. Silver asserts, quite in keeping with earlier research, that film noir seems to be 'a body of films that not only presents a relatively cohesive vision of America but that does so in a manner transcending the influences of auteurism or genre ... film noir is a self-contained reflection of American culture and its preoccupations at a point in time. As such it is a unique example of a wholly American film style' (p. 6). Two of the more interesting issues raised at the end of the book include the relationship of film noir to TV noir, including shows such as *Miami Vice*, and the relationship of recent films – what Jeremy Butler calls 'tech-noir' and 'neo-noir' – to 40s film noir (Butler, 1996: 289–306).

Among other books on film noir in the intervening years,[6] R. Barton Palmer's *Hollywood's Dark Cinema: The American Film Noir* usefully pulls together discussions of film noir, highlighting the status of these films as inexpensive 'B' productions geared towards a reasonably narrow audience and by no means eclipsing the genres with endings that are optimistic and which reinforce American values. Palmer also makes a bridge through Boorman's *Point Blank* (1967) to Verhoeven's *Basic Instinct* (1992) which two of the new essays included here address. Frank Krutnik's *In a Lonely Street: Film Noir, Genre, Masculinity* (1991) builds on feminist work similar to that in our volume in arguing that film noir is a response to a troubled sense of masculinity in the 40s. Ian Cameron's *The Book of Film Noir* (1992) gathers together articles by various scholars on many different aspects of noir, although the approaches deliberately avoid ideological, political or feminist perspectives in favour of addressing matters of style, history, narrative, auteurism. Also deliberately, the book contains in-depth analyses of individual films.

On the whole, though, film noir research has not been one of the 'hot' film topics – such as postmodernism, postcoloniality, ethnicity, and the gay/lesbian issues noted above – that have impacted on film studies in recent years. But the new authors in this volume (as well as myself and Dyer in his Postscript), bring to bear precisely and quite self-consciously these intellectual foci dominating film studies in the 90s. Unlike the 1978 authors, the new contributors make explicit the contemporary intellectual, political and institutional conjunctures. They do this partly by self-consciously building out from (even as they critique) the theories and methods in the original 1978 essays: it is this scholarly manner that attests to film studies as a professional and acknowledged research field, and this is one of the marked differences from 1978.

Joan Copjec's 1993 edited collection, *Shades of Noir*, in some ways anticipates our revised volume, and thus stands out as a major contribution in these years of rather bland noir scholarship when critical paradigms were not themselves self-consciously re-evaluated. Copjec's call for a re-theorisation of film noir and the investigation of what she calls 'another order' is welcome. The essays in her volume, she argues, aim to seize film noir 'from the perspective of the old unanswered question of the genre's "absent cause", that is, of a principle that does not appear in the field of its effects' (Copjec, 1993: xii). The iconoclasm in many of the essays offers a welcome breath of fresh air,[7] but does not evacuate the focus on gender that the 1978 volume introduced. We retain here, then, the categories of race and gender as useful in furthering understanding of the noir universe, but this is not to say that the categories are used in the same ways as in 1978, nor that they are homologous. Far from it. New authors mobilise each category and then discuss the degree to which the categories of sexuality and race displace or work in tandem with that of gender.

It was important to honour the new theories about women in film noir that had been developing in the intervening years, although, as a result of recent theoretical developments noted above, I found that feminist perspectives on film noir, or perspectives dealing with women at all, have been few and far between. In 1984, Jon Tuska applied ideas developed by several of the authors in *Women in Film Noir* to films we had not discussed, as well as to some we had (Tuska, 1984: 200–220); Karen Hollinger's essay in Silver's volume also revisits some of the theories and readings advanced in *Women in Film Noir*, adding a twist enabled by theories of Michel Foucault not fully available to us in 1978 (Silver and Ursini, 1996). James Maxfield, meanwhile, explores women in noir films who are 'fatal' to the hero but who are not themselves evil or deliberate agents of the hero's destruction as the classic *femmes fatales* (such as Brigid O'Shaughnessy in *The Maltese Falcon* or Phyllis Dietrichson in *Double Indemnity*) are seen to be. Maxfield argues that the true theme of these movies could be regarded as 'male anxiety over emotional vulnerability' (Maxfield, 1996). Many of the women, Maxfield claims, do not deliberately destroy the hero, but are themselves manipulated and often victimised by powerful men. In the case of Madeleine/Judy in Hitchcock's *Vertigo*, and Evelyn Mulwray in *Chinatown*, Maxfield says: 'Without intending to be *femmes fatales*, Evelyn and Judy nevertheless qualify as "fatal women" … because of the extremely destructive effects they have on the male protagonist' (p. 10).

Ruby Rich's brief overview of neo-noir in her article 'Dumb Lugs and Femmes Fatales' (1995) includes some discussion of the women characters. Rich points out that there is precedent in classic noir for neo-noir women being 'usually pure evil with sexuality and greed the primary markers of character' (p. 8). But she notes that contemporary audiences (perhaps more than earlier ones) seem to love the new *femmes fatales'* 'rapacious acts, their disregard for human life, their greed and lust and lack of restraint' (p. 9). Rich suggests discomfort with the way that many audiences accept the neo-noir heroine's display of power, however depraved and unmotivated, 'as a new version (albeit warped) of female empowerment'. For Rich, it is a postmodern world 'in which people frequently know too much for their own good' (p. 9). It is just some of these provocative issues that both Chris Straayer and Kate Stables take up in more detail in the essays included here.

Revisioning classical feminist film theory about the *femme fatale* in another way, Elizabeth Cowie challenges the assumption that film noir is always a masculine film form. She points out that these films 'afforded women roles which are active, adventurous and driven by sexual desire' (in Copjec (ed.), 1994: 135). Cowie asserts that the fantasy of a woman's dangerous sexuality is as much a feminine as a masculine one: further, that it is the fantasy itself 'that demands the punishment, for in the punishment the reality of the forbidden wish is acknowledged' (p. 136). Since some of the new essays in this volume take up Cowie's thesis, I will return to her points later on.

Although the term 'film noir' only enters once in the text, Lynda Hart's *Fatal Women: Lesbian Sexuality and the Market of Aggression* works with ideas similar to some of those in the new essays here. In her afterword, Hunt discusses Deb Margolin's *Lesbians Who Kill*: as Hunt puts it, the heroines, May and June, 'know that they are "fallen women", but they like where they have landed' (1994: 160). Hunt goes on to show, through a parody of the classic film noir *Deception,* how 'they re-inhabit the "femme fatale" with a difference' (p. 160). *Lesbians Who Kill,* she says, both reminds man of his dangerous bargain of making woman embody the phallus, and offers hope 'for a place to play that is indifferent to it'. In her discussion of *Basic Instinct,* Hunt refers to it as a 'thriller', defining the genre as a 'transgression of the classic whodunit', which 'exposes the detective/analyst as a fraud. The transference is broken' (p. 126). Here Hunt touches precisely on what characterises a film as noir,[8] and her book complements nicely some of the discussions in our expanded volume, as well as looking back to some ideas in the original book.

I have called the three new perspectives that the authors bring to bear on women in film noir in the new volume postmodernism, gay/lesbian concerns, and issues regarding postcolonialism/race. The question I want briefly to address is how far these perspectives are mobilised in such a way as to be continuous or discontinuous with our 1978 methods and foci; and, in addition, to say a word about the confluence or dissonances among the categories of gender, sexuality and race as these are worked through in the new essays.

As always, a category or concept only has meaning and is in place by virtue of what it represses. The coming-into-consciousness of the concept of 'gender' with 80s feminisms already marked a paradigm shift from the 70s language of male or female 'sex-role'. But both terms connoted a focus on normative *heterosexuality.* As many have since pointed out, the concept of heterosexuality relies on a repressed notion of homosexuality. But of course, in the 70s and 80s, even a self-conscious focus on the construction of heterosexuality and the gender biases in this construction was new. It thus seems logical to me that, as this work proceeded, more and more scholars would bring to consciousness heterosexuality's repressed term, homosexuality, and start to investigate repressed gay/lesbian/queer identities, subjectivities, activities. Richard Dyer had pioneered with a gay reading of *Gilda* in the 1978 volume, and he is partly responsible for legitimising such studies. In this broad sense, then, the focus in Patricia White's and Chris Straayer's essays on lesbian themes in film noir seems to build upon, rather than break from, work in the 1978 book.

However, in their theorising of lesbian themes, inevitably these authors confront and need to contest prior heterosexist readings of the *femme fatale*. Our 1978 theories largely conceived of the *femme fatale* as a *male* fantasy, as serving unconscious male anxieties and forbidden desires. In her analysis of two films in the essay already mentioned, Elizabeth Cowie argues that it is ultimately impossible to tell whose story each film is telling – that of a man or a woman – and that the visual structure of film noir proves how ambiguous its gender fantasies are.

The gay/lesbian perspectives in the new postscript by Richard Dyer, and the essays by Patricia White and Chris Straayer take this idea further. The three authors examine different issues: Dyer extends his earlier work on the gay relationship between Johnny and Ballin in *Gilda* so as to explore more generally 'the role of queers in the construction of women in film noir'. His central point is that, besides all the predictable reasons why queers are seen as evil in noir (homosexuality is abnormal; gays are like women – abhorrent, perverse, etc), 'queers are also evil because the aesthetic gives them access to women that excludes or threatens the normal male'. The typical ordinary noir hero, then, has to contend with 'a whole miasma of femininty spun around them by queers' (p. 6). Dyer shows how lesbian characters are also made unattractive in film noir, and how, while they too threaten the hero because of their access to women and their knowledge of femaleness, 'they don't threaten [the hero's] hold on the world. It is femininity that does this'.

In her essay 'Female Spectator, Lesbian Spectre: *The Haunting*', Patricia White critiques feminist film theory for its lack of attention to lesbian perspectives in general, and goes on to show how this simply replicates what Hollywood and mainstream culture has always done, namely to repress lesbianism. White argues, however, that lesbian perspectives 'haunt' feminist film theory, and that once again, this haunting repeats what she finds in Hollywood films and films noirs. White's reading of *The Haunting* and other noir films shows that the real couples are female – that the films tell women's stories.

Straayer, meanwhile, takes pleasure in the new, active, independent neo-noir heroines, and in their aggressivity. Rightly, she shows that the new *femme fatale* is 'a metonym that travels among a variety of genres, summoning film noirness for atmospheric or hermeneutic effect'. Straayer argues, importantly, that the *femme fatale* has multiplied in meanings and possibilities for socio-historical reasons (such as the Kinsey Report and the feminist movements), but 'also due to an increase in explicit, on-screen sexual imagery and proliferating media representations of fictional and non-fictional female killers'. Straayer is especially fascinated with the explicit featuring of women's sexual desire. The *femme fatale* 'answers sex-based inequity with sexual manipulation,' but whereas the classic *femme fatale*'s lust 'was overwhelmingly for money rather than sexual pleasure … by contrast, the neo-noir *femme* wants sex as well as money'. Her reading of neo-noir films focuses on the explicitness of the heroine's sexuality – in particular the imaging of her many orgasms – and the frequency with which she has sex with women. It is the specific meanings of all this that Straayer tries to explain.

Kate Stables is also interested in 90s neo-noir, and in the portrayal of explicit fe-

7

male sexuality, with emphasis on sadomasochistic practices. Unique to Stables' analysis is her focus on how 'the heavy presence of sexual speech, rather like the repetition of sexual spectacle, presents the audience with marked and novel areas of pleasure in their experience of the screen *fatale*'. Examples of the heroines' 'bluntly sexual speech' provide grist to Stables' argument that such speech provides a special kind of hallucinatory force because the women 'name what should not be mentioned in public – they reveal the truly sexual life'.

Stables is interested in why the *femme fatale* returns in this era in this particular form. For Stables, a vital component of the new heroine's makeup is the postmodern cinema in which she figures. Where classical Hollywood cinema produced homogeneous texts for a supposedly homogeneous audience, the new postmodern cinema 'has to reach a media-literate global audience, composed of wildly diverse cultural groupings'. Stables regards it as important that postmodern cinema's 'polysemic nature allows films to accommodate and privilege radically opposing discourses at the same time'. For this reason, a film such as *Basic Instinct* 'could be variously reviled as a misogynistic fantasy and celebrated as the ultimate cult lesbian movie'. Stables wonders whether there is any longer 'a need to piece together a recuperative reading around the *femme fatale*, when the text can be experienced in multiple fashion?' This is a question that Stables grapples with throughout her essay, which focuses on a reading of *Basic Instinct*.

Angela Martin's study also provides a 'corrective' to our 1978 characterisations of the *femme fatale*, and of noir as a masculine genre. In her essay on 40s pulp thrillers, Martin focuses specifically on those films noirs with central women characters after whom the film is named. She argues that 'films which have central female characters throw back implications for that model of film noir that has emerged *critically* without taking into account the existence of both men *and* women as central characters'. She provides a useful taxonomy of female roles for films with central characters, to demonstrate her point about 'the inability of film noir theory to recognize female characters as performing other narrative functions – as other than expression of female sexuality which threatens the hero'. Martin also provides an appendix which lists films with a central involvement of women, not only as lead characters, but also as writers and producers. The films are separated according to the different combinations of involvement.

Gay/lesbian, and other feminist perspectives like Martin's or Kate Stables' were, interestingly, easier to find than people working on noir and issues of race. Manthia Diawara has very nicely parodied white critics' adoption of the term noir, and commented on the neglect of issues of race in his essay 'Noirs on Noir' (Diawara, 1993), which I discuss in some detail in my essay in this volume. Eric Lott has written an essay about the 'Whiteness of Film Noir', which addresses the racial undertones of the use of shadow in noir films – that is, the way noir lighting renders characters 'black', implicitly commenting on the 'whiteness' of the characters, by inference – which I also discuss in my essay.

My interest in contributing to this volume lies in thinking about the social/historical moment *vis-à-vis* race and gender together, without, however, collapsing the two into the *same* difference. Introducing the category of race, I argue, unsettles prior theories of the *femme fatale*. Race complicates the structure of a film noir's desire to manage male/female difference, to re-assert male heterosexual dominance over the white female. Dominant male culture fears difference from itself. In this minimal way, then, women and people of colour are rendered *structurally* similar – that is, both women and people of colour need to be 'managed', and the boundary of each from the white 'centre' maintained. While the specificity of fears of women, homosexuals, and people of colour are different, all three groups share a similarity as marginalised by the white centre. In reality, fears of black men and of black women have a different structure from fears of white women; fears of gay males have a different structure from that of gay women. Fear also functions on a range of levels – economic, class, cultural and political fears operate alongside purely psychic, fantasmatic ones in relation to all groups. Research on the complex issues of how gender, sexual and racial differences operate in regard to the centre as well as in relation to each other is ongoing. Scholars do not agree about which level should take precedence, or about the specific differences in the mechanisms which control each kind of difference: I argue, however, that Hollywood tends to use a *similar structure in relation to all kinds of difference*. That is, Hollywood puts different kinds of difference into the same position *vis-à-vis* the imaginary white centre.

In my essay I note how the repressed fears regarding race and gender partly account for the dis-ease films noirs are famous for. Feminists have focused on this dis-ease in regard to women returning from the war (Harvey, in Kaplan (ed.), 1978). But the dis-ease was equally to do with the race issues that had emerged as a result of World War II. It was harder to deny racism after the revelation that black and white GIs had segregated quarters when in Europe; as well, the Nazis had embarrassing support among Germans in the US. Thus, race disturbance surfaced in oblique but still dramatic ways in films noirs. During the war, as during the Depression (see John Stahl's 1934 novel *Imitation of Life*), some black women still served as baby-minders and house cleaners for the white women who made up the majority working in factories and making war weapons. However, as Julia Reichert has documented in her film *War Maids*, and as Lucy Fischer has noted (Fischer, 1990), World War II at least opened up possibilities for black women to join white women in the factories. The changing roles of white *and* black women provided a kind of double threat to male culture in the post-war period.

Film noir: whose fantasy?

A theme that runs through all the essays in this volume has to do with whose fantasy is satisfied by the gender 'trouble' of film noir. In the 70s and 80s, theories of the *femme fatale* in feminist film studies seemed to validate Freud's insight, re-articulated strongly by Laura Mulvey and others in the mid-70s, that males feared castration – the 'open wound' that women's genitals apparently presented to the male imaginary. The *femme fatale* figures of the male imaginary (or so we argued), imaged forth males' terror of, but fascinated interest in, that bleeding wound: the play of desire and fear hovered around the castration that might happen if males followed their desire for the beautiful sexual and powerful woman. What many named the phallicisation of these women aimed to reduce male fear of their castration – their own bleeding wound – so as to permit fulfilment of the sexual de-

9

sire the women evoked. Since the *femme fatale* was often evil and deliberately used her sexuality to draw the hero into the enemy's hands, the films were in one sense a message to men to stay away from these sexy women – to settle for the home-girl. Men were trying to convince themselves in this regard, which is why many have argued that films noirs are not really about women at all.

As we saw earlier, this is a thesis that has been challenged in intervening years. Elizabeth Cowie, I noted, asserts that the fantasy of a woman's dangerous sexuality is as much a feminine as a masculine one; further, that it is the fantasy itself 'that demands the punishment, for in the punishment the reality of the forbidden wish is acknowledged'.

But it seems to me that it is still not proven that 'the fantasy of a woman's dangerous sexuality' is a widespread *female* fantasy; or that 'the conjoining of desire and destruction is as much a matter for women as for men' (p. 160). Cowie refreshingly challenges some of the prior theoretical assumptions in our 1978 volume, but I see no convincing evidence for either the prior position or Cowie's later revisionist one. In his Postscript, Dyer also seems so to question Cowie's position when he says: 'If it is powerful to be designated as feminine, it is still not a choice. If (some) women and queers participate in that male construction, is that seizing the opportunity afforded by male desire or colluding with it?' Countering what Ruby Rich reported regarding contemporary audiences feeling empowered by neo-noir heroines, Lynda Hart argues that films like *Basic Instinct* reveal something important about the masculine imaginary, namely 'the systematic homophobia of masculine heterosexual desire'. In making this visible, *Basic Instinct* challenges 'the patriarchal symbolic to own up to what it conceals in order to maintain itself' (1993: 134).

Assuredly, both male and female fantasies take many forms and are far from monolithic. Sexual fantasies are often conditioned by childhood experiences and by the psychological environment a child grows up in. As we know, family environments have changed, and continue to change dramatically as the structures within which children are raised have altered from the 40s to the present day. Feminist spectatorship, or feminists' sexual identification with images in noir and neo-noir films, will therefore never be the same for all individual women. It is possible that there might be more conformity across one age group than between different age groups, but one can not even be certain about that.

Given generational, racial, class, and sexual-orientation differences among women, I would argue that film noir offers a space for the playing out of *various* gender fantasies. If the fantasy is produced by the filmic text, as Cowie argues, and if the text 'must move the spectator to occupy his or her place within it' (p. 137), I assume that the text is producing places for more than one gender fantasy, depending on the needs of the spectator as noted above. The exciting, powerful, sexual woman of 40s noirs can, alternately, be a fantasy that satisfies male unconscious needs (and may be seen by some female spectators as a *male* fantasy because she is not of interest to them as a model); and the same figure can be a fantasy that precisely interests and excites other female spectators, who do not read the figure as a male desire, but as their own fantasy. It all depends on what turns on any specific female spectator.

The 90s neo-noir films that Straayer and Stables discuss also offer a space for the playing out of varied gender fantasies. Only now, as the authors here have argued, the sexual practices of the fatal women are made explicit, and they are often serial killers as well. In neo-noirs, males are lured by the sadomasochistic sexual practices the heroines are skilled in; they become addicted to these practices, and end up sexual pawns in the women's hands, often with fatal results. *Body of Evidence* (Uli Edel, 1993) almost parodies the genre by making Rachel Carlson's body literally the murder weapon, standing in for the phallic gun of the 40s *femme fatale;* or, in Kate Stables' words, 'the *fatale becomes* the murder weapon, when she stands accused of using violent sex to murder an ailing tycoon'. Once again, despite the possibly empowering nature of images of the heroines boldly initiating sex, taking the lead, and controlling all that goes on, given their exaggerated greed (these women are out for the really big money) and their willingness to lie and kill to get their millions, the spectator may conclude with the hero that it might be best to go back to the home-girl and conventional sex.

But of course by the 90s, this proves impossible: the hero has only two choices: to kill the fatal woman or to be killed. If, as in *Fatal Attraction* (Adrian Lyne, 1987), the hero manages to escape and save his threatened 'home-girl', it is by the skin of all their teeth. The neo-noir heroine does, in effect, castrate these male characters. Indeed, the males in neo-noirs are all but parodies of the original noir detective. If, as Krutnik argues, 40s noirs are about the crisis in masculinity following World War II, neo-noirs explore female scorn and derision for men. Neo-noir heroines find no match at all in their men, whether detectives or criminals. While the hero in *Bound* (The Wachowski Brothers, 1996) might be an extreme case, he is really not that much more stupid than are most of these heroes. Contemporary men should beware of the 'gaping wound', the films appear to say, since these women mean business like no 40s heroine could quite conceive of.

Arguably, these images can be read by women as speaking to their anger and perhaps disappointment at what feminist movements have failed to achieve. In recent years, women have carried out their fantasies on the living bodies of men: Lorena Bobitt achieved fame in her celebrated actual castration, as did Amy Fisher in her shooting of Mrs Buttafuco.[9] While Susan Smith's murder of her children is of a different order, nevertheless we were given to understand that her tremendous rage at her husband and her abusive father might have been behind her actions. Women are angrier than ever, partly because of the expectations that feminists of earlier decades promised: they now want explicit fantasies of women overcoming weak, stupid and oppressive men.

Yet despite the unflattering image of men in most neo-noirs, a male spectator might take pleasure in such a film by satisfying some of his forbidden fantasies about S&M sexual practices and about beautiful, young women aggressively initiating sex. Neo-noirs are brilliant, then, as Stables argues, in fulfilling multiple fantasies. Some women feel empowered by the knife-wielding S&M heroines; some are gratified by the explicit expressions of passionate female orgasms, and of women seducing men to limp victims who trail after them, asking for more S&M. But surely others appreciate not so much the form of the heroines as these women's power over men: their ability to outwit male strategies, their creative ideas for releasing themselves from male power, etc. These are not films about morality: no-one is ethical and the larger moral framework that used to be mobilised in the resolutions of 40s noirs is missing. *The Last Seduction* (John Dahl, 1993) may be an extreme example, but, as Straayer shows, it is not alone in showing the heroine coolly getting away with stealing millions of dollars. The *excessive* wealth neo-noir heroines run off with is a kind of symptomatic exaggeration of what women feel they are owed in a culture that has traditionally subjugated them. Money stands in for power in an obvious transference.

In the 90s, neo-noirs seem to be mutating into a new genre, that of the 'Serial Killer'. This usually white male figure (Bernard Rose's 1993 film *Candyman* might appear to be an exception, but the black 'Candyman' is fused with a white female) now replaces the *femme fatale* as the figure most threatening to the hero. Many of these films deal with the sick psychic connection the killer sets up with the hero, and this threatens his love for the good woman as much as did the *femme fatale*. *The Mean Season* (Phillip Borsos, 1985) is a prototype for later films, like *The Vanishing* (George Sluizer, 1993) and many of the *X-Files* episodes. Indeed, in some films the gender roles are reversed: the serial killer fulfils the role of the *femme fatale vis-à-vis* the female heroine as well (see the prototype *Peeping Tom* (Michael Powell, 1957); *Lipstick* (Richard Brooks, 1976); *Silence of the Lambs* (Jonathan Demme, 1990); and Katherine Bigelow's *Blue Steel* (1994) or her *Strange Days* (1996)). In many of these films, as well, the specifically female 'open wound' has been replaced by an interest in what Mark Seltzer (1997) has called 'wound culture', in which interest in the wound of the entire opened body is central. But these are issues that will need to be pursued elsewhere.

A much more promising approach to the dilemma of the *femme fatale* and whose fantasy she is can be found in Susan Streitfeld's *Female Perversions* (1997). Inspired by Louise J. Kaplan's book of the same name, this film parodies male traditions of seeing female sexuality as somehow in itself a 'perversion'. The opening title proclaims that 'All perversions are socially constructed. ... They are the framework for defining the constraints that hamper female sexuality.' The question the film poses is: What would happen if female sexuality were not restrained and uninhibited? If women could act out some of their sexual fantasies? And it proceeds to play with that idea of an unrestrained female sexuality. In so doing it cleverly dispenses with the categories of the 'home-girl' and the '*femme fatale*' in the central character, while parodying them in minor characters. One character, Amy, a mother, parodies the home-girl in pushing her boyfriend into marriage; another parodies the whore stereotype. In a brilliant scene, this woman 'masquerades' as female in order to teach Ed how to be a woman!

The film does not idealise the new free female sexualities that might emerge if constraints were taken away. Far from it: the heroine, played by Tilda Swinton, is an aggressive, highly successful and competitive lawyer, whose obsessional neuroses and aggressive sexual practices are ultimately seen (psychoanalytically) to derive from an early childhood experience with her parents' sexuality. Her sister is equally disturbed, and, unmarried and without sexual partners, she finds eroticism in stealing. The one sane and balanced sexual woman is a lesbian and (not incidentally) a psychoanalyst. Film noir and neo-noir films, as many have argued, largely depict female sexualities as males fantasise them. Streitfeld's film, like Kaplan's book, opens up a long-neglected terrain about the nature of female sexualities as women constitute them, or know them, themselves.

Notes

1. I refer here, as most readers will know, to Fredric Jameson's now classic notion of the 'postmodern' as that which recirculates past aesthetic and cultural modes in a way that is neither irony nor satire, but what he termed 'pastiche'. See Jameson, 1985.

2. I discuss the 'NoirNet' in a later note, but let me comment on the 'Noir York' image that accompanied the story. The image was of a novel, titled *Noir York;* the picture on its cover was of an aging, slightly greying detective, conspicuously lacking the *de rigueur* 1940s hat. The usually clear, firm lines of the city scape in the 1940s images are blurred and softened. It's still shadowy, but it's a shaky set of shadows now, instead of the clean, hard ones of yore. The detective is looking scared, too; and instead of staring out at the viewer, his head is turned toward a shadow to his left. Meanwhile, his hands are in his pockets, but not apparently fingering a gun! This is a vastly weakened hero in today's 'Noir York'. Interest in noir continues: *New York* magazine (7 July 1997: 61–62), blazed its 'Weekly Guide to Entertainment' front page with a brightly coloured poster for Joseph H. Lewis' *Gun Crazy.* The line at the bottom read: 'Attack of the Killer B's' and announced a retrospective of sixty films noir being to be shown at New York's Film Forum Cinema in July and August 1997. On 19 July1997, *The New York Times Book Review* displayed on its dusky cover an image in huge letters, such as those used to advertise films shown in cinemas, which read 'DARK GENIUS: THE LIVES OF TWO GREAT DIRECTORS', referring to new biographies of Howard Hawks and Fritz Lang, reviewed by Diane Jacobs and Stanley Kauffmann in the issue. That is, the editors of *The New York Times Book Review* turned this into a noir occasion! On 26 September 1997, *The New York Times* featured a column by Bernard Weintraub including a section titled 'Saved by Film Noir', which detailed Martin Scorsese's inspiration from the 40s genre: 'Film noir created an image of the world for me because of its brooding nature, because of its sense of fatalism', Scorcese says, and notes that 'the films were more my vision of life than Andy Hardy' since people around him resembled those in film noir. The interview emerged in the context of a fundraising tribute to Film Noir in Los Angeles.

3. This is not to deny that gender and race were issues in the intervening decades, but just that the intensity and cultural self-consciousness about these issues seem to link the 40s and 90s.

4. Joan Copjec notes that in film noir 'The world no longer unfolds in nonsimultaneous fragments … it breaks up into inconsistent and always alien fragments' (Copjec, 1993: ix).

5. For instance, Silver himself debates with Marc Vernet over whether noir is an American or European style. I am not sure what's at stake here – national pride? – but Silver gets angry with Vernet's mistake over the spelling of his name (with some justification, I suppose). But what are the real issues here and their importance for understanding film noir? Why is there the need to insist on this American-ness? Surely most artistic endeavours are multi-determined and international, or at least in dialogue with other aesthetic modes? To deny the influence of German expressionism or French existentialism seems extreme. I do not know what to make of Silver's comment that 'Vernet's revisionism is like any of the neo-Freudian, semiological, historical, structural, socio-cultural and/or auteurist assaults [!] of the past' (p. 6), except perhaps to imagine that our volume is being alluded to? It's interesting that *Women in Film Noir* is not mentioned in the bibliography, except in reference to Janey Place's essay.

6. I have in mind here books like Foster Hirsch's *The Dark Side of the Screen: Film Noir* (New York: Ada Capo, 1981); and Bruce Crowther's *Film Noir: Reflections in a Dark Mirror* (New York: Frederick Ungar, 1989).

7. For instance, Vernet seems to say that 'film noir is a collector's idea that for the moment can only be found in books' (Copjec, 1993).

8. It would take too long to recapitulate Hunt's complex, psychoanalytically based argument. The important statement here is her noting that 'If the formal movement from the whodunit to the thriller may be understood as a transformation of the detective from a subject-supposed-to-know to a subject-desupposed-of-knowledge, we might simply hypothesise that these conventions invite a spectatorial response that shifts from love to hate. … The thriller would, then, not be about love, or about hate, but rather about their proximity' (p. 127). Perhaps most important for issues in our new volume is Hunt's statement that 'The thriller, then, would seem to command a particular shape to the representation of the "deadly woman". And the shape in which this ubiquitous figure appears in the thriller will be intimately bound to the status of the detective, as the subject-desup-

posed-of-knowledge.' Interestingly, similar ideas, if working with somewhat different language, may be found in essays by Gledhill, Dyer and Johnston in our original volume, which Hunt does not refer to.

9. These thoughts emerged in discussion with Kate Stables. Stables noted that there is a 'compulsion of the body', in the 1990s – a desire to enact fantasies on living bodies which she jokingly referred to as 'bobitting'. We both agreed that neo-noirs are a symptom of what changes still need to be achieved. We also agreed that we need better fantasies than these in neo-noirs.

Introduction to 1978 Edition
E. Ann Kaplan

Looking at the place of women in film noir means the study of an essential aspect of this group of films, and constitutes a useful contribution, as evidenced by the essays here, to our understanding of the placing of women within cultural production. The BFI Summer School in 1975, which I attended, had been concerned with the area of film noir as genre, and the idea for this project resulted from that work and from a paper by Sylvia Harvey (revised for this monograph).

One of the depressing aspects of the study of women in art works is the repetition of the same structures, showing the strong hold of patriarchy. The cinema is no exception and in her two-part essay on *Klute*, Christine Gledhill illustrates the development of those structures from the 40s thrillers in contemporary cinema. She shows that the alterations in the conventions reflect a continuing 'ideological struggle within patriarchy to maintain control over female sexuality and to assimilate its new, would-be liberating manifestations'; yet within this structure 'are enmeshed fragments that refer forcefully to the images and problems of a struggling feminism'. Her analysis of *Klute* demonstrates the need to place contemporary cinematic developments within the traditions that condition them.

All our writers except Janey Place consider these films noirs as a *genre* in one form or another – that is, in terms of thematic concern, narrative structure, iconography etc., a number of recognisable conventions run through them. Christine Gledhill, for example, writes:

> genre production tended both to foreground convention and stereotypicality in order to gain instant audience recognition of its type – this is a Western, a Gangster, a Woman's Picture, etc. – and to institute a type of aesthetic play among the conventions in order to pose the audience with a question that would keep them coming back – not 'what is going to happen next?' to which they would already have the answer, but 'how?'

Janey Place, on the other hand, argues that because of the highly specific visual style and narrative concerns of film noir, its relatively short period (Sylvia Harvey suggests between *The Maltese Falcon* in 1941 and *Touch of Evil* in 1958), and its appearance at a historical moment of crisis (post-World War II), these films – rather than constituting a genre, which is rarely defined in terms of a recognisable visual style and whose conventions very much bend with societal changes – instead represent a *movement*.

However, in discussing the 70s film *Klute*, Christine Gledhill illustrates how the conventions of film noir have been employed in conjunction with traditions drawn from the European art movie to treat a 'modern theme'. This particular trend within the *thriller genre* can be seen in other 70s films and can be distinguished from the different permutation of the genre, of which Clint Eastwood's police thrillers are an example. In other words film noir can perhaps better be seen as a *sub-genre* or a *generic development* emerging from the earlier gangster genre than as a genre by itself.

Whether one sees this group of films as a genre or a movement, however, they are also very much products of Hollywood – even with its German Expressionist influences (Lang, for example) – and it is perhaps useful to signal here two terms used to refer to Hollywood films – 'the *classic text*' and 'the *classic genre film*'; while they are not necessarily mutually exclusive it is useful to bear in mind that there is a difference.

All the contributors in some way imply the notion of 'the classic film' in the sense of *genre*, by their reference to the visual/narrative/iconographic conventions through which one recognises a film to be of this group. (There is also a sense, in this term, of a perfect genre film against which others can be measured.)

The 'classic text' (applicable to genre and non-genre films) describes a *dominant mode of production*, which masks its own operation – either in terms of covering over ideological tension and contradiction, thereby giving dominance to a metadiscourse, which represents the Truth *vis-à-vis* the film's content and meaning; or in terms of giving the impression that it gives access to the 'real world'. There is a continuing debate around this notion in terms of the mechanisms through which the metadiscourse/Truth is carried, and Christine Gledhill discusses aspects of it in relation to feminist film theory in the first part of her essay on *Klute*.

This particular period of the thriller genre – film noir – is, however, recognisably different from other films, in that where there is a metadiscourse, as discussed above, it exists at great cost, through considerable narrative and visual contortion. Film noir is particularly notable for its specific treatment of women. In the films of another genre, the Western – for example, Ford's *My Darling Clementine* or *The Searchers* – women, in their fixed role as wives, mothers, daughters, lovers, mistresses, whores, simply provide the background for the ideological work of the film which is carried out through men.

Since the placement of women in this way is so necessary to patriarchy as we know it, it follows that the displacement of women would disturb the patriarchal system, and provide a challenge to that world view. The film noir world is one in which women are central to the intrigue of the films, and are furthermore usually not placed safely in any of the familiar roles mentioned above. Defined by their sexuality, which is presented as desirable but dangerous to men, the women function as the obstacle to the male quest. The hero's success or not depends on the degree to which he can extricate himself from the woman's manipulations. Although the man is sometimes simply destroyed because he cannot resist the woman's lures (*Double Indemnity* is the best example), often the work of the film is the attempted restoration of order through the exposure and then destruction of the sexual, manipulating woman.

In her close visual analysis of a number of films noirs, Janey Place illustrates (through frame enlargements) some of the ways in which the dislocation of women from their 'proper place' under patriarchy is expressed visually. She shows the play on women's sexuality and sensuality, the way in which parts of their bodies are focused on in their presentation as objects of desire. But women also visually dominate the men in many frames, reflecting the danger and the threat that they assume because of their overpowering sexuality, the control of which must equally be attempted in visual terms.

Clearly, as Sylvia Harvey shows, one way to evoke the threat of female sexuality is to exclude from the films that situation of the family in which it would otherwise be contained. Sylvia Harvey links the appearance of these films, with their new negative attitudes to the family, to the post-World War II period, when the previous ideology of national unity began to be eroded. The depressed peace-time economy brought an end to myths central to the American Dream and caused widespread disillusionment among veterans. There were also sudden fluctuations in the numbers of women entering (during the war) and then leaving (post-war) the job market. Thus the film noir *expresses* alienation, locates its cause squarely in the excesses of female sexuality ('natural' consequences of women's independence), and punishes that excess in order to re-place it within the patriarchal order.

It is largely because of this interplay of the notion of independent women *vis-à-vis* patriarchy that these films are of interest to feminist film theory. Christine Gledhill points out the problems genre films pose for feminists often caught between arguing against stereotyping, and therefore dismissing films clearly within the realm of artifice, and arguing for films which 'show women in real (i.e., recognisable) situations' – *Alice Doesn't Live Here Any More, Klute*. As she points out, the former position ignores the potentiality of genre films to play on ideological tension and contradiction; the latter ignores the existence of a 'realist' *aesthetic* (of the 'classic text' – applied not only to Hollywood, but also European art films), which equally structures tension and contradiction, but, as indicated above, is not seen to be doing so.

The theoretical project of identifying a mode of dominant ideological representation goes along with the impulse to find inconsistencies in a film through which ideological contradiction and tension may be seen to be manifested:

> Thus a criticism operating according to a perspective at odds with the ideology privileged as the film's 'message' or 'world-view' may be able to animate these effects to produce a progressive reading of an apparently reactionary film, or (as I attempt with *Klute*) an ideological reading of an apparently radical film. (Gledhill)

This brings us to the question of reading, which is clearly pertinent in the context of this monograph. There is no single position here on whether film noir as such is progressive or not. Both Christine Gledhill, in Part I of her essay, and Sylvia Harvey talk about both the *potential* progressiveness and the *potential* repression of film noir, the latter writer locating this potential in absence of *family relations* or their negative or distorted treatment.

Klute introduces the notion of family at the beginning of the film and shows how illicit sex has destroyed its unity; Mildred Pierce attempts to take over the place of the father as head of the family, thereby disturbing the balance of the 'normal' family unit; and in *Double Indemnity*, Phyllis Dietrichson has, we learn, already impaired the normal family unit by disposing of and then replacing the wife/mother, before she begins to destroy it by murdering her husband.

Through the operation of the film noir genre and European art film, writes Christine Gledhill, Bree, who is not a conventional *femme fatale* since she is *not* guilty of the family's or the man's destruction, can be saved from her own sexual confusion by Klute. And, writes Pam Cook,

> through an explicit manipulation of genre conventions, by which a hierarchy of discourses is established, suppressing the female discourse in favour of the male; [and by,] on another level, the organisation of the narrative around complicated 'snares' and 'equivocations' [which] increases the desire for a resolution which represents the Truth.

Mildred Pierce is returned to her proper place within patriarchy (i.e., playing out the passage within patriarchal mythology from mother-right to father-right), since she too is innocent (the guilt of excess which she has initiated is carried by Veda), but also because her husband finds his allotted place which she had attempted to take over.

It is interesting to compare the film noir, with its negative or absent family, with melodrama, a genre in which the family and its relations are the focus of ideological representation. While the family melodrama could be seen to deal with the ideological contradictions within patriarchy in terms of sexuality and patriarchal right within the family, the film noir as exemplified by *Double Indemnity* stresses precisely the ordering of sexuality and patriarchal right, the containment of sexual drives with patriarchy as Symbolic Order. Thus there is a sense in which film noir could be seen to close off the ideological contradictions of patriarchy which the family melodrama opens up. Using a framework of psychoanalytic theory, Claire Johnston shows that as the 'fault' in the Symbolic Order, woman must either be found guilty and punished (Barbara Stanwyck/Phyllis Dietrichson) or else restored as good object to her rightful place within patriarchy as a Symbolic Order – within familial relations. Alongside the work of placing woman within patriarchy can be seen the work of repression of homosexuality, considered abnormal and non-masculine – as Richard Dyer describes its operation in *Gilda* – and as narcissistic identification (Neff) with the idealised father (Keyes) – as Claire Johnston discusses it in *Double Indemnity*.

One of the most important theoretical notions in a discussion of the classic text and of film noir is that of *discourse*, and a number of the contributions deal with the question here. It is particularly interesting where there is a discrepancy between one voice and another. For example, in *Mildred Pierce*, as Pam Cook points out, the Truth of the narrative does not reside in what we see and hear but in the Law which provides the missing information necessary to establish Mildred's innocence of the murder. We are torn between Mildred's apparent guilt of an actual crime and clear guilt of a crime against Patriarchy for which she must be made accountable to the Law, represented in the film by the detective, and the Symbolic Order of the Law of Patriarchy, manifested in the narrative structure and the use of lighting codes.

While Pam Cook claims that here the female discourse is totally relocated within the patriarchal order and, therefore, that the film lies *within* patriarchal ideology, my reading of *The Blue Gardenia* intends to show how the film establishes two conflicting discourses in the place of the normal monolithically male one of the traditional film noir. In allowing a space to Nora's discourse, Lang subverts the noir genre, and permits criticism and exposure of male attitudes towards women that the genre assumes. The progressive placing of women is revealed, as is also Nora's passivity in relation to male definitions of her. While in the end Nora herself has not moved beyond her placing in patriarchy, the work of the film has revealed to viewers the way in which men distort women and also offered a warning against too ready acceptance of male ways of seeing.

Richard Dyer, too, by referring to the interplay of genre, character and stars, is concerned, in his discussion of *Gilda*, to show that the female discourse, because of the use of Rita Hayworth and Glenn Ford, and because of the particular conjunction of voice-over and image, manifests itself in spite of the apparent control located in Ford/Johnny's voice-over.

The point about *Gilda*'s use of Rita Hayworth and the character of Gilda herself is similarly made by Janey Place about a number of films noirs. Ultimately, she suggests, what we retain from many of these films is not the repressive treatment of women – in narrative and visual terms – but the strength of the image of the women in the face of textual repression. As she clearly recognises, however, it is important to understand the visual and narrative *work* of the repression of that image of women within film noir if we are to better understand the work of patriarchy and the possibilities for our work as feminists against it.

* * *

I wish to thank especially Sylvia Harvey, without whose initial work this book would not have emerged, and Angie Martin, whose contribution has gone far beyond mere editing. Her thoughtful suggestions and constant support are largely responsible for the success of this project.

1
Klute 1: A Contemporary Film Noir and Feminist Criticism
Christine Gledhill

In the second part of this book I have attempted an analysis of *Klute* – a 'new American cinema'[1] production starring Jane Fonda and supporting a reputedly 'liberated' heroine within a thriller plot structure – in terms of film noir. What my analysis attempts to describe is the ideological effect of the structural interaction between the two apparently contradictory film-making traditions implied in this description. On the one hand the film's modernity and seriousness of theme, linking prostitution, psychotherapy and the problem of woman, places it within a humanist realist tradition of European art cinema. On the other hand, the film's themes are cast within the plot structure and stylistic appeal of the noir thriller – an invocation of this period of the genre characteristic of the 70s – for example, *Chinatown* (Polanski, 1974), *The Long Goodbye* (Altman, 1973), *Farewell My Lovely* (Richards, 1975), *Marlowe* (Bogart, 1969).

As film noir has been largely discussed in terms of a highly elaborated visual style, of baroque stereotypes – among which a particularly virulent form of the *femme fatale* stands out – and of tangibly artificial, often incomprehensible plot structure, the capacity for *Klute* to make claims for the authenticity and progressiveness of what it says about women is worth investigating. Since my analysis is largely descriptive, what I want to do here is reflect on some of the problems such a film poses for feminist film theory. These problems turn on the different ways the critical notions 'realism' and 'genre' have been taken up by ideological analysis both in film theory and feminist criticism.

The real world and fictional production

For much feminist criticism of the cinema – especially that coming from the Women's Movement rather than from a background of film study – the notions of realism and genre are totally opposed. While realism embraces such cultural values as 'real life', 'truth' or 'credibility', genre production holds negative connotations such as 'illusion', 'myth', 'conventionality', 'stereotypes'. The Hollywood genres represent the fictional elaboration of a patriarchal culture which produces macho heroes and a subordinate, demeaning and objectified place for women.[2]

In the first instance then, if feminist criticism is not simply to set generic convention against 'reality', yet at the same time is to avoid a formalism that evades the issue of society with the edict 'films refer to films', the problem it faces is how the operation of such conventions and stereotypes are to be understood in feminist terms – at what level their meanings and ideological effect are located.

At this point two different approaches emerge, the one deriving from a humanist literary tradition, the other arising from a more recent revival of Marxist aesthetics. Criticism deriving from liberal approaches to the humanities tends to treat an art product's fictional structures as providing aesthetic access to the work's truth which is then evaluated in terms of how it illuminates the world. In these terms conventions and stereotypes can be read metaphorically for their immanent meaning. In the second part of my discussion of *Klute*, I see Diane Giddis' analysis of the film[3] as an example of such a metaphoric treatment of genre. However, recent neo-Marxist developments in feminist film theory effectively reverse the values of 'real life' and stereotype, *changing the project of criticism from the discovery of meaning to that of uncovering the means of its production*. This change in direction is set out in Claire Johnston's seminal 'Women's Cinema as Counter-Cinema'[4] and informs much of the writing in this contribution.

In the first instance the aim of this new critical project is greater rigour and demands that closer attention be paid to the specificities of artistic production, and particularly how character is produced by other textual operations such as narration, plot, *mise en scène* etc. But it also implies investigation of a different order of meaning, something I will discuss in more detail shortly.

Behind this new perspective lies a change in the epistemological status of reality and fictional production respectively. In Marxist-feminist terms reality is understood not as phenomenal forms that present themselves to our immediate perceptions but as the historical product of socio-economic forces; it is a social product of which we, as feminists, our knowledge and ideas are an equally constructed part. To understand the real world, then, it is not enough to observe life as it is lived on a day-to-day basis; nor can we call on the values preserved by human civilisation to penetrate phenomenal appearances. What we need is to conceptualise from a feminist standpoint the historical forces at work in the social formation which have produced and are continuing to produce both our material world and those phenomenal forms which appear to constitute reality.

Individual, concrete experience of oppression leads us to resist aspects of our world and provides the motive to interrogate it; but only the developing conceptual framework of feminism will enable us to locate the sources and assess the nature of patriarchy and so formulate the conditions necessary for change. In this sense feminist meaning is not immanent in the world waiting to be revealed. It is a social-sexual dynamic being produced by history.

Thus a change in the status of the real requires a corresponding change in conception of the aesthetic practice which seeks to represent the real. Language and signifying systems in general as part of a socially produced reality are similarly conceived as social products. Language, fiction and film are no longer treated as expressive tools reflecting a transparent reality, or a personal world view, or truths about the human condition; they are seen instead as socially-produced systems for signifying and organising reality, with their own specific histories and structures and so with their own capacity to produce the effects of meaning and values. Thus

21

the 'convincing' character, the 'revealing' episode, or 'realistic' image of the world is not a simple reflection of 'real life', but a highly mediated production of fictional practice.

A critical practice for which meaning is already constituted in the world, stored up in 'the highest achievements of mankind', is clearly dangerous for feminism, which understands such achievements as posited on the oppressive location of woman as the unknowable other, outside history, in the realm of nature and eternal truth, man's mysterious *alter ego* against whom he achieves his definition, and symbolically controls in artistic production. Thus it is arguably more important for feminist film criticism to analyse not what a film means in terms of its 'image of women' – measured against some supposedly objective reality or the critic's personal predilections – but rather those mediations which produce and place that image within the total fictional structure of the film with particular ideological effects.

In other words there are two levels at which meaning can be located: one as revelation read off metaphorically as the immanent content of the film's devices and style – of which I argue Diane Giddis' article is an example – the second as the set of structured effects produced by the dynamic interplay of the various aesthetic, semiotic and semantic processes which constitute the 'work' of the film. The second level of analysis asks, according to the now familiar phrase, not 'what is this film's meaning?', but 'how is its meaning produced?'

Whereas the first approach tends towards the validation of ideology in giving meaning the status of a 'truth', the latter attempts to locate behind the manifest themes of a film a second order of meaning which lies not in thematic coherence but rather in the implications the structural relationships of the text have for the place of woman in patriarchy. In other words the critic does not examine the relation between a narrative device, such as male voice-over, and the heroine for its equivalence to some symbolic meaning, but rather for the way it organises the female image into a patriarchal location. What this shows us is not the expression of a truth individual women can translate in terms of an inner world, but rather an aspect of how patriarchy works. It is under this rubric that I have attempted my analysis of *Klute*.

The second point which emerges from the foregoing is the refusal to conceive of meaning as a static quantity residing inside the art work, waiting to be revealed by the ultimate, 'correct' interpretation. If meaning is a production, then the reader/critic plays a part in this production by bringing to bear on the work her/his own cultural knowledge and ideological perspective. A feminist reading reworks the text and produces meanings that would have been impossible prior to the development of the conceptual framework of feminism.

Within this context of a broad change in feminist film criticism, from the interpretation of immanent meaning to the interrogation of the production of meaning, I want now to look more closely at the way the opposition between realism and genre has been reworked in neo-Marxist feminist aesthetics.

Bourgeois ideology, artistic practice and realism

In much 1970s theoretical work on cultural production,[5] the task of bourgeois ideology in western capitalist society is seen as that of masking those socio-economic contradictions which are the driving force of history – the contradictions between the forces and relations of production and consequent division of the social formation into opposing class interests. The result of such masking is to obscure the fact of society as an interrelated totality grounded on contradiction, and as a historical and social production. In bourgeois ideology the members of the social formation find themselves as isolated individuals who confront over and against them society as a pre-constituted given which appears to derive from nature. The bourgeois concept of the human condition or of human nature thus serves to 'naturalise' and so put beyond human control those socio-economic forces which produce the social formation, and its contradictions. Besides masking the social origins of those contradictions, bourgeois ideology finds means to produce their illusory unification through such notions as the 'common interest'; or fundamentally antagonistic material contradictions are displaced on to idealist contradictions within bourgeois ideology which are amenable to resolution – such as the conflict between love and honour in neo-classical drama.

Having proposed the function of bourgeois ideology it is necessary to ask how this takes place in practice.

Ideology, in much recent cultural analysis, is understood in Althusser's terms as 'a system (with its own logic and rigour) of representations (images, myths, ideas or concepts, depending on the case) endowed with a historical existence and role within a given society'.[6] In other words, the work of masking, unifying or displacing contradiction goes on at one level in the circulation of pre-formed ideas, common-sense understandings, the conventional wisdom of a given social group or society. On another level, according to Althusser's arguments, this conventional wisdom is materialised in the way we live our daily lives. If ideology is to be defined as a system of representations that have a material organisational force in society, the issue for film theory is the role in this of art as a practice specifically developed for the purposes of aesthetic representation and distinct from other forms of signifying practice.

In this context, the notion of a realist practice takes on a sinister aspect. On one level the issue is: what is the epistemological status of the 'reality' that the realist artist represents? Given that the 'representations' of bourgeois ideology attempt to present reality as a phenomenal, unified, naturalised entity to which the individual must adapt, there is clearly an ideological pressure on the artistic producer to identify reality with the *status quo*. On another level, if we grant that this is frequently the case in so-called realist production, our task is to identify in particular realist practices those conventions and devices which serve both to reproduce an ideological sense of reality – masking and naturalising contradiction – and to mask their own work of artistic production. Current film theory has developed an analysis of the so-called classic text constituted in a monolithically conceived realism embracing Hollywood genres, European art cinema and TV naturalism, which claims to demonstrate how this inevitably and always takes place in any attempt to represent reality. In the end the project of representation itself is said to be based on the denial of contradiction.[7]

This is not the place to argue the pros and cons of a potential progressive realist practice – something I feel needs urgently to be done. But what anti-realist theory rightly draws attention to is that traditional humanist criticism, which reads artistic texts in terms of their immanent revelation of the meaning of life and the human condition, is reactionary in that it posits a reality outside the action of social forces and so outside human control and the possibility of change; and that the iconic media of the twentieth century perpetuate this epistemology in the interests of the dominant ideology by promulgating a natural view of themselves as a 'window on the world', or as an expression of human life. It is in these terms that contemporary Hollywood's European look can be approached and similarly its need to take account of the contemporary phenomenon of Women's Liberation.

Ideology, genre and subversion

What has been described above is in a sense the *ideal project* of the dominant ideology in its attempt to turn artistic practice to its own ends. Realist artistic practice clearly can provide ample ground for bourgeois ideology to seed itself in because of the epistemological ambiguity surrounding the concept of 'reality'. However, due to a complex of contradictions in the socio-economic and cultural conditions of the mass media and aesthetic production, the hegemony of the dominant ideology is always in question. Despite the claim that all mainstream production is tainted with realist reaction, genre has been seized on by radical cultural analysts as the ground on which 'progressive' appropriations may be made of bourgeois and patriarchal products. It is here that neo-Marxist aesthetic theory can make use of the specificities of fictional production which get lost in the description of the realist text as a form of production whose aim is precisely to disguise that fact.

The economic rationale of this compromise with the ideological requirements of 'realism' is found in the studio system. The formulaic plots, stereotypes and stylistic conventions of the different genres were developed in response to the needs of a mass industry to predict market demand in order to standardise and so stabilise production. A contradictory demand of the market, however, is for novelty, innovation. So, unlike the concern with artistic exploration of the human condition which became the dominant themes of the European art cinema, Hollywood genre production tended both to foreground convention and stereotypicality in order to gain instant audience recognition of its type – this is a Western, a Gangster, a Woman's Picture, etc. – and to institute a type of aesthetic play among the conventions in order to pose the audience with a question that would keep them coming back – not 'what is going to happen next?' to which they would already have the answer, but 'how?'[8]

Thus genre provides neo-Marxist criticism with suitable territory on which to develop the more progressive possibilities of the notion of fictional production. Behind this approach lies the Russian formalist Victor Shklovsky's theory of 'art as device', in which he proposed that the function of aesthetic form should be to distort or 'make strange' everyday, 'normal' appearances, in order to impede our automatic perception of them, and so return them to our vision anew.[9] For Marxist aesthetics, because the means of artistic production are not simply formal devices any more than they are mere expressive devices, but rather determinate and determining structuring principles, Shklovsky's notion of 'making strange' is located in the contradictions that may arise between the structuring activity of art – which may produce its own effects of meaning – and the ideological themes of its subject matter. This is more likely to happen, however, where form is foregrounded rather than transparent.

In these terms the generic conventions and stereotypes of classic Hollywood can be seen as offering highly formalised and foregrounded sets of codes which can be set into play one against another, or against the grain of the film's thematic material, to expose the contradiction it is the film's project to unify, in a kind of *aesthetic subversion*.[10] Thus a criticism operating according to a perspective at odds with the ideology privileged as the film's 'message' or 'world-view' may be able to animate these effects to produce a progressive reading of an apparently reactionary film, or (as I attempt with *Klute*) an ideological reading of an apparently radical film.

Feminist readings of Hollywood genre

Claire Johnston and Pam Cook[11] have developed progressive feminist readings of this kind for the classic decades of Hollywood in the 40s and 50s – the period of film noir. Possibly this period is particularly amenable to subversive analysis in that what has been called the cinema's recapitulation of the embourgeoisement of the novel had reached the stage of discarding a purely emblematic and heroic mode of characterisation and event and was grappling with contemporary issues and larger themes in the interests of a more mature and demanding realism, but still within the confines of a highly codified studio-based mode of generic production.

For feminists such a formulation has interesting possibilities for analysis of patriarchal ideology in cultural production. The twentieth century has seen an acceleration in the process of the emancipation of women and an intensification of the contradictions surrounding the sexual division of labour and reproduction, so that women perhaps more crucially than before constitute a consciously perceived social problem. At the same time feminists have discerned how women occupy a tangential position in relation to production and culture, and, as guardians of reproduction, or a reserve labour force, or the mythical 'other' against which man takes his definition, are defined as constitutive functions in society rather than among its producers.

In such terms the attempt of much Hollywood production in its classic decades to handle the issue of women as a growing social force can be read as foregrounding the problem of the 'image' of woman not simply as a reflection of an economically constituted problem – the post-war impulse, for instance, to punish the independent female image as a reflex of the economy's need to push women out of production and back into the home – but also as a crisis in the function of that image of defining male identity. Thus the analyses of Pam Cook and Claire Johnston seek to demonstrate how the attempt of the 40s and 50s to produce the independent woman stereotype repeatedly founders against the role of the female image in the fictional and iconic systems of the cinema.

Character, discourse

The *progressive or subversive reading*, which shifts the focus of criticism from the interpretation of immanent meaning to analysis of the means of its production, seeks to locate not the 'image of woman' centred in character, but the woman's voice heard intermittently in the female discourse of the film.[12]

The problem for feminist analysis of the impulse of traditional criticism to locate meaning in character is first that it leads the critic into moralistic assessment of the heroine and her subjectivity in terms of its truth to the actual condition of women, or to supposed female aspiration, or to a feminist perspective on either. The problem with this is that ideological myths about women are as much a part of the real world as any other construct. Thus to use a particular individual's notion of 'the realistic' as a criterion of truth can only lead to disagreement, and if used simply to dismiss what is defined as stereotypical, to the elimination of the chance to examine the power of recognition which certain character structures or stereotypes may invoke.[13]

Second, as I have already suggested, the character becomes the dominant element in the text, the focus of its 'truth' in terms of which all other aesthetic structures are read. Such a procedure ignores the fact of character as a production of these mechanisms and of its structural location within the narrative.[14] As I hope to show in terms of film noir, these structural determinants can be crucial in affecting the degree or otherwise of ideological control over the character. If a positive heroine is to be created, who can speak from and for the woman's point of view, then there has to be a change in the structures of fictional production and these have first to be identified for their patriarchal determinations.

The concept of the *woman's discourse* avoids this collapse of text into character; it is equally valuable in that it cuts across the form/content division and similarly the division fiction/society. A discourse is shared by a socially constituted group of speakers or particular social practice, provides the terms of what can or cannot be said and includes all those items, aesthetic, semantic, ideological, social which can be said to speak for or refer to those whose discourse it is. It is to be distinguished from point of view in that the latter is attached to a particular character or authorial position, while a discourse stretches across the text through a variety of different articulations of which character is only one; it need not be coherent but can be broken by a number of shorter or longer gaps or silences.

A filmic text is composed of a variety of different discourses which may be organised along class, racial or gender lines, to name a few. The structural coherence of the text arises from the interrelations of its discourses while ideological hegemony is gained by the power of the discourse carrying the dominant ideology to place and define the 'truth' of the others. Within patriarchal culture the various discourses that interweave through a specific text are so organised along gender lines as to give priority to the 'male discourse'. One form of subversion that feminists will look for, then, are those moments when in the generic play of convention and stereotype the male discourse loses control and the woman's voice disrupts it, making its assumptions seem 'strange'. From this perspective the question the feminist critic asks is not 'does this image of woman please me or not, do I identify with it or not?'[15] but rather of a particular conjuncture of plot device, character, dialogue or visual style: *what is being said about women here, who is speaking, for whom?'*

Women and film noir

In this context film noir stands out as a phase in the development of the gangster/thriller of particular interest to feminist film criticism, which seeks to make progressive or subversive readings of Hollywood genre films. Film noir is a purely critical term (as opposed to an industrial category of studio production) and interest in the films it designates is itself fairly recent, arising as part of the 60s revaluation of classic Hollywood genres and concern with *mise en scène* as opposed to auteurs and thematic analysis.

Film noir is commonly identified as a particular period in the development of the thriller in the 40s and 50s during which certain highly formalised inflections of plot, character and visual style dominated at the expense of narrative coherence and comprehensible solution of a crime, the usual goal of the thriller/detective film. *Mise en scène* criticism has tended to interpret the aberrant style of film noir metaphorically, as aiming at the production of a certain mood – angst, despair, nihilism – within which are rearticulated perennial myths and motifs such as the deceptive play of appearance and reality, the eternal fascination and destructiveness of the *femme fatale*, the play of salvation and damnation.

However, my analysis, which follows, of the location of women in film noir will not attempt to interpret the genre's themes but rather to identify some of those devices, the effects of which structure, in an intermittent commentary, a discourse about women and sometimes, perhaps subversively, for women.

Five features of film noir

In my viewing experience there are five main structural features of film noir that together produce a specific location for women and somewhat ambiguous ideological effects. These are:

1. The investigative structure of the narrative
2. Plot devices such as voice-over or flashback, or frequently both
3. Proliferation of points of view
4. Frequent unstable characterisation of the heroine
5. An 'expressionist' visual style and emphasis on sexuality in the photographing of women.

Investigative narrative structure

In the mainstream thriller the investigative structure presupposes a male hero in search of the truth about an event that either has already happened or is about to come to completion. This premiss has two consequences. The plots of the thriller/detective story offer a world of action defined in male terms; the locales, situations, iconography, violence are conventions connoting the male sphere. Women in this world tend to split into two categories: there are those who work on the fringes of the underworld and are defined by the male criminal ambience of the thriller – barflies, nightclub singers, expensive mistresses, *femmes fatales*, and ruthless gold-diggers who marry and murder rich old men for their money; and then there are on the outer margins of this world, wives, long-suffering girl-friends, would-be fiancées who are victims of male crime, sometimes the objects of the hero's protection, and often points of vulnerability in his masculine ar-mour. The second consequence is an epistemological one in so far as the investi-gation assumes truth to be a goal attainable by tracing a logical process of cause and effect, and that to every puzzle there is a key through which a complex but co-herent pattern will emerge within seemingly anarchic events.

In the film noir cycle of thrillers both these features are inflected through the intervention of its other defining characteristics. To take the second first: the plots of noir thrillers are frequently impossible to fit together even when the criminal secret is discovered, partly through the interruptions to plot linearity and the breaks and frequent gaps in plot produced by the sometimes multiple use of flash-back, and partly because the processes of detection are for the most part displaced from the centre of the film by other features.

This brings us to the roles of women in the male world of the thriller, and to a kind of dual inflection of these roles, in which the norm of the bourgeois family becomes markedly absent and unattainable, at the same time as the female figure becomes more central in the plot than usual.[16] Frequently the female figure exists as a crucial feature within the dangerous criminal world which the hero struggles with in the course of his investigation, and as often as not constitutes the central problem in the unravelling of truth. Woman becomes the object of the hero's in-vestigation. Thus the place of the female figure in the puzzle which the hero has to solve often displaces solution of the crime as the object of the plot; the pro-cesses of detection – following clues and deductive intellection – are submerged by the hero's relations with the women he meets, and it is the vagaries of this re-lationship that determine the twists and turns of the plot.

Rather than the revelation of socio-economic patterns of political and financial power and corruption which mark the gangster/thriller, film noir probes the se-crets of female sexuality and male desire within patterns of submission and dom-inance. Thus the enquiries of the police or private detective come eventually to concentrate on the state of the hero's, and more frequently, the heroine's, heart.

These inflections set up a conflict in the treatment of women in film noir. On the one hand their image is produced in the course of male investigation and moral judgment. On the other the suppression of the bourgeois family and cen-trality of women in the male world of action produces female representations out-side family definition and dependency. This means that questions of economic survival have to be broached. Two options are available to women – work or living off a man. In film noir both options emphasise the sexual objectification of women, for its criminal ambience situates working women in bars and night-clubs rather than in professions or factories. But sexuality and money are brought into explicit juxtaposition – a contradiction for bourgeois morality in that female sexuality is supposed to be sanctified by love given freely, which is hidden within marriage and the family. Moreover, the heroine often shares the hard-boiled cynicism of the hero, which further undermines conventional sexual ideology. But this does not imply an unambiguously progressive approach in the noir treatment of women, for female sexuality is also juxtaposed within the investigative structure to the law and the voice of male judgment, and in many ways it is the underside of the bourgeois family that is brought to the surface for investigation.

One final feature of the investigatory structure of film noir consequent on its almost consistent use of flashback is that the investigation need not necessarily be carried through the agency of police or private detective, but often takes the form of a confession either to another person (*Out of the Past, Double Indemnity*) or to oneself/the audience (*Detour, The Postman Always Rings Twice*).

Flashback and voice-over

These two plot devices frequently work together in film noir, though their effects seem to remain the same even if they are used separately. The voice-over technique is usually an authoritative mode, either invoking the authority of the nineteenth-century, omniscient story-teller (see *The Magnificent Ambersons*) or pronouncing with a documentary 'voice-of-God' (see *The House on 92nd Street*). However, within an investigative narrative with a flashback – and sometimes multiple flashback – structure, the voice-over loses some of its control over events which are locked in the past and which the investigative or confessional voice-over seeks to unravel.

Two consequences arise from this. First, the story-teller is put on much more of an equal footing with the audience, the temporal separation of the moment of telling and the event told leading to something of a dislocation between sound and image and leaving a gap within which an audience can judge between what they observe and the story-teller's account of it. This aspect is intensified in that the story-teller is often proved wrong by subsequent events and may even be lying (see, for example, *Gilda, Crossfire*). Second, the whole process of story-telling is itself foregrounded in the noir thriller in that the investigation proceeds through a complex web of stories told by the characters to each other or by the narrator to the audience.

Both these consequences are intensified by the fact that the centre of the plot is dominated by questions about female sexuality, and sexual relationships involving patterns of deception, seduction and unrecognised revelations rather than by deductions of criminal activity from a web of clues. An extreme version of the story-telling structure of the film noir narrative is found in *Crossfire*, where three accounts of the same event are given, only one of which is true, and where, in a purely gratuitous scene, a mysterious and unidentified stranger offers to the hero three different versions of his relationship to the bar hostess they are apparently both involved with, without ever confirming which if any of the stories is true.

One way of looking at the plot of the typical film noir is to see it as a struggle between different voices for control over the telling of the story. This feature of the noir thriller is important to feminist criticism and perhaps offers the key to a feminist analysis of this cycle of films.

In film noir the voice-over is generally male – (*Mildred Pierce* is a notable exception and very interesting for this reason, but it also represents an attempt to fuse two genres; the Woman's Film and the noir thriller) – something Molly Haskell sees as the ultimate sexist structure,[17] and it is true that in some versions of the cycle the heroine is almost totally robbed of a speaking voice (see *Laura*, where the possessor of the voice-over, Lydecker, struggles to retain control over his protégée's story against the investigations of the detective, McPhearson, who silences his controlling voice halfway through the film when he reveals the mistake on which Lydecker's version of Laura's story is based). However, the tendency of the flashback structure to put a distance between the narrating voice-over and the story narrated also means that a distance sometimes appears between the expressed male judgment and the woman who is being investigated and judged – leaving room for the audience to experience at least an ambiguous response to the female image and what is said about her. A good example of this is Gilda's strip routine song 'Put the Blame on Mame, Boys' (in the film which is named after her) which is discussed in this monograph by Richard Dyer and Janey Place.

Thus the woman's discourse may realise itself in a heroine's resistance to the male control of her story, in the course of the film's narration. To be clear, this has little to do with a conscious struggle on the part of the film's *characters* but is to do with effects structured in by the interaction of different generic and narrative conventions.

Point of view

Point of view may be a visual or a fictional factor in the cinema. In fiction the term refers to the subjective perspective within which the story and its meaning is being conceived and from which the viewer should ideally interpret it. This perspective may belong to the narrator, more difficult to identify in films than in novels, to the consciousness of a particular character, or it may be divided across several characters. In fiction, where there are several different points of view operating, coherence and harmony are usually maintained by one point of view carrying more weight than the others – often, in the nineteenth-century novel, the omniscient author's.

As was evident in the preceding discussion of voice-over, in film noir there is a proliferation of points of view and a struggle within the text for one viewpoint to gain hegemony. For the image of women in these films this may have a number of different implications. Where a single woman is seen from several viewpoints – either by different characters (*Laura*) or at different moments in time (*Double Indemnity, Out of the Past*), what is produced is a fractured, incoherent image. This is taken up again in terms of characterisation below.

The struggle between different viewpoints may be between men for control of the image (*Laura*) or, more usually in the 40s noir thriller, between the man and the woman (*Gilda*). The generic features of the noir thriller which locate strong women in image-producing roles – nightclub singers, hostesses, models etc. – encourage the creation of heroines whose means of struggle is precisely the manipulation of the image which centuries of female representations have provided.

Thus, though the heroines of film noir, by virtue of male control of the voice-over, flashback structure, are rarely accorded the full subjectivity and fully expressed point of view of psychologically realist fiction, yet their *performance* of the roles accorded them in this form of male story-telling foregrounds the fact of their image as an artifice and suggests another place behind the image where the woman might be. So when in *Double Indemnity*, Phyllis Dietrichson comes to Walter Neff's flat there is at least a sense of discrepancy between his vilification of her duplicity and the power of her sexual appeal to him. In reverse, in *Out of the Past* a similar discrepancy might seem to arise between Jeff's sentimental romanticising of his first meeting with Kathie – 'She walked out of the moonlight' – and her 'playing' of the role.

Characterisation of the heroine

The material for the film noir heroine is drawn from the stereotypes of the *femme fatale* or evil woman and the good–bad girl, and generally contrasted in the film with a marginal female figure representing the good woman, who is worthy of being a wife, and often the victim. But the processes of narration in film noir described above modify this stereotypical material and the conventions of characterisation, particularly in terms of coherence and motivated development. The *femme fatale* is noted for changeability and treachery (see Sternberg's films with Marlene Dietrich). But in the noir thriller, where the male voice-over is not in control of the plot, and on the contrary represents a hero on a quest for truth, not only is the hero frequently not sure whether the woman is honest or a deceiver, but the heroine's characterisation is itself fractured so that it is not evident to the audience whether she fills the stereotype or not.

Rather than a coherent realisation of the unstable, treacherous woman, we tend to find in film noir a series of partial characterisations juxtaposed, not necessarily in continuity but separated by gaps in time (see *Out of the Past*) and often in blunt contradiction with each other. So, for instance, in *The Postman Always Rings Twice* Cora exhibits a remarkable series of unmotivated character switches and roles something as follows: (1) sex-bomb; (2) hardworking, ambitious woman; (3) loving playmate in an adulterous relationship; (4) fearful girl in need of protection; (5) victim of male power; (6) hard, ruthless murderess; (7) mother-to-be; (8) sacrifice to law.[18] Such a mode of characterisation, needless to say, is in marked contrast to the consistent moral trajectory of the male, who, although he may be confused or uncertain as to the relation of appearances and reality, at least maintains a consistency of values.

The ultimate ideological effect of this unstable and fractured characterisation of women depends on the organisation of each particular film. As an aspect of the genre's theatricality such characterisations contribute to the instability and uncertainty of the hero's world, to the ever-deceiving flux of appearance and reality. In this sense they express a male existential anguish at the failure of masculine desire. But in the course of this, noir female characterisations, while they superficially confirm popular stereotypes about women, in their stylisation and play with the surfaces of the cinematic image they arguably foreground some of the

31

features of that image. This is not to claim the progressiveness of the cycle but merely to assert its ideological interest for feminists.

Visual style

The visual style of film noir is commonly seen as its defining characteristic through which its formal excesses carry and submerge the incomprehensibility of plot and contradictoriness of characterisation – or rather turn these features into a further expression of the existential angst carried by the films' 'expressionist' lighting schemes and camera angles.

Within this context the female image is frequently part of this visual environment, just as she is part of the hostile world of the plot in which the hero is enmeshed. The noir heroine frequently emerges from shadows, her harsh white face, photographed without softening filters, part of the abstract lighting schemes. More crucially, of course, she is filmed for her sexuality. Introductory shots, which catch the hero's gaze, frequently place her at an angle above the onlooker, and sexuality is often signalled by a long, elegant leg (*The Postman Always Rings Twice, Double Indemnity, Deadlier Than the Male*). Dress either emphasises sexuality – long besequined sheath dresses – or masculine independence and aggression – square, padded shoulders, bold striped suits.

Film noir – a subversive genre?

From this account of film noir we see that it exists in highly foregrounded generic terms, exhibiting as its principal features conventionalisation, stylisation, theatricality, stereotypicality. As a sub-genre its mode has been described as determinedly anti-realist. To understand what produced this and its significance for women, it would be necessary to analyse the conjuncture of specific aesthetic, cultural and economic forces; on one hand the ongoing production of the private eye/thriller form of detective fiction; on the other the post-war drive to get women out of the workforce and return them to the domestic sphere; and finally the perennial myth of woman as threat to male control of the world and destroyer of male aspiration – forces which in cinematic terms interlock to form what we now think of as the aberrant style and world of film noir. What this means for women is the focusing of a number of contradictions, for the films both challenge the ideological hegemony of the family and in the end locate an oppressive and outcast place for women.

Klute and film noir

The issue, then, that my analysis of *Klute* will try to explore, is the relation between the claims made for the film in terms of a so-called progressive realism, and the potentially subversive elements it might incorporate in its recourse to the generic features of film noir. In fact the 'realism' of *Klute* is derived from a Europeanised Hollywood which, while it seeks stylishness – a certain cinematic elaboration on the surfaces of the contemporary world – also eschews the notion of the conventional, the stereotype, and looks for a contemporary authenticity and psychological truth.

It is perhaps significant that its explicit generic affiliations are to a phase of the thriller that is firmly locked away in history. Their distance in time enables the noir conventions to be used less conventionally and more as metaphor, and so to comply with the aesthetic needs of the European tradition which the film is assimilating. In this respect *Klute* joins other examples of the 70s noir revival such as *Chinatown* or *The Long Goodbye* whose Europeanised mode distinguishes them from the more orthodox line of development of the gangster/thriller into the Clint Eastwood police movie such as *Dirty Harry* or *Magnum Force*.

Such a view of the film's generic affiliation is supported by Alan Pakula's account of his aims:

> At the outset *Klute* has all the characteristics of a forties thriller. For me, starting to direct quite late, the attraction was in using a genre for my own ends; it wasn't pastiche which interested me but, on the contrary, making a contemporary exploration through the slant of a classic form. What's also marvellous about the suspense film is it allows for stylisation or theatricalisation, which is not possible in more simple films like *The Sterile Cuckoo* (*Pookie*).[19]

Thus the conventions, which in the classic film noir affect a structural distortion to plot and character and present a dislocated world, are now used consciously to offer a metaphoric revelation of a modern social and psychic malaise. What I will want to argue in my analysis of the significance of this for women is that, under pressure of the psychologism of the European tradition, the contradictions around woman animated by the dislocated world of film noir are thematically relocated and made amenable to resolution in the name of contemporary authenticity.

Notes

1. For a discussion of this notion, see Steve Neale, 'New Hollywood Cinema', *Screen*, vol. 17, no. 2, Summer 1976, pp. 117–122.
2. For examples of early film criticism close to the Women's Movement and concerned with the opposition of generic stereotype and realism, see the first issues of *Women and Film* (now discontinued). For instance, in the first issue, Christine Mohanna, in her article 'A One-Sided Story: Women in the Movies', poses against the stereotypes of male-dominated mass cinema – mostly Hollywood – individual 'works of art' – mostly European cinema – which support heroines, defined not in 'romantic or sexual terms' but in their own terms, as people. Thus Dreyer's '*The Passion of Joan of Arc*', she says, 'evokes an image of woman so powerful it evades all stereotypes.'
3. Diane Giddis, 'The Divided Woman: Bree Daniel in *Klute*', *Women and Film* vol. 1, nos. 3/4, 1973, pp. 57–61; anthologised in Bill Nichols (ed.), *Movies and Methods* (Berkeley: University of California Press, 1976).
4. Claire Johnston, 'Women's Cinema as Counter-Cinema' in *Notes on Women's Cinema*, Screen Pamphlet No. 2, SEFT, London 1973.
5. The account of bourgeois ideology given here is largely drawn from Stuart Hall, 'Culture, the Media and the "Ideological Effect"', in James Curran et al. (eds), *Mass Communication and Society* (London: Edward Arnold, 1977).
6. Louis Althusser, 'Marxism and Humanism', *For Marx* (Harmondsworth: Penguin, 1969), p. 231.

7. For different examples of the anti-realist polemic, see Paul Willemen, 'On Realism in the Cinema', *Screen*, vol. 13, no. 1, Spring 1972; Colin MacCabe, 'Realism and the Cinema: Notes on some Brechtian Theses', *Screen*, vol. 15, no. 2, Summer 1974; and Peter Wollen, '*Vent d'est*: Counter-Cinema' in *Afterimage* 4, Autumn 1972. For a feminist development of this position, see Eileen McGarry, 'Documentary, Realism and Women's Cinema', *Women and Film*, vol. 2, no. 7, Summer 1975; and *Camera Obscura*, 1, Fall 1976.

8. For seminal accounts of the function of convention and stereotyping in the cinema see Erwin Panofsky, 'Style and Medium in the Moving Pictures', in Daniel Talbot (ed.), *Film: An Anthology* (Berkeley: University of California Press, 1969); Robert Warshow, 'The Gangster as Tragic Hero', *The Immediate Experience* (New York: Atheneum, 1970); and Lawrence Alloway, 'The Iconography of the Movies' in Ian Cameron (ed.), *Movie Reader* (London: November Books, 1972).

9. Victor Shklovsky, 'Art as Technique', in Lee T. Lemon and Marion J. Reis (eds), *Russian Formalist Criticism* (Lincoln: University of Nebraska Press, 1965).

10. For an early elaboration of a theory of ideological subversion in the cinema, see Jean-Louis Comolli and Jean Narboni, 'Cinema/Ideology/Criticism', translated in *Screen*, vol. 12, no. 1, Spring 1971, and reprinted in *Screen Reader*, 1. For a feminist adaptation, see Claire Johnston, 'Women's Cinema as Counter-Cinema' in Claire Johnston (ed.), *Notes on Women's Cinema*, op. cit.

11. See Claire Johnston and Pam Cook's essays in Claire Johnston (ed.), *The Work of Dorothy Arzner: Towards a Feminist Cinema* (London: BFI, 1975); and Pam Cook, '"Exploitation" Films and Feminism', *Screen*, vol. 17, no. 2, Summer 1976.

12. See, for example, Claire Johnston's discussion of Dorothy Arzner in *The Work of Dorothy Arzner*, op. cit.

13. For discussion of the function and value of stereotypes for oppressed groups, see Richard Dyer, 'Stereotyping' in Richard Dyer (ed.), *Gays and Film* (London: BFI, 1977).

14. See Richard Dyer, *Stars: New Edition* (London: BFI, 1998), which includes an account of the star image of Jane Fonda.

15. Julia Lesage comments on Joan Mellen's *Women and their Sexuality in the New Film*: 'Mellen rejects women characters she finds "unpleasant". Thus Chloe in Rohmer's *Chloe in the Afternoon* is "plain, with shaggy, unwashed hair falling in her eyes. Her complexion is sallow and unaided by make-up. Her sloppiness is intensified by a decrepit raincoat without style."', 'Whose Heroines', *Jump Cut*, no. 1, May–June 1974, pp. 22–24.

16. See Chapter 2, by Sylvia Harvey, in this book, 'Woman's Place: The Absent Family of Film Noir'.

17. Molly Haskell, *From Reverence to Rape* (New York: Holt, Rinehart and Winston, 1974), p. 198: 'The guilt for sexual initiative, and faithlessness was projected on to woman; she became the aggressor by male design and in male terms, and as seen by the male in highly subjective narratives, often recounted in the first person and using interior monologue, by which she was deprived of her point of view.'

18. Richard Dyer has analysed in detail the role of Lana Turner as Cora in *The Postman Always Rings Twice* in 'Four Films of Lana Turner', *Movie*, no. 25, Winter 1977/78.

19. Pakula: in 'Entretien avec Alan J. Pakula' by Michel Ciment in *Positif*, no. 36, March 1972, p. 36.

2
Woman's Place: The Absent Family of Film Noir
Sylvia Harvey

The world view generated within the film noir entitles this group of films to be considered as a distinct and separate entity within the history of American film.[1] What this world view reflects is a series of profound changes which, though they are not yet grasped or understood, are shaking the foundations of the established and therefore normal perceptions of the social order. Like an echo chamber, film noir captures and magnifies the rumbles that preceded one of those earthquakes in human history that shift the hidden foundations of a society, and which begin the displacement of its characteristic and dominant systems of values and beliefs. Like the world of Shakespeare's *King Lear*, in which the ingratitude of children towards their parents is at once the cause and effect of an immense disorder within the human universe, film noir offers us again and again examples of abnormal or monstrous behaviour, which defy the patterns established for human social interaction, and which hint at a series of radical and irresolvable contradictions buried deep within the total system of economic and social interactions that constitute the known world.

Despite the presence of most of the conventions of the dominant methods of film-making and story-telling – the impetus towards the resolution of the plot, the diffusion of tension, the circularity of a narrative that resolves all of the problems it encounters, the successful completion of the individual's quest – these methods do not, in the end, create the most significant contours of the cultural map of film noir. The defining contours of this group of films are the product of that which is abnormal and dissonant. And the dissonances, the sense of disorientation and unease, while frequently present at the level of plot and thematic development are, more importantly perhaps, always a function of the visual style of this group of films. Disequilibrium is the product of a style characterised by unbalanced and disturbing frame compositions, strong contrasts of light and dark, the prevalence of shadows and areas of darkness within the frame, the visual tension created by curious camera angles, and so forth. Moreover, in film noir these strained compositions and angles are not merely embellishments or rhetorical flourishes, but form the semantic substance of the film. The visual dissonances that are characteristic of these films are the mark of those ideological contradictions that form the historical context out of which the films are produced.

This principled claim that seeks to establish the importance of style and *mise en scène* as, materially, that which produces meaning in these movies, is not to be adequately followed up in this article.[2] The piece attempts an approach to the problem of defining the contours of this group of films from a different angle.[3] The essay, that is, tries to understand the process whereby the depiction of women in these films, by a complex and circuitous network of mediation, reflects such social changes as the increasing entry of women into the labour market.

It is the representation of the institution of the family, which in so many films serves as the mechanism whereby desire is fulfilled, or at least ideological equilibrium established, that in film noir serves as the vehicle for the expression of frustration. On the thematic level, one of the defining characteristics of film noir is to be found in its treatment of the family and family relations. However, there is another level of analysis beyond that of theme where things are not what they seem at the surface level of narrative and plot. One of the fundamental operations at this concealed level has to do with the non-fulfilment of desire. The way in which this underlying frustration or non-fulfilment is translated into, or expressed at, the thematic level in film noir is through the representation of romantic love relations, the family and family relations.

The repressed presence of intolerable contradictions, and the sense of uncertainty and confusion about the smooth functioning of the social environment, present at the level of style in film noir, can be seen also in the treatment of social institutions at the thematic level, and most notably in the treatment of the family. Moreover, the kinds of tension characteristic of the portrayal of the family in these films suggest the beginnings of an attack on the dominant social values normally expressed through the representation of the family.

In so many of the major and so-called 'non-political' American films, it is the family which has served a crucial function in inserting within the film narrative the established values of competitive, repressive and hierarchical relationships. The presence of the family has served to legitimate and naturalise these values: that is, to present them as the normal, natural and unthought premise for conducting one's life. Moreover, the representation of women has always been linked to this value-generating nexus of the family. The value of women on the market of social exchange has been to a large extent determined by the position of women within the structure of the family. Woman's place in the home determines her position in society, but also serves as a reflection of oppressive social relationships generally. As Engels suggested, within the family 'she is the proletarian, he the bourgeois'.

All movies express social values, or the erosion of these values, through the ways in which they depict both institutions and relations between people. Certain institutions are more revealing of social values and beliefs than others, and the family is perhaps one of the most significant of these institutions. For it is through the particular representations of the family in various movies that we are able to study the processes whereby existing social relations are rendered acceptable and valid.

Through its manifestation of a whole series of customs and beliefs, the family functions as one of the ideological cornerstones of western industrial society. It embodies a range of traditional values: love of family, love of father (father/ruler), love of country, are intertwined concepts, and we may see the family as a microcosm containing within itself all of the patterns of dominance and submission that are characteristic of the larger society.

We might summarise here some of the most important concepts that are dealt with through and in the representation of the family. First, the concepts of reproduction and socialisation: the family is the arena that is sanctified by society for the reproduction and preliminary education of the human race, for the bringing up of children. In the free labour that it requires the mother to perform in raising the child, the family serves to legitimate a whole series of practices that oppress women. Moreover, in its hierarchical structure, with the father as the head, the mother as subservient, and the children as totally dependent, it offers us a legitimating model or metaphor for a hierarchical and authoritarian society. The internal, oppressive, often violent relations within the family present a mirror image of oppressive and violent relations between classes in the larger society.

Second, the family is sanctified as the acceptable location of a sexuality defined in extremely limited terms. Western industrial society has regarded marriage, and hence the family, as the only legitimate arena for the fulfilment of sexual needs, though this legitimacy has been somewhat modified to allow for the double standard, that is, for the separate codes of sexual practice to be adhered to by male and female. What is most interesting is that in general in the movies, as in society, the family at the same time legitimates and *conceals* sexuality. Although marriage is the only place where sexual activity is to be sanctioned, oddly enough (or perhaps it is not so odd) mothers and fathers are seldom represented as sexual partners, especially in those movies of the 40s and 50s when censorship demanded that only bedrooms with separate beds were to be shown on the screen. So that, although married couples – that is, mothers and fathers – are the only ones allowed to engage in erotic activity, these parents or potential parents are normally presented in a totally de-eroticised way.

A final concept dealt with through the representation of the family is that of romantic love. Though so many movies go to extreme lengths to keep the two apart (a function of ideology working overtime to conceal its contradictions), romantic love and the institution of the family are logically and inevitably linked. The logical conclusion to that romantic love which seeks always the passionate and enduring love of a lifetime is the family, which must serve as the point of termination and fulfilment of romance. And if successful romantic love leads inevitably in the direction of the stable institution of marriage, the point about film noir, by contrast, is that it is structured around the destruction or absence of romantic love and the family.

Moreover, since we are engaged in analysing the ideological systems of movies, and not those of novels or newspapers, it is important to note that in film noir it is not only at the level of plot and narrative resolution that lovers are not permitted to live happily ever after,[4] but it is at the additional and perhaps more important level of *mise en scène* or visual style that the physical environment of the lovers (whether created by landscape/set, or by camera angle, framing and lighting) is presented as threatening, disturbing, fragmented.

The ideological significance of lovers living happily ever after lies in the unspoken, and usually invisible, metamorphosis that is implied to take place at the end of every happy ending. By means of this metamorphosis lovers are transformed into fathers and mothers, into families. This magic circle of transformation is broken in film noir which, in presenting family relations as broken, perverted, peripheral or impossible founds itself upon the absence of the family.[5]

In certain ways, the representation of women in this group of films reflects the 'normal' status of women within contemporary social relations. The two most common types of women in film noir are the exciting, childless whores, or the boring, potentially childbearing sweethearts. However, in other respects, the normal representation of women as the founders of families undergoes an interesting displacement. For it is the strange and compelling absence of 'normal' family relations in these films that hints at important shifts in the position of women in American society. Among these changes must be listed the temporary but widespread introduction of women into the American labour force during World War II, and the changing economic and ideological function of the family that parallels the changing structures and goals of an increasingly monopolistic economy. These economic changes forced certain changes in the traditional organisation of the family; and the underlying sense of horror and uncertainty in film noir may be seen, in part, as an indirect response to this forcible assault on traditional family structures and the traditional and conservative values which they embodied. The astounding Mildred Pierce (*Mildred Pierce*, 1945), a woman of the world, a woman of business, and only secondarily a mother, is a good example of this disruption and displacement of the values of family life. The image of Mildred, in a masculine style of dress, holding her account books and looking *away* from her lover, typifies this kind of displacement.

The appearance of the early film noir coincides with the rise and fall of nationalistic ideologies generated by the period of total war. It may be argued that the ideology of national unity which was characteristic of the war period, and which

Mildred Pierce.

tended to gloss over and conceal class divisions, began to falter and decay, to lose its credibility, once the war was over. The encounter with a depressed peacetime economy, with its threat of high prices and rising unemployment, began a process of general disillusionment for many of those returning home after the war, in search of values which they had fought to defend. It is this breakdown also, this erosion of expectations, that finds its way into the film noir by a series of complex transmutations. The hard facts of economic life are transmuted, in these movies, into corresponding moods and feelings. Thus the feelings of loss and alienation expressed by the characters in film noir can be seen as the product both of post-war depression and of the reorganisation of the American economy.

With the increasing size of corporations, the growth of monopolies and the accelerated elimination of small businesses it became increasingly hard for even the petit bourgeoisie to continue to believe in certain dominant myths. Foremost among these was the dream of equality of opportunity in business, and of the God-given right of every man to be his own boss. Increasingly, the petit bourgeoisie were forced into selling their labour and working for the big companies, instead of running their own businesses and working 'for themselves'. It is this factor of being forced to work according to the goals and purposes formulated *by someone else* which accounts in large measure for the feelings of alienation and helplessness in film noir.

It is no accident that Walter Neff in *Double Indemnity* (1944) seeks an escape from the dull routine of the insurance company that he works for, in an affair with the deadly and exotic Phyllis Dietrichson. The possession of Dietrichson, as of any of the other film noir women who function as sexual commodities, is, in the

Scarlet Street.

magic world of the movies, held up as a tempting means of escape from the boredom and frustration of a routinised and alienated existence. Nor is it accidental that Neff, on his way up to his office to make his final confession, encounters the elevator man who tells him that he never could buy medical insurance from the company that he has worked for all of his life, because he has a bad heart. It is this feeling of being lost in a world of corporate values (represented in different films by big business, the police, the mob etc.) that are not sensitive to the needs and desires of the individual, that permeates film noir.

In the world of symbolic searches, exchanges and satisfactions created by these movies, women are accorded the function of an ideological safety valve, but this function is ambivalent. Presented as prizes, desirable objects, they seem to offer a temporary satisfaction to the men of film noir. In the (false) satisfactions that they represent, they might be seen to prevent the mood of despondency and loss, characteristic of these films, from being translated into an understanding and analysis of the conditions that *produce* the sense of alienation and loss. However, the ideological safety valve device that operates in the offering of women as sexual commodities breaks down in probably most of these films, because the women are not, finally, possessed. Walter Neff, in *Double Indemnity*, summarises the position of many of the film noir men when he concludes: 'I didn't get the woman and I didn't get the money.' The same statement would be true for the men of *Scarlet Street* (1945), *They Live By Night* (1949), *Sunset Boulevard* (1950), *The Lady From Shanghai* (1949) and *Gun Crazy* (1949).

One of the recurrent themes of film noir is concerned with the loss of those satisfactions normally obtained through the possession of a wife and the presence of

Woman in the Window.

40

a family, though this theme is manifested in different ways. At the simple level of the organisation of the plot, *Woman in the Window* (1944) is one of the most obvious examples of the multifarious evils that befall a man who is left alone without his family. At the beginning of the film, the wife and children of the professor, who is the central character of the film, depart for a summer vacation, leaving him alone with only the company of his male friends. Left to his own devices he gets involved with a woman whose portrait, displayed in the window of a gallery, has mesmerised him. The woman turns out to be the mistress of another man, and because of his relationship with her the professor is involved in a murder.

As he sits at home, terrified that the police are closing in on him, he is surrounded by the photographs of his family, which seem to reproach him for the life that he is leading while they are absent.

At the end of the movie we discover that these lurid events have been enacted only in the professor's dream. But it is none the less significant that this masochistic dream is triggered by the departure of the protagonist's wife and children. Moreover, in the images of this departure – the family farewells at the station – we are given certain visual clues about the operation of the marriage. The children in the foreground of the scene, engrossed in their comic books, ignore both their mother and father. The father fumbles awkwardly with his hat, the wife, with an extremely restrained gesture, touches him with one hand; both clutch at objects (the hat, the pile of glossy magazines) which prevent them from embracing each other. There is no warmth in the farewell, no hint of the erotic. Even the polished marble floor adds an element of coldness to the scene.

In the world of film noir both men and women seek sexual satisfaction *outside*

Double Indemnity.

The Lady from Shanghai.

marriage. This is true, for example, for the characters of *Woman in the Window*, *Double Indemnity* and *The Lady From Shanghai*. However, a fundamental ideological contradiction rises to the surface in these movies, for the noir lovers are not permitted the socially acceptable practice of quiet 'adultery' (an ideological operation which, like that of prostitution, reconfirms the primacy of monogamy), rather they are required to carry out the violent destruction of the marriage bonds. Paradoxically (and it is through this paradox that the dominant ideology attempts to reassert itself), the destruction of the sanctity of marriage, most notable in *Double Indemnity*, results in placing the relationship of the lovers under such strain, so beyond the boundaries of conventional moral law, that the relationship becomes an impossibility, and transforms itself into the locus of mutual destruction.

In *Double Indemnity* the act of killing the husband serves as the supreme act of violence against family life, and has, in some sense, to be atoned for through the mutual destruction of the lovers in the macabre shoot-out, at the family house, which ends the film. It is perhaps most clear in this movie that the expression of sexuality and the institution of marriage are at odds with one another, and that both pleasure and death lie outside the safe circle of family relations.

Moreover, there is clearly an impetus in film noir to transgress the boundaries of this circle; for the presence of husbands on crutches or in wheelchairs (*Double Indemnity*, *The Lady From Shanghai*) suggests that impotence is somehow a normal component of the married state. Other imagery in these films suggests that a routinised boredom and a sense of stifling entrapment are characteristic of marriage. A large birdcage looms in the foreground of the family home in *Scarlet Street*, separating husband and wife, and the husband hovers uncertainly at the

42

edge of the frame, holding in one hand the paint brushes which signify for him his escape into the fantasy world of his paintings. The family home in *Double Indemnity* is the place where three people who hate each other spend endlessly boring evenings together. The husband does not merely not notice his wife, he ignores her sexually; so that it is only under Neff's gaze that her long legs become the focal point of both the room as Neff sees it and the composition of the frame. While Neff looks at her, the husband looks at the insurance papers which function as his own death warrant, in the sense that they are the device through which the lovers plan to benefit from the large insurance payments on his death. Neff is subsequently caught up in the inescapable cycle of desire, death and retribution.

By contrast, the man in *The Lady From Shanghai*, Michael, does not kill, and does not die, but neither is he satisfied. He watches as husband and wife kill each other, realising at last that she has betrayed him as well as her husband. It is at the end of the movie a condition of the lonely and frustrating freedom of Michael (as well as for the crusading private eye in *The Maltese Falcon*, 1941) that he is not married, that marriage is an impossible state for him. The men of film noir tend to be the chief protagonists, the chief movers of the plot, the locus from which the point of view of the film proceeds, and the central narrative consciousness which retells the events of the past, and controls the unfolding of the tale. However, this dominance is not total. For the 'black widow' women, for example in *Double Indemnity* and *The Lady From Shanghai*, are actively involved in the violent assault on the conventional values of family life.

If many of the films noirs depict a boredom and sterility associated with the married state, others present married couples who create a kind of anti-family. Most obviously, lovers on the run are unable to conform to the normal stereotypes of family or married behaviour. The lovers on the run of *Gun Crazy* and *They Live By Night* are, technically, married; they go through the marriage ceremony. However, their position outside the law does not permit them to function as normal couples acceptable to the dominant ideology. Their marriages function as the nexus of destruction, not as the showcase of desire fulfilled. Even the marriage ceremony has a slightly threatening quality to it in *They Live By Night*. The left foreground of the frame is taken up by the looming figure of the man performing the ceremony; the lovers face the camera in the centre and behind them, seeming to encircle and dominate them, hover the two stern-faced witnesses. Moreover, the man who performs the ceremony appears again later in the film as the one who can most clearly foresee the rapid approach of the tragic end. In refusing with an unexpected honesty to take the money that he is offered to help the young couple across the border into Mexico, he is the one who makes clear to them, at last, the impossibility of their situation and the inevitability of a violent climax.

In *Gun Crazy* the isolation of the couple as well as their nonconformity to certain social norms is emphasised by the way in which they are presented as outsiders to the family and family life. Taking refuge with Bart's family at the end of the film, they so clearly do not belong; they constitute a violent eruption into the ordered patterns of family life. Moreover, as in *They Live By Night*, it is through the organisation of the *mise en scène* that their final doom is foretold. The scene in the deserted railway shack where they plan their final heist is characterised by

They Live by Night.

Sunset Boulevard.

a series of unsettling frame compositions: by such things as the obsessive presence in the composition of a large lamp, which dwarfs the human subjects; or by the blacking out of portions of the screen, caused by the intervention of objects in the foreground. As in *Double Indemnity* and *The Lady From Shanghai*, the relationship of the lovers turns to mutual destructiveness. At the end of *Gun Crazy*, in the terrible dawn scene in the marshes, with the mist rising and the police encircling the couple, Bart shoots his wife in order to stop her from shooting his male friends – the cop and the newspaper man. Destructive passion characterises the central male/female relationship, while the more protective gestures of loving are exchanged, as in *Double Indemnity*, between men.

The sterility, in conventional family terms, of the central male/female relationships in film noir (and often these relationships are unfavourably contrasted with male/male relationships) is further emphasised by the childlessness of the couples. *Sunset Boulevard* offers an interesting example of this emphasis. The absence of the family and the failure of romantic love are central thematic elements. Joe Gillis, by becoming involved in the unsanctified relationship of gigolo (the paid and kept lover) to Norma Desmond, loses whatever chances he might have had of finding a successful romantic relationship. His failure is matched by hers, and the presence of the butler (Stroheim), her ex-husband, now her servant, ministering to her relationships with men like Joe, is a permanent reminder of the failure of romance and marriage in her life. The macabre incident in which the butler and Norma officiate at the nocturnal, candle-lit burial of the chimpanzee which is Norma's substitute for a child, seems to summarise the sterile state of a world which floats adrift from the normalcy of a society normally governed by the institution of marriage and the relations of family life.

The family, within a capitalist economy, has functioned both objectively and subjectively as the locus of women's particular oppression. Its internal relations have *produced* those ideological entities, daughters, wives and mothers, that are so familiar a part of our world. It is the absence of normal family relations (of the network of relationships between mother–father–wife–husband–daughter–son) that forms one of the distinctive parameters of film noir. If we can say that familial *entities* are the ideological fictions called into being by family relations, then the absence of these *relations*, which are by definition normal in capitalist society, creates a vacuum that ideology abhors. This terrible absence of family relations allows for the production of the *seeds* of counter-ideologies. The absence or disfigurement of the family both calls attention to its own lack and to its own deformity, and may be seen to encourage the consideration of alternative institutions for the reproduction of social life. Despite the ritual punishment of acts of transgression, the vitality with which these acts are endowed produces an excess of meaning which cannot finally be contained. Narrative resolutions cannot recuperate their subversive significance.

Notes

1. The film noir period can be taken to coincide approximately with the appearance of *The Maltese Falcon* in 1941 and of *Touch of Evil* in 1958.
2. The polemic for this position, and for the primacy of this method, is developed in Bill Nichols' article, 'Style, Grammar and the Movies', *Film Quarterly*, vol. XXVII, no. 3, Spring 1975, pp. 33–49.
3. The methodological inadequacy of this article lies in its failure to conceptualise the relationship between its own (only partly articulated) method, and the primary hypothesis already postulated, namely that of the primacy of visual style. Moreover, the attempt at analysing ways in which certain structures within the movies reflect certain (changing) structures within the society that is contemporary with the movies is insufficiently theorised.
4. In a few of the films noirs, for example *Pick-up On South Street* (1953), the ending suggests that the lovers are to live happily ever after. However, it can be argued that the mood created and the knowledge produced by the visual style of the film negates or undercuts the apparent happiness of the ending.
5. The notion of a 'structuring absence' is developed by the editors of *Cahiers du cinéma* in their article on 'John Ford's *Young Mr. Lincoln*'; they write:

> What will be attempted here through a re-scansion of these films in a process of active reading, is to make them say what they have to say within what they leave unsaid, to reveal their constituent lacks … they are structuring absences, always displaced … the unsaid included in the said and necessary to its constitution. (*Cahiers du cinéma*, no. 223, 1970, translated in *Screen*, vol. 13, no. 3, Autumn 1972, pp. 5–44 and reprinted in the *Screen Reader*, No. 1, 1978.)

Thanks for practical assistance to David Bradley (UCLA) and the Stills Department at the British Film Institute. Thanks for intellectual stimulus to members of the doctoral seminars in film, UCLA (on the basis of which work this article was originally written in 1975): Ron Abramson, Jacoba Atlas, Joe McInerney, Bill Nichols, Janey Place, Bob Rosen, Eileen Rossi and Alain Silver.

3
Women in Film Noir
Janey Place

The dark lady, the spider woman, the evil seductress who tempts man and brings about his destruction is among the oldest themes of art, literature, mythology and religion in western culture. She is as old as Eve, and as current as today's movies, comic books and dime novels. She and her sister (or *alter ego*), the virgin, the mother, the innocent, the redeemer, form the two poles of female archetypes.

Film noir is a male fantasy, as is most of our art. Thus woman here as else-where is defined by her sexuality: the dark lady has access to it and the virgin does not. That men are not so deterministically delineated in their cultural and artis-tic portrayal is indicative of the phallocentric cultural viewpoint; women are de-fined *in relation to* men, and the centrality of sexuality in this definition is a key to understanding the position of women in our culture. The primary crime the 'liberated' woman is guilty of is refusing to be defined in such a way, and this re-fusal can be perversely seen (in art, or in life) as an attack on men's very exist-ence. Film noir is hardly 'progressive' in these terms – it does not present us with role models who defy their fate and triumph over it. But it does give us one of the few periods of film in which women are active, not static symbols, are intelligent and powerful, if destructively so, and derive power, not weakness, from their sexuality.

Myth

Our popular culture functions as myth for our society: it both expresses and re-produces the ideologies necessary to the existence of the social structure. Mythol-ogy is remarkably responsive to changing needs in the society: in sex roles for example – when it was necessary for women to work in factories during World War II and then necessary to channel them back into the home after the war.[1]

We can look at our historic film heroines to demonstrate these changing atti-tudes: the strong women of 40s films such as Katharine Hepburn and Rosalind Russell (whose strength was none the less often expressed by their willingness to stand *behind* their men in the last reel) were replaced by the sex goddesses (Mar-ilyn Monroe), virtuous wife types (Jane Wyman), and professional virgins (Doris Day) of the 50s as the dominant cultural heroines. This is not to assert that these were the *only* popular movie stars of their times, but by the shift in relative im-

'It is not their inevitable demise we remember but rather their strong, dangerous, and above all, exciting sexuality.' Barbara Stanwyck in Double Indemnity.

portance of an archetype can be observed the corresponding change in the needs of the culture which produced them all.

Myth not only expresses dominant ideologies, it is also responsive to the *repressed* needs of the culture. It gives voice to the unacceptable archetypes as well; the myths of the sexually aggressive woman (or criminal man) first allows sensuous expression of that idea and then destroys it. And by its limited expression, ending in defeat, that unacceptable element is controlled. For example, we can see pornography as expressing unacceptable needs which are created by the culture itself, and allowed limited (degraded) expression to prevent these socially induced tensions from erupting in a more dangerous form.

Two aspects of the portrayal of women in film noir are remarkable. First, the particular mix and versions of the more general archetypes that recur in films noirs; and second the style of that expression. Visually, film noir is fluid, sensual, extraordinarily expressive, making the sexually expressive woman, which is its dominant image of woman, extremely powerful. It is not their inevitable demise we remember but rather their strong, dangerous and, above all, exciting sexuality. In film noir we observe both the social action of myth which damns the sexual woman and all who become enmeshed by her, and a particularly potent stylistic presentation of the sexual strength of woman which man fears. This operation of myth is so highly stylised and conventionalised that the final 'lesson' of the myth often fades into the background and we retain the image of the erotic, strong, unrepressed (if destructive) woman. The style of these films thus overwhelms their conventional narrative content, or interacts with it to produce a remarkably potent image of woman.

This expression of the myth of man's 'right' or need to control women sexually

48

'A particularly potent stylistic presentation of the sexual strength of women which man fears.'
Jane Greer in Out of the Past.

is in contrast to the dominant version of it in 'A' films of the 30s, 40s and 50s, which held that women are so weak and incapable that they need men's 'protection' to survive. In these films, it is the woman who is portrayed benefiting from her dependence on men; in film noir, it is clear that men need to control women's sexuality in order not to be destroyed by it. The dark woman of film noir had something her innocent sister lacked: access to her own sexuality (and thus to men's) and the power that this access unlocked.

Movement and genre

Any claims for film noir's special significance in portraying fear of women (which is both ancient and newly potent, today and during the period which produced film noir) must account for the particularly valid ties between film noir and the cultural obsessions of the United States during the 40s and early 50s. Film noir has been considered a genre, but it has more in common with previous film movements (e.g., German Expressionism, Soviet Socialist Realism, Italian neo-realism) and, in fact, touches every genre. For a consideration of women in film noir, this is more than a semantic dispute. Film movements occur in specific historical periods – at times of national stress and focus of energy. They express a consistency of both thematic and formal elements which makes them particularly expressive of those times, and are uniquely able to express the homogeneous hopes (Soviet Socialist Realism and Italian Neo-Realism) and fears (German Expressionism and film noir) brought to the fore by, for example, the upheaval of war.

The attitudes towards women evidenced in film noir – i.e., fear of loss of stability, identity and security – are reflective of the dominant feelings of the time.

Genres, on the other hand, exist through time: we have had Westerns since the early 1900s and, in spite of rises and falls in their popularity, Westerns are with us today. Genres are characterised more by their subject matter and their iconography than movements, and they can express a wide and changing range of ideologies. The convention of the railroad in the Western, for example, has changed radically from 1924 (*The Iron Horse*) when it symbolised man's hopes for progress, the uniting of the continent, and the building of a peaceful community in the West, to 1972 (Sergio Leone's *Once Upon a Time in the West*), when it was the economic imperative causing exploitation of the poor. Many gangster pictures now champion the criminals, and Westerns depict the West as corrupt and lawless instead of an innocent refuge from corrupt Eastern values and a pure environment in which to build a virtuous society.

Unlike genres, defined by objects and subjects, but like other film movements, film noir is characterised by the remarkably homogeneous visual style with which it cuts across genres: this can be seen in the film noir influence on certain Westerns, melodramas (even musicals) and particularly the detective genre. This style indicates a similarly homogeneous cultural attitude, and is only possible within an isolated time period, in a particular place, in response to a national crisis of some kind.

The characteristics of film noir style, however, are not 'rules' to be enforced,[2] nor are they necessarily the most important aspects of each film in which they appear; and no attempt to fix and categorise films will be very illuminating if it prescribes strict boundaries for a category. This leads to suppression of those elements which do not 'fit', and to exclusion of films which have strong links but equally strong differences from a particular category. Often the most exceptional examples of these films will be exceptional *because* of the deviations from the general 'norms' of the movement.

For example, in the classic film noir, *They Live By Night*, the strain of romanticism is far more important than that of the spider woman, who is in this film a minor character. The 'evil' Mattie who turns Bowie over to the police is even psychologically sympathetic – through love and loyalty to her imprisoned husband she is 'trading' Bowie for him. On the other hand, in as equally central a film, *Kiss Me Deadly*, no one, male or female, enjoys any of the transcending benefits of the romantic aspects of film noir. Only the victims Christina (Cloris Leachman) and Nick (the mechanic) are sympathetic: the rest are doomed only by their own greed. But after acknowledging that *every* film worth discussing is going to be 'exceptional' in *some* way and that their visual styles are going to vary, we can then go on to identify the visual and narrative themes that dominate film noir and influence countless other films made during the 40s and early to mid-50s in the United States.

The detective/thriller genre, whose subjects are generally the lawless underworld, the fringes of society, crimes of passion and of greed, is particularly well suited to the expression of film noir themes. The movement affected other genres: melodrama particularly, but there are Westerns and even musicals that have distinctly noir elements. When the themes of the genre are not conducive to the noir mood, an interesting and confused mix results. *Ramrod* (1947, directed by André de Toth) is one such Western. Veronica Lake plays the typically aggressive, sexual 'dark lady' of film noir who causes the murders; Arleen Whelan is her opposite, the nurturing, stay-at-home good woman. The usual stable moral environment of the typical Western is lacking, and the noir influence is evident in the murky moral confusion of the male characters and in their inability to control the direction of the narrative. *Ramrod* has the open, extreme long shots characteristic of the genre, but the clarity they generally signify is undercut by the noir ambiguity.

The dominant world view expressed in film noir is paranoid, claustrophobic, hopeless, doomed, predetermined by the past, without clear moral or personal identity. Man has been inexplicably uprooted from those values, beliefs and endeavours that offer him meaning and stability, and in the almost exclusively urban landscape of film noir (in pointed contrast to the pastoral, idealised, remembered past) he is struggling for a foothold in a maze of right and wrong. He has no reference points, no moral base from which to confidently operate. Any previous framework is cut loose and morality becomes relative, both externally (the world) and internally (the character and his relations to his work, his friends, his sexuality). Values, like identities, are constantly shifting and must be redefined at every turn. Nothing – especially woman – is stable, nothing is dependable.

The visual style conveys this mood through expressive use of darkness: both real, in predominantly underlit and night-time scenes, and psychologically through shadows and claustrophobic compositions which overwhelm the character in exterior as well as interior settings. Characters (and we in the audience) are given little opportunity to orient themselves to the threatening and shifting shadowy environment. Silhouettes, shadows, mirrors and reflections (generally darker than the reflected person) indicate his lack of both unity and control. They sug-

Expressive use of darkness in Double Indemnity.

'The dark woman is comfortable in the world of cheap dives, shadowy doorways and mysterious settings.' Googie Withers in Night and the City.

The family home in The Big Heat – *in 'contrast to the fringe world'.*

gest a *doppelganger*, a dark ghost, *alter ego* or distorted side of man's personality which will emerge in the dark street at night to destroy him. The sexual, dangerous woman lives in this darkness, and she is the psychological expression of his own internal fears of sexuality, and his need to control and repress it.

The characters and themes of the detective genre are ideal for film noir. The moral and physical chaos is easily expressed in crime: the doomed, tortured souls seem to be at home in the violent, unstable milieu of the underworld. The dark woman is comfortable in the world of cheap dives, shadowy doorways and mysterious settings. The opposite archetype, the woman as redeemer, as agent of integration for the hero into his environment and into himself, is found in the innocent victim who dies for the hero (*The Big Combo*), the longsuffering and faithful lover of the loser hero (*Pick-up on South Street, They Live By Night, Night and the City*) or as a contrast to the fringe world itself (*The Big Heat, On Dangerous Ground, Out of the Past*).

The Spider Woman

The meaning of any film image is a complex function of its visual qualities (composition, angle, lighting, screen size, camera movement, etc.), the content of the image (acting, stars, iconography, etc.), its juxtaposition to surrounding images, and the context of the narrative. Even more broadly, meaning is affected by ever-enlarging contexts, such as the conventions of a particular genre, of film generally, and of the time in which the film is made and in which it is viewed. It would be presumptuous and an impossible undertaking to attempt to establish a 'dictionary' of meanings within a system which is so bound for specific meaning to such complex elements and their interaction. Nevertheless, film noir is a movement, and as such is remarkably stylistically consistent. It thus becomes possible to identify recurrent visual motifs and their general range of meanings. Within these recurrent patterns, some drawn from conventions not specifically filmic, others specific to film generally, and still others to film noir or the detective film genre, the source and operation of the sexual woman's dangerous power is expressed visually.

The following illustrations are all made up of these visual motifs, but the consistent meaning is not necessarily the entire meaning in any single image. A director – consciously or unconsciously – can use a convention against its usual meaning for expressive effect, as for example in *Laura*. The power to incite murder which is visually ascribed to Laura's magnificent portrait is revealed to be a product of the neuroses of the men around her, not of the power she wields. Norma Desmond in *Sunset Boulevard* is the most highly stylised 'spider woman' in all of film noir as she weaves a web to trap and finally destroy her young victim, but even as she visually dominates him, she is presented as caught by the same false value system. The huge house in which she controls camera movement and is constantly centre frame is also a hideous trap which requires from her the maintenance of the myth of her stardom: the contradiction between the reality and the myth pull her apart and finally drive her mad. The complete meaning of any single image is complex and multidimensional, but we can identify motifs whose meaning proceeds initially from common origins.

Gloria Swanson as Norma Desmond in Sunset Boulevard, *emphasises the perverse, decaying side of film noir sexuality, with her claw-like hands, dark glasses and bizarre cigarette holder.*

The source and the operation of the sexual woman's power and its danger to the male character is expressed visually both in the iconography of the image and in the visual style. The iconography is explicitly sexual, and often explicitly violent as well: long hair (blond or dark), make-up, and jewellery. Cigarettes with their wispy trails of smoke can become cues of dark and immoral sensuality, and the iconography of violence (primarily guns) is a specific symbol (as is perhaps the cigarette) of her 'unnatural' phallic power. The *femme fatale* is characterised by her long, lovely legs: our first view of the elusive Velma in *Murder My Sweet* (*Farewell My Lovely*) and of Cora in *The Postman Always Rings Twice* is a significant, appreciative shot of their bare legs, a *directed* glance (so directed in the latter film that the shot begins on her calves, cuts to a shot of her whole body, cuts back to the man looking, then finally back to Lana Turner's turban-wrapped angelic face) from the viewpoint of the male character who is to be seduced. In *Double Indemnity* Phyllis's legs (with a gold anklet significantly bearing her name) dominate Walter's and our own memory of her as the camera follows her descent down the stairs, framing only her spike heels and silk-stockinged calves. Dress – or lack of it – further defines the woman: Phyllis first is viewed in *Double Indemnity* wrapped in a towel, and the sequinned, tight, black gown of the fantasy woman in *Woman in the Window* and the nameless 'dames' of film noir instantly convey the important information about them and their role in the film.

The strength of these women is expressed in the visual style by their dominance in composition, angle, camera movement and lighting.[3] They are overwhelmingly the compositional focus, generally centre frame and/or in the foreground, or

John Garfield and Lana Turner in The Postman Always Rings Twice.

Barbara Stanwyck in Double Indemnity.

pulling focus to them in the background. They control camera movement, seeming to direct the camera (and the hero's gaze, with our own) irresistibly with them as they move. (In contrast, the 'good' women of film noir and many of the seduced, passive men are predominantly static, both within the frame and in their ability to motivate camera movement and composition.) The *femme fatale* ultimately loses physical movement, influence over camera movement, and is often actually or symbolically imprisoned by composition as control over her is exerted and expressed visually: sometimes behind visual bars (*The Maltese Falcon*), sometimes happy in the protection of a lover (*The Big Sleep*), often dead (*Murder My Sweet, Out of the Past, Gun Crazy, Kiss Me Deadly, Double Indemnity*), sometimes symbolically rendered impotent (*Sunset Boulevard*). The ideological operation of the myth (the absolute necessity of controlling the strong, sexual woman) is thus achieved by first demonstrating her dangerous power and its frightening results, then destroying it.

Often the original transgression of the dangerous lady of film noir (unlike the vamp seductress of the 20s) is ambition expressed metaphorically in her freedom of movement and visual dominance. This ambition is inappropriate to her status as a woman, and must be confined. She wants to be the owner of her own nightclub, not the owner's wife (*Night and the City*). She wants to be a star, not a recluse (*Sunset Boulevard*). She wants her husband's insurance money, not her comfortable, middle-class life (*Double Indemnity*). She wants the 'great whatsit', and ends up destroying the world (*Kiss Me Deadly*). She wants independence, and sets off a chain of murders (*Laura*). She wants to win an uninterested lover, and ends up killing him, herself, and two other people (*Angel Face*). She wants money, and suc-

Rita Hayworth in Gilda: *'... self-absorbed narcissism: the woman gazes at her own reflection in the mirror'.*

The attention that Norma Desmond pays to herself, as opposed to the man, is the obvious narrative transgression of Sunset Boulevard.

ceeds only in destroying herself and the man who loves her (*Gun Crazy, The Killers*). She wants freedom from an oppressive relationship, and initiates events that lead to murder (*The Big Combo, The Postman Always Rings Twice*). Whether evil (*Double Indemnity, Gun Crazy, Kiss Me Deadly, Night and the City, The Maltese Falcon, The Postman Always Rings Twice*), or innocent (*Laura, The Big Combo*), her desire for freedom, wealth or independence ignites the forces which threaten the hero.

Independence is her goal, but her nature is fundamentally and irredeemably sexual in film noir. The insistence on combining the two (aggressiveness and sensuality) in a consequently dangerous woman is the central obsession of film noir, and the visual movement which indicates unacceptable activity in film noir women represents the man's own sexuality, which must be repressed and controlled if it is not to destroy him.

The independence which film noir women seek is often visually presented as self-absorbed narcissism: the woman gazes at her own reflection in the mirror, ignoring the man she will use to achieve her goals.[4] This attention to herself instead of the man is the obvious narrative transgression of Norma Desmond whose images – both reflected and pictures – dominate her mansion in *Sunset Boulevard*. She hires Joe Gillis to work on her script for her comeback, and she continues to insist he participate in her life rather than being interested in his. He dreams he is her pet chimp, and he actually becomes a victim of her Salome. Joe finds an acceptable lover in Betty, the young woman who types while he dictates, smells like soap instead of perfume, dreams of *his* career, and is content to be behind the camera instead of in front. Self-interest over devotion to a man is often the original sin of the

'Mirror images ... seen in odd, uncomfortable angles help to create the mood of threat and fear.' The Big Heat.

film noir woman and metaphor for the threat her sexuality represents to him.

Another possible meaning of the many mirror shots in film noir is to indicate women's duplicitous nature. They are visually split, thus not to be trusted. Further, this motif contributes to the murky confusion of film noir: nothing and no one is what it seems. Compositions in which reflections are stronger than the actual woman, or in which mirror images are seen in odd, uncomfortable angles, help to create the mood of threat and fear.

In some films the 'spider women' prove not to be so and are thus redeemed. Gilda and Laura are validated as individuals (Gilda was simply acting out the paranoid fantasies of her true love, Johnny, and Laura was an innocent catalyst for men's idealisations), but the images of sexual power they exhibit are more powerful than the narrative 'explanation'. The image of Gilda we remember is the close-up introduction to her, with long hair tossed back over her head to reveal her beautiful face. Her song, 'Put the Blame on Mame, Boys' (for every natural and economic disaster to hit the world), is ironic, but stripping as she performs, the power she possesses as a sexually alive woman seems almost up to the task. Laura's beautiful, dominating portrait that haunts the characters and determines the action of the film when she is believed dead is the strongest visual image even when she reappears alive.

The framed portrait of a woman is a common motif in film noir. Sometimes it is contrasted with the living woman: in *Night and the City* Helen is a nagging, ambitious, destructive bitch, but her husband gazes longingly at her 'safe' incarnation in the framed portrait – under control, static and powerless. Laura's portrait is compositionally dominating, inciting Mark's fantasies and giving visual expression to Waldo's idealised vision of her, but only when she unexpectedly turns

The image of Gilda we remember.

'Laura's beautiful, dominating portrait that haunts the characters.'

up alive does further trouble ensue as she refuses to conform to the fantasies inspired by the portrait. In *Woman in the Window*, an elderly, respectable professor puts his wife and children on a train and, longing for adventure, dreams a beautiful portrait comes to life and involves him in murder. He is about to take his own life when he wakes up, cured of his longing for adventure. The lesson is obvious: only in a controlled, impotent, powerless form, powerless to move or act, is the sexual woman no threat to the film noir man.

On the rare occasions that the normal world of families, children, homes and domesticity appears in film noir it is either so fragile and ideal that we anxiously anticipate its destruction (*The Big Heat*), or, like the 'good' but boring women who contrast with the exciting, sexy *femme fatales*, it is so dull and constricting that it offers no compelling alternative to the dangerous but exciting life on the fringe.

The nurturing woman

The opposite female archetype is also found in film noir: woman as redeemer. She offers the possibility of integration for the alienated, lost man into the stable world of secure values, roles and identities. She gives love, understanding (or at least forgiveness), asks very little in return (just that he come back to her) and is generally visually passive and static. Often, in order to offer this alternative to the nightmare landscape of film noir, she herself must not be a part of it. She is then linked to the pastoral environment of open spaces, light, and safety characterised

Out of the Past: *Robert Michum as Jeff and Virginia Huston as Ann, who is 'firmly rooted in the pastoral environment'.*

Out of the Past: *Jeff with Kathie (Jane Greer) – 'exciting, criminal, very active and sexy'.*

by even, flat, high-key lighting. Often this is an idealised dream of the past and she exists only in memory, but sometimes this idealisation exists as a real alternative.

Out of the Past is one of the best of the latter type: one woman (Ann) is firmly rooted in the pastoral environment, static, undemanding and rather dull, while the other (Kathie) is exciting, criminal, very active and sexy. In this film the lack of excitement offered by the safe woman is so clearly contrasted with the sensual, passionate appeal of the other that the detective's destruction is inevitable. Kathie appears out of the misty haze of late afternoon in a little Mexican town, walking towards the detective hero as he sits in a bar, waiting for this woman whose image has already been set up for him by the man she shot and ran away from, who wants her back at any cost. They later embrace against the tumultuous sea, a sudden rainstorm, and the dark, rich textures created by low-key lighting.

The independent, active woman is often the primary noir element of noir-influenced films in other genres. In *Ramrod*, a Western, and *Beyond the Forest*, a melodrama, the initial cause of the drama which results in death is a woman who will not 'stay at home' – Connie (Veronica Lake) on her father's ranch and Rosa (Bette Davis) in her small town with her doctor husband. Each woman is characterised sexually as aggressive and dangerous by the iconography and by the results of her actions. But because neither is centrally film noir, in *Ramrod* the quiet, waiting woman gets the man instead of aggressive Connie, and in *Beyond the Forest* Rosa's 'unnatural' ambition is powerful enough to cause only her own destruction. The intersection of the Western and its noir influence is particularly interesting because in Westerns women are generally genre objects representing home and stability rather than actors in the drama. Other examples of noir-influ-

They Live by Night: *Bowie and Keetchie are visually confined by lighting and composition as the outside world makes their love impossible.*

On Dangerous Ground: *'Mary is ... cut off from the corruption of greed, money and power of the urban environment by living in a rural setting.'*

enced Westerns are also characterised by active women and noir visual style: *Johnny Guitar, Rancho Notorious,* and *Forty Guns.*

The redemptive woman often represents or is part of a primal connection with nature and/or with the past, which are safe, static states rather than active, exciting ones, but she can sometimes offer the only transcendence possible in film noir. *They Live By Night* and *On Dangerous Ground* (both directed by Nicholas Ray, 1949 and 1951) are characterised by the darkly romantic element that can exist with the cynical. In the former, the young lovers are doomed, but the possibility of their love transcends and redeems them both, and its failure criticises the urbanised world that will not let them live. Their happiest moments are outdoors in the sunlight, with 'normalcy' an ideal they can never realise because there is no place for them in the corrupt world. Mary (*On Dangerous Ground*) is not only cut off from the corruption of greed, money and power of the urban environment by living in a rural setting, she is further isolated (and purified) by her blindness. She teaches the badly disturbed and violent Jim to feel, and her reliance on him releases him from his emotional prison. Both characters are crippled – he emotionally and she physically – and need each other to achieve the wholeness of health. This interdependence keeps both characters and their relationship exciting, while other 'innocents' of film noir who exist only to contrast with the dangerous woman simply fade into forgetfulness.

* * *

Film noir contains versions of both extremes of the female archetypes, the deadly seductress and the rejuvenating redeemer. Its special significance lies in the combination of sensuality with activity and ambition which characterises the *femme fatale*, and in the mode of control that must be exerted to dominate her. She is not often won over and pacified by love for the hero, as is the strong heroine of the 40s who is significantly less sexual than the film noir woman. Indeed, her strength is emphasised by the general passivity and impotence which characterises the film noir male, making her a far greater threat to him than the career woman of the 40s was, and thus only actual or symbolic destruction is an effective control. Even more significant is the form in which the 'spider woman's' strength and power is expressed: the visual style gives her such freedom of movement and dominance that it is her strength and sensual visual texture that is inevitably printed in our memory, not her ultimate destruction.

The tendency of popular culture to create narratives in which male fears are concretised in sexually aggressive women who must be destroyed is not specific to the 40s to mid-50s in the United States, but is seen today to a degree that might help to account for the sudden popularity of these films on college campuses, on television, and in film retrospectives. But despite their regressive ideological function on a strictly narrative level, a fuller explanation for the current surge of interest in film noir must acknowledge its uniquely sensual visual style which often overwhelms (or at least acts upon) the narrative so compellingly that it stands as the only period in American film in which women are deadly but sexy, exciting and strong.

The stills on pages 64–7 provide further illustrations of the sylistic and iconographical motifs identified in this chapter. They fall into eight groups.

I – 'the iconography is explicitly sexual …: long hair (blond or dark), make-up and jewellery'.

Googie Withers in Night and the City.

Ava Gardner in The Killers.

II – 'Cigarettes with their wispy trails of smoke can become cues of dark and immoral sensuality.'

Jean Peters in Pick-up On South Street.

*III – 'Dress – or lack of it …
defines the woman'.*

Gloria Grahame in The Big
Heat.

*IV – 'the iconography of vi-
olence (primarily guns) is a
specific symbol … of her
"unnatural" phallic power'.*

Gaby Rodgers in Kiss Me
Deadly.

Gloria Grahame in The Big
Heat.

V – 'The framed portrait of a woman is a common motif in film noir'.

Joan Bennett in Woman In The Window.

VI – Mirrors indicate narcissism or duplicity.

Gloria Grahame in The Big Heat.

VII – Women 'are overwhelmingly in the compositional focus, generally centre frame and/or in the foreground or pulling focus to them in the background. They control camera movement, seeming to direct the camera (and the hero's gaze, with our own) irresistibly with them as they move.'

Googie Withers in Night and the City.

Barbara Stanwyck in
Double Indemnity.

VIII – 'The visual style conveys ... mood through ex-
pressive use of darkness:
both real, in predominantly
underlit and night-time
scenes, and psychologically
through shadows and claustrophobic compositions
which overwhelm the char-
acter in the exterior as well
as the interior settings. ...
The sexual, dangerous
woman lives in this dark-
ness.'

Rita Hayworth in Gilda.

Jane Greer in Out of the
Past.

Notes

1. See the contributions to this volume by Sylvia Harvey and Pam Cook.
2. Often it is the films made from Raymond Chandler's novels, or films made by a director such as Fritz Lang, that have the most characteristic visual and narrative themes. Indeed, a film noir made by a strong director such as Nicholas Ray may have more in common with one of his films that is not squarely in the film noir style than with other films noirs.
3. Lighting and chiaroscuro can express the moral relationship between characters; in the still of Phyllis Dietrichson and her stepdaughter from *Double Indemnity* (p. 94) the women are contrasted and morally characterised.
4. See, for example, the still from *Double Indemnity* (p. 93) where Phyllis is putting on her lipstick.

4
Duplicity in *Mildred Pierce*
Pam Cook

We live in a society ruled by the father, in which the place of the mother is suppressed. Motherhood and how to live it, or not to live it, lies at the roots of the dilemma. (Laura Mulvey, 'Riddles of the Sphinx: a film by Laura Mulvey and Peter Wollen', *Screen*, vol. 18, no. 2, Summer 1977.)

To write about *Mildred Pierce* (Michael Curtiz, 1945) as an example of film noir poses more problems than are immediately apparent. In spite of the fact that several articles about the film[1] place it as typical of the 1940s genre characterised by a prevailing mood of pessimism and paranoia, a visual style dependent upon 'expressionist' lighting and décor, systematic use of geometric patterns of light and shadow, distortion produced through camera angles and wide-angle lenses and a convoluted organisation of narrative, *Mildred Pierce* does not fit easily into the self-contained, homogeneous world created by those formal strategies now accepted as characteristic of film noir.[2]

The difficulties of establishing and maintaining the boundaries of genre are obvious. Elements of film noir can be found in films as far removed in time and place as *Pursued* (Raoul Walsh, 1947), *Vampyr* (Carl Dreyer, 1932) and *Nostalgia* (Hollis Frampton, 1971). It is not the intention of this article to discuss *Mildred Pierce* in terms of the representation of women in film noir, nor to try to prove that the film is not a good example of film noir. I would claim instead that the film deals explicitly with questions of genre as part of its project, that the ideological work of the film is to articulate the necessity for the drawing of boundaries and to encourage the acceptance of the repression which the establishment of such an order entails. *Mildred Pierce* is interesting for the ways in which it signifies its problematic: the historical need to reconstruct an economy based on a division of labour by which men command the means of production and women remain within the family, in other words the need to reconstruct a failing patriarchal order. This reconstruction work is problematic precisely because it is based on the brutal and enforced repression of female sexuality, and the institutionalisation of a social place for both men (as fathers and husbands) and women (as mothers and wives) which rests uneasily on this repression, aware of the continual possibility of the eruption into the present of the submerged past.

On one level this work of repression is signified through an explicit manipulation of genre conventions, by which a hierarchy of discourses is established, suppressing the female discourse in favour of the male; on another level, by the organisation of the narrative around complicated 'snares' and 'equivocations' to increase the desire for a resolution which represents the Truth, whatever the cost. On every level the film works on audience expectation and response in order to produce audience subject positions based on defence, and elements of these positions are necessarily retained, even in the face of the re-establishment of Order and Truth, thus emphasising the need for work, sacrifice and suffering in the process of reconstruction. The aim of this article is to suggest some of the ways in which *Mildred Pierce* articulates this problematic, avoiding if possible the idea that the film simply reflects the historical needs of post-war America. The drama of the institution of the patriarchal order, the familiar Oedipal story, is enacted and re-enacted throughout history in many and various forms; in the context of the transition to a post-war economy, an impaired masculine population, the disintegration of the family unit and the increased economic and sexual independence of women, the Oedipal structure is threatened: the system which gives men and women their place in society must be reconstructed by a more explicit work of repression, and the necessity for this repression must be established unequivocally, by resolving equivocation. The ideological work of the film then is the way in which it articulates its project, encouraging certain subject positions rather than others, signifying a problem which is not only specific to *Mildred Pierce* itself, and the conditions in which it was produced, but also general in so far as the institution of patriarchy is a historical problem.

The extent of the problem of the institution of patriarchy is indicated in the work of J. J. Bachofen[3] who, in his scholarly and imaginative study of ancient myths and symbolism, traces the historical transition from mother-right to father-right, a transition articulated by a number of myths of which the Oedipus story is only one. From his studies Bachofen insists that there is universal evidence for the historical existence of a matriarchal society which preceded our patriarchal system, a claim which has brought his ideas into question.[4] Nevertheless, his work remains fascinating for its revelation of the extent to which the idea of a society based on mother-right persists in mythology, a society which was forcibly overturned in the transition to a 'higher' form of civilisation: patriarchy. I would argue that *Mildred Pierce* draws extensively on this mythology, and on the symbolism which Bachofen identifies as specific to the myth: that the project of the film is to re-present the violent overthrow of mother-right in favour of father-right[5] through the symbolic use of film lighting and the organisation of its narrative structure.

In an interesting article on *Mildred Pierce*,[6] Joyce Nelson discusses the film in terms of its narrative structure, drawing attention to the device of the 'false suture'[7] used to structure audience response, to lead the audience to concentrate on the need to resolve the enigma rather than to speculate on the possibility of alternative readings. The 'false suture' involves the masking, through the work of other filmic and cinematic codes, of the exclusion of a reverse-shot in order to create an enigma which the film will answer for the viewer, later, in the final flashback, when the missing shot is reinserted and the truth about the murder is revealed.

Nelson points out an apparently obvious fact, which is nevertheless not always mentioned in discussions of the film as film noir: the scenes which take place in the present are significantly more suggestive of film noir than are the two segments comprising Mildred's version of her own story. She goes on to show that

Mildred's discourse is markedly different from the framing discourse of the detective, in that he is simply concerned with establishing the Truth, with resolving the enigma, while Mildred's story contains complexity and ambiguity, showing a concern for feelings rather than facts. The detective's discourse is directed towards cleaning up the past, and this involves the invalidation of Mildred's version of the story, in terms of form *and* content. At the end of the second flashback the detective reveals that he knew the truth all the time, that Mildred was 'only the key'. This initiates the final flashback in which the enigma is resolved, shot almost entirely in noir style (see below).

Nelson goes on to discuss the representation in the film of the relationship of similarity between Veda and Mildred, suggesting that the film asks us, through the device of metaphorical substitution, to confuse the wicked Veda with the honest Mildred, thus establishing Mildred's innate guilt, even though she is not guilty of the actual murder.

I find Joyce Nelson's reading of *Mildred Pierce* interesting because it uses a theoretical approach which assumes that the ideological work of the film lies in its structure, and in the structures in which it engages its audience. Although I disagree with some of her conclusions, this reading offers some useful insights into *Mildred Pierce* which I should like to use as a starting point for my own discussion of the film, and develop a little further. I shall draw on the structure of the film itself, its use of narrative and filmic codes of lighting, but also on those non-cinematic elements already indicated: the mythology outlined by Bachofen, and the sexual structure of the Oedipus complex appropriated from mythology by Freud. What follows is not intended to be a textual analysis; rather, I am trying to suggest a way of reading the film which opens up the question of the working of patriarchal ideology and the place it holds for women and men, and the implications of this question for sexual politics as well as for feminist film criticism.

Mildred Pierce and genre

As I indicated in my opening paragraph, the film does not fit easily into the category of film noir. Although the opening and closing sequences, and two short interruptions during the film, are shot in 'classic' noir style, the first two long flashback sequences in which Mildred tells the story of her past are significantly different, more evenly lit, few variations in camera angle, etc., except towards the end of the second flashback when Mildred realises that Monty has betrayed her and she 'confesses' to the murder, when noir *mise en scène* takes over Mildred's discourse as well. The first flashback sequences are also concerned with different subject matter: the family, sexual and emotional relationships, property, work and investment. Mildred's discourse is the discourse of melodrama, her story is the stuff of which the 'Woman's Picture' was made in the pre-war and war years when women were seen to have an active part to play in society and the problems of passion, desire and emotional excess articulated by melodrama[8] could be tolerated. The difference between the two forms of discourse (Mildred's story and the framing noir discourse) is marked enough for some account of the function of this marking to be necessary.

It seems that a basic split is created in the film between melodrama and film noir, between 'Woman's Picture' and 'Man's Film', a split which indicates the presence of two 'voices', female and male, which in itself is a mark of excess since 'classic' film is generally characterised by the dominance of a metadiscourse, which represents the Truth. *Mildred Pierce* is constituted as a sexually ambiguous film, an ambiguity founded on duplicity which is eventually resolved by the reassertion of the patriarchal metadiscourse. In the process of resolution, melodrama, Mildred's point of view, is displaced by film noir (in which female discourse is suppressed but remains in the form of threatening shadows and man-killing Amazonian women), when in the final flashback narrative and lighting codes combine with extreme camera angles and music to connote imminent chaos, and the truth about Monty's murder is revealed. The consequences of the retreat from patriarchy are represented as the complete upheaval of social order leading to betrayal and death, in the face of which the reconstitution of the patriarchal order is seen to be a necessary defence.

The question of the retreat from patriarchy brings me to Bachofen's theory of the relationship between mother-right and father-right. From his study of myth he establishes two basic cultural levels: a primitive level of swamp generation where the union of water and land brings about birth which swiftly becomes death and returns to the land. This level is telluric, associated with sexual promiscuity and characterised as female. The second level is luminous and transcendent, associated with light and the sun, a higher intellectual and spiritual level, characterised as male. The second (patriarchal) level is the one to which all human life aspires, and therefore the more primitive level (called hetaerism by Bachofen) must constantly be overcome. The schema is more complex than this, taking in various stages between the two levels. Demetrian matriarchy, for instance, occupies a position midway between hetaerism and patriarchy, and is therefore an area of struggle since it stands in opposition both to the excesses of hetaerism and to the institution of patriarchy, which signals the loss of matriarchal rights and privileges. In the transition from mother-right to father-right there is a further stage: the Dionysian, which heralds the founding of patriarchy, undermining the Demetrian principle by an alliance with hetaerism and a return to the sensual frenzy of a more primitive era, characterised as an era of sexual freedom in which women are held in common by men. Against the abuse of women's bodies which hetaerism implies the man-killing Amazon arises, yet another stage in the transition to patriarchy.

Bachofen isolates a symbolic grid which supports the basic division between female (matriarchal)/male (patriarchal), a shortened version of which could be set out as follows:

Female	Male
Tellurian	Uranian
Material/Corporeal	Spiritual/Intellectual
Night	Day
Dark	Light
Passive	Active
Left	Right
Mass solidarity	Individuality
Womb	Phallus

It is not arbitrary to apply Bachofen's schema of the struggle between mother-right and father-right to *Mildred Pierce*. Apart from the film's thematic concern with a mother who attempts to gain control of family and business, the classic struggle between Mother and Father, and its 'inevitable' resolution is multiply coded in the film in the narrative organisation and the symbolic use of film lighting.

Film noir

In accordance with Bachofen's schema the contrast dark/light in the film noir sections of *Mildred Pierce* is taken to connote sexual ambiguity: the presence of male and female in the text, the struggle between two symbolic orders. In film noir generally, the protagonist, usually male, moves unhappily through this world of sexual ambiguity (against which his paranoia is a defence) until it is resolved, either by his own death at the hands of the Father, or by his taking over from the Father as the agent of death. Although there are exceptions, women who are represented as the agents of death usually turn out to be only instruments when the duplicity is resolved by the narrative. It is unusual for film noir to have a female protagonist narrating her own story; in *Mildred Pierce* Mildred's story is revealed as duplicitous, thus foregrounding the work of repression involved in narrative resolution.

As already indicated, the noir sections of the film are situated in the present, a present therefore characterised by violence and death, uncertainty and duplicity. Duplicity is underlined in the text of the film by the use of contrasting light and shadow and by the use of a 'snare' in the narrative: the exclusion of the reverse shot which would reveal the true murderer encourages the audience to believe that Mildred is the murderer/agent of death, especially when, in true noir heroine style, she proceeds to set Wally Fay up as the murderer, apparently to protect herself, using her sexuality as bait. 'You make me shiver, Mildred,' says Wally, reinforcing the belief that it is Mildred who is the location of duplicity.

Later, at the police station, the brisk, orderly atmosphere makes Mildred nervous as she waits to be questioned: again she is seen as the location of uncertainty, this time in the face of the Law which will tolerate no uncertainty or ambiguity.

The first flashback ends at the point where Mildred is at the height of her economic success and Bert gives her the divorce she wanted. We return to the present in the police station, and the lighting (shadows) on Mildred's face suggest her guilt in the present when she has just been seen as successful in her own right in the past. The function of this interruption seems to be to encourage the audience to anticipate the fate of independent successful career women, and to force a separation or distance between audience and any sympathy or identification with Mildred's success. Towards the end of the second flashback, when Mildred's story draws to its (false) conclusion and closer to present time (when the murder takes place), deceit and betrayal, represented by Wally, Veda and Monty are rife, and Mildred has lost everything that was dear to her. Film noir conventions invade Mildred's discourse and she confesses to the murder.

Mildred's confession does not introduce any contradiction into her discourse. On the contrary, it allows her to insert herself into the present as a woman still in control of her destiny, with the power of death over the men who betray her. In the face of this assertion of power, based on duplicity, since Mildred is not the real murderer, the detective's response is to remove all possibility of duplicity by invalidating Mildred's confession. He reveals the truth, which he knew all the time anyway, confronting Mildred with Veda, who confesses, believing that Mildred has betrayed her, and is taken away from Mildred into the custody of the Law.

In this final cleaning-up process all power is seen to return into the hands of the Law. The paternalistic detective, who has secretly always controlled the progress of the narrative because of his foreknowledge of the truth, dispels duplicity by throwing light upon the scene: his assertion of the Truth is supported symbolically when he opens the blinds to let in the dawn – light is the masculine principle which heralds the dawn of patriarchal culture and the defeat of matriarchy. This defeat is accomplished by the forcible and final separation of Mildred and Veda, thus making it possible for Mildred to live with Bert in a 'normal' couple relationship. She is returned to point zero, completely stripped, rehabilitated. To understand why such violent repression had to be seen to be necessary it is important to look at the use of melodrama in the film.

Melodrama

The melodramatic sections of the film are set in the past, Mildred's own account of her history in terms of her rejection of her class (represented by Bert, who is critical of Mildred's petit bourgeois aspirations, but is down on his luck, unemployed, his masculinity impaired) and her rejection of the patriarchal symbolic order (she expels Bert from the family and rejects Wally Fay as a substitute, taking over the place of father/provider herself). The crucial question quoted at this point is, of course, 'Has Mildred the right to rule the family?' At first the answer seems to be positive: she is strong, hard-working, honest and single-minded, not to mention ambitious. She seems to possess precisely those characteristics lacking in the men. Mildred attempts to return to the Demetrian stage of matriarchy in which women command home and state, represented here by her family and her restaurant business. However, her retreat from patriarchy leads 'inevitably' through the cause and effect of narrative to the primitive stage of hetaerism and the deterioration of all social order, represented by Veda and Monty, whose relationship implies the Dionysian stage characterised by Bachofen as heralding the coming of patriarchy.

The first sign of deterioration comes when Mildred's one night of illicit passion with Monty is followed by Kay's death. The loss of one daughter strengthens Mildred's obsession with Veda, and with making a success of her business, in the course of which she forms a relationship of mutual solidarity with her friend Ida who helps her to run the business, while men (Wally and Monty) are relegated to the secondary status of instruments.

In the second flashback deterioration sets in, revolving around Veda's problem with finding a sexual identity, since she has no father, and a mother who is also a father. Sexual ambiguity is compounded by Veda's sexual blackmail of the Forrester family (aided by Wally), and the implication of a sexual relationship between Veda and Monty. Veda and Mildred separate after a confrontation, but Mildred cannot live without Veda, and finally marries Monty in order to get her back. While Veda and Monty enjoy themselves at a party, Mildred discovers that she has lost her business because Monty and Wally have done a deal without telling her. When she discovers that Veda and Monty have gone to the beach house together she follows them with the gun. At this point Mildred confesses to the murder of Monty.

Mildred's take-over of the place of the father has brought about the collapse of all social and moral order in her world: Monty and Veda are on the point of breaking the ultimate taboo: that against father incest. In the face of impending chaos and confusion the patriarchal order is called upon to reassert itself and take the Law back into its own hands, divesting women completely of any power they may have gained while the patriarchal order was temporarily impaired. This involves establishing the truth without a doubt, restoring 'normal' sexual relationships and reconstituting the family unit, in spite of the pain and suffering which such repressive action must cause. Pain and suffering are a necessary part of the work of reconstruction (represented by Bert, who has earned his right to take the place of the father again through suffering and self-sacrifice).

The split between melodrama and film noir is overcome by the force of the Law, and Bert and Mildred walk into the dawn together, reconstituted as a couple, the image bearing the marks of repression in the form of another couple from the past: two women who work together, this time to support the patriarchal institution by scrubbing the steps of the police station. They remain as a reminder of the consequences which would ensure should 'illicit' or ambiguous couplings become a possibility again.

The 'snare'

Barthes has emphasised the importance of *delay* to the unfolding of narrative.[9] In *S/Z* he isolates several forms of 'reticence' which are used to hold back the resolution of the enigma. The 'snare' is identified as a deliberate evasion of the Truth.

The act of involvement in 'classic' narrative is for the reader/viewer an act based on misrecognition. The reader suspends knowledge of the Truth for the required length of time: 'I know, but …'. Pleasure is generated by the possibility of the return of infantile wishes and phantasies repressed by the passing through the Oedipus complex. In the 'classic' narrative knowledge is suspended for a limited amount of time and Truth is re-established at the end through the resolution of the enigma: thus 'classic' narrative re-enacts the Oedipal drama itself: the passage from misrecognition (the pre-Oedipal stage of bisexuality when both male and female are thought to possess a penis and the mother is the love-object of both male and female children) to knowledge (the discovery of the fact of castration through sight of the mother's body without a penis, at which point boys must identify with the father, who has the power of castration, and give up (temporarily) their desire for the mother, and girls must identify with the mother in her (already) castrated state, also giving up their desire for her. Thus boys and girls become 'sexed' human beings, relinquishing bisexuality in favour of the choice of a love-object from the

opposite sex). 'Classic' narrative affirms this heterosexual structure, the mainstay of the family unit and of social reproduction, again and again.

Bachofen's description of the transition from mother-right to father-right corresponds in many ways to Freud's Oedipus complex, since the transition rests on the suppression of motherhood and the constant struggle of patriarchy to resist the return of an earlier matriarchal symbolic order characterised by greater sexual freedom and democracy.

In *Mildred Pierce* the Oedipal drama is re-enacted in an explicitly repressive form, since the 'snare', the deliberate withholding of the reverse-shot, which is the basis for the audience's 'misrecognition' of Mildred as an agent of death, is reinforced on several levels in the film, and the knowledge that Mildred is not the murderer is withheld from the viewer, so that the resolution of the enigma, the progress to 'knowledge', rests entirely with the detective as the representative of the Law.

As Monty dies, whispering 'Mildred', the next shot shows a car drawing away from the beach house, in long-shot so that we cannot see who is driving. A dissolve leads us into a shot of Mildred walking on the pier in a suicidal state. Film noir lighting suggests duplicity: an unknown threat which might emerge from the shadows. Joan Crawford, who plays Mildred, is an ambiguous sexual figure as a star with a history of playing 'independent women' roles, emphasised in this scene by the broad shoulders of her coat. The fundamental misrecognition has been established as we are led to believe that Mildred is the murderer, that she has exercised the power of life and death which only the Father holds.

The 'snare' is compounded further when, in the following sequence, Mildred attempts to set Wally up for the murder, since we assume from what we 'know' so far that she is protecting herself from discovery. It is probable that she is the un-castrated mother, and the spectator is invited to enter into a pre-Oedipal phantasy, a recollection of a repressed, but not forgotten, time when much more sexual freedom was possible. At the same time, the phantasy is represented as increasingly threatening, encouraging the spectator to take up a defensive position and to wish for the resolution of ambiguity, to put an end to feelings of anxiety.[10]

The function of the first flashback is to articulate the phantasy by recreating the circumstances in which Mildred denies her own castration by taking over as head of the family, and building up her own business. She invades the territory of men: that of property and investment, and after Kay's death rejects men as sexual partners, becoming obsessed with Veda and her work. Her relationship with Veda,[11] coupled with her close friendship with Ida (played by Eve Arden, another actress who is an ambiguous sexual figure), represents an attempt to return to the pre-Oedipal bisexual state, a regression from patriarchy. This regression includes the men too, who are represented as weak and dissipated, untrustworthy, except for Bert, who grows to maturity during the film.

Veda represents the consequences of this retreat from patriarchy. Her close physical resemblance to Mildred emphasises her function as a 'double', created by Mildred as a defence against castration.[12] She is, however, all the things that Mildred is not: deceitful, promiscuous, greedy and hysterical; she represents the threat of chaos, the excess which Mildred's discourse calls into being and which it cannot resolve.

The threat of chaos extends to the world of business as well. The evasion of the patriarchal law produces a situation in which nothing is stable, since business relationships are closely tied to sexual relationships in the film, and Mildred's business rests on the goodwill of her two partners, Wally and Monty, both less than reliable. These are hardly the best circumstances in which to rebuild an economy; in order to create a stable economic situation suitable for investment, sexual order must be re-established, excess and ambiguity must be resolved through a 'necessary' repression.

In her false confession Mildred claims to have resolved the excess herself by killing Monty. As I have already suggested, however, if Mildred had killed Monty this would perpetuate the situation in which the mother is seen to have the power of life and death, in this case explicitly the power to enforce the taboo against incest. The situation of unresolved excess would remain, since Veda would go free.

The resolution of excess is achieved when the detective invalidates Mildred's confession, revealing that he knew the true murderer all the time. The existence of the 'snare' is made explicit, thus putting Mildred *and* the audience in the same position, at the mercy of the Law.[13] The resolution is articulated by the scene in which Veda confesses, believing that Mildred has betrayed her, and mother and daughter are separated for ever – Veda, the representative of excess, being removed for imprisonment or death. The final flashback, the 'true' story of the murder, confirms the resolution: when Mildred comes to the point of killing Monty she is incapable of doing so. Veda, however, is not, and kills Monty (surrogate father) in a frenzy of libidinal excess. The final flashback is shot in 'classic' noir style: it is not until Mildred and Bert are finally reunited under the aegis of the Law that ambiguity is resolved and the shadows dispersed by the light of the new day.

The body of the film[14]

I have tried to show that the problematic articulated by the film *Mildred Pierce* is one of uncertainty and duplicity, centred on Mildred's body as the location of sexual ambiguity, and the return of an infantile phantasy about the body of the mother, a phantasy which allows for a potentially more democratic structure of sexual relationships based on bisexuality, a structure repressed by the heterosex-

Mildred as the location of duplicity.

Veda: the sign of excess.

ual division which the Oedipus complex attempts to enforce. The problematic is signified on one level by the relationship between Veda and Mildred: Veda is seen as a part of Mildred's body, an extension of herself, the phallus she will not relinquish. 'Veda is a part of me', Mildred says to Ida at one point, and publicity photographs of the film inevitably show Mildred holding Veda (and sometimes Kay as well) close to her.

I have tried to indicate that this phantasy of the mother's body, with its connotations of sexual excess and the erosion of the patriarchal order, cannot be tolerated by the film, and is resolved by a brutal act of repression in which Mildred is castrated, not only through the invalidation of her discourse, but by her enforced separation from Veda (which allows for no possibility of emotional reconciliation) which amounts to an act of mutilation perpetrated by the police on Mildred's body.

I should like to suggest some ways in which I think an analogy is drawn between the 'body' of the film, its material structure, and Mildred's body as the location of duplicity.

The 'snare' utilised in the opening section serves a double function: it omits something (a reverse-shot), and then proceeds to mask the omission by the use of a long-shot of the car driving off, and a dissolve to Mildred on the pier. There is an absence, or lack, in the film which the film itself masks in the same way as Mildred masks her own 'lack'.

Masking also takes place on the level of *mise en scène*, in the use of film noir conventions of lighting: sharp contrasts of light and shadow suggest partial truth; something is missing, but whatever it is remains hidden. Since the enjoyment of the phantasy rests on the temporary masking of the truth, the insertion of the film noir segments into the structure of the film both reinforces the phantasy and reminds the spectator that something is to be revealed.

The use of even lighting and more classic shot compositions in Mildred's discourse indicate a plenitude, a situation in which nothing is missing and which belongs to the past, as the mother's body represented plenitude for the child in the pre-Oedipal situation. Again, the interruptions by the film noir segments serve both to confirm the ambiguity upon which the phantasy of plenitude is based, and to remind us that something is hidden. The presence of two markedly different styles of film genre underlines the sexual ambiguity in the structure of the film itself, since each genre is specifically associated with a different audience and market: melodrama with women and film noir with men.

What is hidden in the body of the film is eventually revealed as the presence of the father as agent of the Law, represented by the detective, who was actually in control of the structure of the film all the time, who unmasks the gap and then proceeds to fill it with the missing reverse-shot, thus revealing the 'lack' in the mother's body (the body of the film), into which he inserts his own discourse, the Truth. The enigma is resolved by dispelling ambiguity in favour of patriarchy and a symbolic order based on heterosexuality which it implies, explicitly suppressing matriarchy and reconstituting Bert and Mildred as a 'normal' heterosexual couple.

As Mildred and Bert walk off into the light of the new dawn from which all shadow and duplicity has been erased, they turn their backs on another couple, two women in the classic position of oppression, on their knees: an image of sacrifice which closes the film with a reminder of what women must give up for the sake of the patriarchal order.[15]

Notes

1. See, for instance, Stephen Farber, 'Violence and the Bitch Goddess', *Film Comment*, Nov/Dec 1974; and John Davis, 'The Tragedy of Mildred Pierce', *Velvet Light Trap*, no. 6.
2. Described in J. A. Place and L. S. Peterson, 'Some Visual Motifs of Film Noir', *Film Comment*, Jan 1974; and Paul Schrader, 'Notes on Film Noir', *Film Comment*, Spring 1972.
3. J. J. Bachofen, *Myth, Religion and Mother Right*, 1861 (New Jersey: Princeton University Press/ Bollingen Foundation, 1973).
4. See, for instance, Frederick Engels in *The Origin of the Family, Private Property, and the State*, 1884 (New York: Pathfinder Press, 1973).
5. James Cain's novel *Mildred Pierce*, which appeared in 1941, is significantly different from the film in that it presents Mildred's story in terms of her economic, emotional and sexual problems after the break-up of her marriage to Bert. The film draws more on myth and less on naturalistic detail than the novel.
6. Joyce Nelson, '*Mildred Pierce* Reconsidered', *Film Reader*, no. 2.
7. Nelson takes the term 'suture' from the influential article by Daniel Dayan: 'The Tutor-Code of Classical Cinema', in *Film Quarterly*, Fall 1974. The concept has been the subject of much debate (see 'Notes on Suture' by Stephen Heath in *Screen*, vol. 18, no. 4), but can be briefly defined as the system by which, in classic cinema, the spectator is bound into the image-frame and narrative.
8. Interesting attempts to define melodrama in terms of excess have been made by Laura Mulvey in 'Notes on Sirk and Melodrama', *Movie*, no. 25, and by Geoffrey Nowell-Smith in 'Minnelli and Melodrama', *Screen*, vol. 18, no. 2.
9. Roland Barthes, 'Delay', *S/Z* (London: Jonathan Cape, 1975), p. 75.
10. Anxiety feelings similar to those which cause us to wake up when a dream threatens to go beyond the pleasure principle. The detective's action in opening the blinds could be interpreted as a metaphor for waking up.
11. In the novel, Mildred's relationship with Veda is represented as explicitly sexual, in the physical and emotional sense.
12. The relationship of physical similarity between Mildred and Veda represents in Freudian terms Mildred's choice of a love object based on narcissism, the dyadic relationship which the Oedipus complex attempts to resolve. The 'wicked' side of Veda seems to represent the underside of Demetrian matriarchy, the unregulated excesses of hetaerism.
13. When the 'snare' is made explicit, the meaning of Monty's dying whisper, 'Mildred ...', changes: Mildred now becomes the 'lost object', relegated to the past, a memory (cf. 'Rosebud' in *Citizen Kane*), rather than the agent of death.
14. Two articles which discuss the concept of film as 'body' are 'Minnelli and Melodrama' (see Note 8) and Mark Nash, 'Notes on the Dreyer-text', *Dreyer* (London: BFI, 1977).
15. It is worth noting that Bachofen associates the number 2 with the feminine principle of justice in the section on Egypt in *Myth, Religion, and Mother Right* (see Note 3). The two women on the steps of the police station could be said to represent the subjugation of matriarchal Law.

5

The Place of Women in Fritz Lang's *The Blue Gardenia*

E. Ann Kaplan

In the typical film noir, the world is presented from the point of view of the male investigator, who often recounts something that happened in the past. The investigator, functioning in a nightmare world where all the clues to meaning are deliberately hidden, seeks to unravel a mystery with which he has been presented. He is in general a reassuring presence in the noir world: we identify with him and rely on him to use reason and cunning, if not to outwit the criminals then at least to solve the enigma.

By contrast, the female characters in film noir stand outside the male order and represent a challenge to it.[1] They symbolise all that is evil and mysterious. Sexuality being the only weapon women have in relation to men, they use it to entrap the investigator and prevent him from accomplishing his task. Dangerous because their sexuality is so openly displayed and so irresistible, women become the element that the male investigator must guard against if he is to succeed in his quest.

The Blue Gardenia is a challenge to critics,[2] because in it Lang does not simply follow noir conventions in the manner that he does in two other films (*The Big Heat* and *Human Desire*) made about the same time. Lang rather turns noir conventions upside down in *The Blue Gardenia* by presenting two separate discourses – that is, two modes of articulating a vision of reality.[3] There is the usual male discourse familiar from noir films and represented here by Casey Mayo, a journalist playing investigator, and the police; but alongside this, Lang has inserted the discourse of Norah, a young telephone operator – a discourse that presents the confusion and alienation of women in a male world. As I'll show, Lang's treatment of Norah exposes male assumptions about women in noir films; by juxtaposing the male discourse, with its noir conventions, to Norah's point of view, Lang reveals elements of that discourse which generally go unquestioned.[4]

The film opens in an apparently traditional manner, with Mayo driving up to the West Coast Telephone Company and leaving his sleepy photographer in the car. Inside, we find Prebble flirting with Crystal, a friend who lives with Norah and who is also a telephone operator. Prebble, called to the phone, is irritated with demands being made by a hysterical woman. Visually, the men dominate the frames in the expected manner. Prebble is shot lounging beside Crystal, sitting above her and facing the camera. Mayo dominates by standing up and both men act seductively to the women, Mayo in a less sinister and offensive way than Prebble.

The second scene, set in the apartment that Crystal, Norah and Sally share, is in striking contrast to the first. The female discourse is now evident, although the women are still placed symbolically in a subordinate way to men. The cosy relationships among the working women and the sense of a female world recall Dorothy Arzner's films and other so-called 'women's films', such as Gregory La-Cava's *Stagedoor* and Lloyd Bacon's *Marked Woman*. Visually, the women occupy the centre of the frames and face the camera. Within the privacy of their home, they have more confident gestures and body postures, and freely extend themselves in a way that was not possible when men were *physically* present. There is friendly repartee between the women and obvious support and caring for each other.

But, as in the 'women's films' mentioned, the symbolic importance of men assures their domination even when absent. Men provide the main topic of interest and, although presented from the women's point of view, their centrality to the women's lives is clear. Each woman has made her own accommodation to the need to have a man: Sally finds real men boring, and lives a vicarious but passionate love life through pulp fiction; Crystal is dating her ex-husband, Homer, having discovered that she gets much more out of the relationship this way; Norah at the beginning of the scene is in love with her soldier in Korea, and lives for his return.

Norah's sudden discovery of her soldier's infidelity sets the narrative in motion and conditions her behaviour on the fatal night of Prebble's murder. Earlier on in the evening, her friends had ridiculed Norah for preferring a lonely birthday supper with her fiancé's photograph to a night out. Anticipating that the letter she has saved for this moment will be full of his love for her, Norah is cruelly disappointed by an abrupt announcement of the soldier's imminent wedding to a nurse. At this point, Prebble telephones for a date with Crystal, whose number he had finally obtained earlier in the day. Pretending to be Crystal, Norah accepts the date herself, out of a desperate need to drown her hurt.

Taken aback at first to see Norah instead of Crystal, Prebble quickly adjusts to the situation, the implication being that the particular girl does not matter that much to him. He sees that Norah gets thoroughly drunk at the Blue Gardenia club, where Cole Porter sings the 'Gardenia' song and a blind woman sells gardenia flowers. He then takes Norah back to his apartment where he begins to make love to her. Norah goes drunkenly along at first, pretending her lover is her fiancé, but on realising her mistake, she wants to leave. Prebble insists, and in defence against being raped, Norah grabs a poker and strikes out at him, fainting before she can see what she has done. Waking up some time later, she rushes out of the house without her shoes, and goes home.

When Norah gets up the next morning, she has no memory of the events that took place in Prebble's apartment. While on the level of the surface narrative, this is a clumsy device for providing the enigma that has to be solved, it has symbolic importance in relation to the placing of women. Norah's inability to 'remember' or to say what actually happened represents the common experience of women in patriarchy – that of feeling unable to reason well because the terms in which the culture thinks are male and alien. Women in patriarchy do not function competently at the level of external, public articulation, and thus may appear 'stupid' and 'uncertain'.[5] Norah's 'forgetting' dramatically symbolises her lostness in the male noir world of the film; she experiences a nightmare-like feeling of not knowing whether she is innocent or guilty, and of being therefore vulnerable to male manipulation.

The *mise en scène* of the opening sequences underscores Norah's vulnerability; the male world is presented visually as a labyrinth through which she cannot find her way and which is fraught with danger for her. There is a dramatic contrast between the *mise en scène* in scenes representing the women's worlds (the telephone company, the women's apartment), and that in the male worlds (The Blue Gardenia club, Prebble's apartment and, later on, Mayo's office). While the scenes in the telephone company and the apartment are brightly lit, the atmosphere cheerful and bustling, those in the male locations are shot in noir style, with looming shadows, unusual camera angles, objects awkwardly placed in the frame, etc., to create a sinister, claustrophobic atmosphere.[6] The first scene in the women's apartment demonstrates the threatening aspect of the male world for Norah in the dramatic change that takes place once the other women have left, and Norah discovers her soldier's betrayal.

Even before we know this, however, Lang has prepared us for something unpleasant. Norah is dressed in a black taffeta dress, and has darkened the room, supposedly to create a romantic candlelit atmosphere, but as she sits down the shadows loom ominously. She sits opposite her fiancé's picture almost as if before an icon, the candle light adding to the sense of something unnatural going on. Lang seems to be deliberately exposing the excessive nature of Norah's devotion here, as if to increase the shock of the soldier's infidelity. Once his voice is heard, Norah translating the letter to her lover's spoken speech, the scene becomes even more sinister and ominous, the shadows darkening to the point of seeming almost to invade the light. When the phone rings, and Norah crosses the room to answer it, the music becomes sinister and the screen is almost black.

The women's apartment, thus, is seen to change dramatically, to become sinister and threatening, once men symbolically invade it. The Blue Gardenia club next presents the male world as manipulative, seeking to trap unaware women. We first see Prebble at the club setting up his seduction and making jokes about women with Mayo, who is at the bar on the pick-up. As Norah enters, she is seen in long shot, a tiny figure lost in the maze of the elaborate Hawaiian décor of the club. Guided to Prebble's secluded table, she is seated in a wicker chair with an enormous back that seems to swallow her up. Things become more sinister again as the couple drive home in the pouring rain and a thunderstorm. The shots of the car hood closing over the couple suggest that Norah is being trapped, as does the corresponding shot of the skylight window in Prebble's apartment with the rain beating down on it from the outside. Once the couple move into the living room, the *mise en scène* becomes even more sinister; there is a large mirror on the wall, surrounded by plants that cast eerie shadows over the room. It is as if Norah is lost in a jungle, the décor symbolising male traps and wiles.

It is important to note that it is only at this point that Prebble begins to appear in a sinister light. The section of the film up to this point has merely presented the alternating discourses of the men, on the one hand, and Norah (and to a degree the other women) on the other, both being shown as equally 'valid'. As the film

The Blue Gardenia.

goes on, however, and as we come to identify increasingly with Norah rather than the men, so the male discourse begins to be undercut by that of Norah. Reversing the situation in most noir films, where women are seen only within the male discourse, here that discourse is demystified through the fact that Norah is allowed to present herself directly to us. There are three main ways in which the male discourse is challenged.

The first way in which the male discourse is undercut is through Norah's knowing more than the male investigators about what went on on the night of the murder. As already noted, in most noir films we identify with the male investigator and rely on him to bring at least some coherence in an essentially chaotic world. Here, however, we identify with Norah and have been present, as Mayo and the police have not, in Prebble's apartment the night of the murder. Although neither we nor Norah know all the facts, we at least know that she was the girl in Prebble's room who left her shoes and handkerchief there, and who was wearing a taffeta dress. On the evidence we have, it seems likely that Norah did kill Prebble in self-defence, but we are sympathetic to her hesitation in giving herself up to the police. Because we are seeing from Norah's point of view, we identify with her, not the investigators, whom we perceive from the outside trying to piece together parts of a puzzle that already fit for us.

A second way in which the male discourse is undercut is through the perspective we acquire, by being placed in Norah's consciousness, on the hypotheses that Mayo and the police develop about the woman who was with Prebble on the night of the murder. They automatically assume that she was no good (most likely a prostitute, since what decent woman would go out with Prebble), and that she deserves all she will get for murdering Prebble. (There is, however, no condemnation of Prebble's seductions, no suggestion that he may have exploited women for his own ends, or taken advantage of women's loneliness.) The disjunction between Norah, whom we experience as a gentle, warm and honest person, and the 'fictional' woman the men and society in general conjure up, highlights the harsh stereotype that women must deal with and the sexual double standard.

Particularly painful for Norah is the way even her close friends assume that the woman with Prebble was no good, and is to be despised and punished. Through the device of Norah's increasing identification with the heroines of Sally's pulp fiction, Lang notes Norah's growing self-hatred as she hears the comments about the 'Prebble woman'. Earlier on, Sally discussed with zest her latest book about a 'red debutante [who] is hit on the head, stabbed in the back, and shot in the stomach'. Norah's increasing identification with these pulp fiction women is made clear after an upsetting conversation with Sally and Crystal about the murderess. When the two friends leave Norah in the kitchen, she picks up a knife and holds it suggestively toward her stomach. We cut to a cover of one of Sally's books, showing a woman brandishing a knife with a terrible grimace on her face; the image echoes Norah's growing frustration as she feels condemned, trapped and helpless.

Norah's increasing sense of being trapped comes from her inability to withstand a definition of herself imposed by an alien and indecipherable male discourse. She does not trust her own sense of what she is, or is not, capable of, uncertain as to where male definitions end and her own begin. As the events of her night with Prebble are reconstructed for her by the police, Norah suffers a ter-

85

rifying dislocation from reality. Not having evidence to the contrary, she comes to accept their definition of her as a murderess, despite an underlying sense that something is amiss. She is reduced to a state of hysteria, acting like a criminal, jumping when she sees the police, burning evidence like the taffeta dress, listening secretly to the radio in the dead of night. Her personality changes, and she becomes irritable with her friends. She thus folds up under the weight of the male structuring of things, succumbs to their view of her, and takes the guilt upon herself.

The third way in which the male discourse is undercut is through the perspective we develop on Casey Mayo. Identified as we are with Norah, the alternation between the discourses 'places' what Mayo is doing and allows us to see it for what it is. In the ordinary noir film, the investigator's trapping of the murderess would be a demonstration of his triumph over sexuality and evil. Here, Mayo is seen to engineer a despicable betrayal of the murderess whose dilemma he exploits for a publicity stunt. He pretends to be the killer's friend, seductively offering help and secrecy but all along intending to give the girl up to the police once she has revealed herself to him. Norah resists Mayo's appeals for a long time (while, by the way, the audience is 'entertained' by a series of false responses by desperate women, who are made ridiculous), but her isolation finally wears her down. She is unable to confide in her women friends (although we sense that at least Crystal would be sympathetic), partly because they have spoken so badly of the Prebble 'woman', but also because Norah presumably does not see them as being able to help. She assumes that only men, those in the place of power, can get her out of her fix. She thus turns to Casey Mayo, who has been presenting himself over the radio as someone able to make reason out of chaos.

Because of the total trust with which Norah turns to Mayo, his treatment of her is shocking. When she comes to him posing as the murderess' friend, Mayo responds warmly to her, partly because he is attracted to her but also because he is anxious to be the first to discover the murderess. When Norah finally reveals that she is herself the supposed murderess, Mayo's response is terrifying: she is now repulsive to him, someone to be shunned, cast off. He does not quite decide to turn her in himself as originally planned – because of his attraction – but is glad to be sent off on another job.

Lang's visual treatment of the meeting between Mayo and Norah underscores her vulnerability, and Mayo's manipulation. He asks Norah to meet him late at night in his office. Norah's arrival is shot from Mayo's point of view: when he hears the elevator coming, he shuts off the lights, presumably so that he will be able to size her up before she has a chance to see him. Also, perhaps, to frighten her. We see Norah emerge from the lit elevator in the back of the frame; she is a tiny figure in black, in the lit corridor, with the threatening blackness of Mayo's office looming in front of her. Mayo watches silently as she slowly makes her way up the dark room, lit only from outside. The visual presentation of the scene expresses Mayo's power over Norah, her dependence on him and his unworthiness to be trusted, since he thinks only in terms of power and not of human vulnerability. Mayo is exposed as incapable of pity or empathy, and as bound by stereotypes of women as either 'good' or 'bad' girls.

The progressive elements of *The Blue Gardenia* that I've been discussing are, as so often, undercut by the way the film ends. Mayo has to be 'redeemed' by being the one who finally *does* solve the mystery of who murdered Prebble. By noticing a discrepancy between the record Norah said was on the phonograph at the time of the murder and that found by the police on the turntable when they arrived, Mayo tracks the murderess down; she turns out to be the hysterical woman Prebble had rejected at the start of the film. Mayo's reward for liberating Norah is of course to win her for himself; he now has the 'good' woman and can throw over his black book to his delighted photographer.

Although by the end of the film all the structures defining men and women are safely back in place, Lang's achievement remains. In turning noir conventions upside down, *The Blue Gardenia* has revealed the place that women usually occupy in these films. We see that the view men have of women is false in that the set of implications about Norah generated from the male world turn out to be invalid. While the male discourse tried to define Norah as a *femme fatale*, we see rather that she is a victim of male strategies to ensnare her for something she did not do. Norah's submissive placing of herself in relation to the male world is also exposed. She accepts the male view of her and then experiences the world as a riddle that she cannot solve. In this way, *The Blue Gardenia* exposes the essential contradiction between the dominant male discourse and the subordinate (repressed) discourse of women in patriarchy.

Notes

1. Relevant here is the statement that Laura Mulvey makes in *Riddles of the Sphinx* in the second section where she is reading directly into the camera. Looking to the world of mythology for an understanding of women's place in patriarchy, Mulvey describes the Sphinx as representing the unconscious and women. Mulvey says: 'The sphinx is outside the city gates, she challenges the culture of the city, with its order of kinship and its order of knowledge, a culture and a political system which assign women a subordinate place.' (*'Riddles of the Sphinx:* a film by Laura Mulvey and Peter Wollen', *Screen*, vol. 18, no. 2, Summer 1977, p. 62.) Women in film noir in particular are placed in the position of the Sphinx, mysterious, sinister and challenging to men but assigned a place outside the order of the film.
2. There has been little extended treatment of *The Blue Gardenia*, and the film has in the main been dismissed as a poor example of Lang's work. Paul Jensen, for instance, says that Lang's 'rejection of the narrative qualities of mystery and suspense is so complete that it must be intentional', concluding that 'the film's sole distinction remains its introduction of the theme song'. In *The Cinema of Fritz Lang* (New York: A. S. Barnes, 1969), p. 181.
3. I am using the notion of 'discourse' as developed firstly by Colin MacCabe in 'Realism and the Cinema: Notes on some Brechtian Themes', *Screen*, vol. 15, no. 2, Summer 1974, pp. 7–27, and later on by Claire Johnston and Pam Cook in *The Work of Dorothy Arzner* (London: BFI, 1975). Its use here is similar also to that of Pam Cook in her piece on *Mildred Pierce*, also included in this volume.
4. This is not the first time that Lang has worked in a 'progressive' (cf. MacCabe) manner in a classic text. Noel Burch's analysis of *M* ('De *Mabuse* à *M*: Le travail de Fritz Lang', in *Revue d'esthétique*, numéro spécial, 1973) shows how Lang used techniques to distance viewers in order to present an extraordinarily complex image of the child murderer and the society he lived in. According to Burch, Lang abandons literary conceptions of character and narrative, and works rather through 'la langage sans langue' that Metz calls cinema. In an unpublished dissertation on Lang, Julian Petley notes that in *The Return of Frank James*, Lang seems interested in exploring the processes in the Western genre by which the outlaw becomes a hero, rather than in simply presenting the hero

without question: *The Films of Fritz Lang: The Cinema as Destiny* (unpublished thesis, Exeter 1973, p. 22).

5. Here again Mulvey's words in *Riddles* illuminate the point usefully. If women in traditional film noir are in the Sphinx position, in Lang's film what Mulvey has to say about women within patriarchy applies:

> To the patriarchy, the Sphinx as woman is a threat and a riddle, but women within patriarchy are faced with a never-ending series of threats and riddles – dilemmas which are hard for women to solve, because the culture within which they must think is not theirs. We live in a society ruled by the father, in which the place of the mother is suppressed. ... And meanwhile the Sphinx can only speak with a voice apart, a voice off. ('*Riddles of the Sphinx*', p. 62)

6. In Pam Cook's 'Duplicity in *Mildred Pierce*', she notes a similar contrast between the flashback sequences, that have to do with Mildred's subject matter – the family, sexual and emotional relationships, work, property and investment and the noir parts of the film related to men. Mildred's story, Cook says, is the 'stuff of which the "Woman's Picture" was made ...'. The style here is different from that in the rest of the film, scenes being 'evenly lit, few variations of camera angle, etc.' In contrast the framing noir discourse is marked by classic noir style. She concludes that there are two voices, female and male within the film, each roughly corresponding to the Woman's Picture and the Man's Film and with its own style. The divisions, interestingly enough, roughly correspond to those I've noted in *The Blue Gardenia* between Norah's discourse and that of the male, noir discourse, also filmed in classic noir style.

6
Double Indemnity
Claire Johnston

Double Indemnity, based on James M. Cain's *roman noir* of the same title, is the story of an insurance agent, Walter Neff, who plots with Phyllis Dietrichson to kill her husband by making it appear that he died falling from a moving train, thus allowing them to claim double the insurance money on his life. In attempting to retain Cain's first person interior monologue, director Billy Wilder and Raymond Chandler, the scriptwriter, used the narrative device, extremely rare in classic Hollywood cinema in the 40s, of having Neff recite the past events into a dictaphone, so that the plot resolution is known from the outset, the film taking the form of a memory. Such a device at one level would seem to constitute an attempt to preserve the essence of the *roman noir* as a sub-genre of the detective genre as a whole.

As Todorov notes,[1] while retaining the structure of the enigma, the narrator displaces its centrality and relativises its structuring function within the narrative. In that the narrator does not know whether he will remain alive at the end, he becomes problematic for the reader. The *roman noir* fuses two narrative codes, suppressing the code of the detective story which offers the possibility of sense and believability for the reader in terms of an enigma resolved by the Law, and giving life to the first person narration spoken in the present coinciding with the action in the form of a memory. Essentially the *roman noir* as a sub-genre presents a particular social milieu of immorality and sordid crime in which the narrator risks his life and sanity.

The believability of the detective genre as a whole is a particular one founded on questions relating to the social construction of social reality – it is the character who is not suspected who is, in fact, guilty. Such a systematic process of inversion of social reality within the genre necessitates that social reality be reaffirmed through resolution and closure for the reader in terms of the Law. Far from opening up social contradictions, the genre as a whole, through such a process of naturalisation, performs a profoundly confirmatory function for the reader, both revealing and simultaneously eliminating the problematic aspects of social reality by the assertion of the unproblematic nature of the Law.

The use of the 'novelesque' in *Double Indemnity* as a continuous, first person narrative discourse co-extensive with the image track – semi-diegetic speech[2] – undoubtedly draws the film closer to literary speech, but within the filmic discourse its function within the text is displaced and transformed. While the film poses a first person narrating discourse which takes the form of a memory, the filmic/diegetic image is always in the present. Far from displacing the enigma in revealing the plot resolution at the beginning of the film, the first person narrative discourse, in its play of convergence/divergence with the visible, produces an enigma at another level for the viewer: a split relationship to knowledge. The first person narration presents itself as a 'confession' which reveals the truth of the narrative of events by which we can talk of the various characters in the film – it purports to provide the knowledge of how things really happened. But as the film unfolds, a divergence emerges between the knowledge which the first person narrative discourse provides and that which unfolds at the level of the visible. Finally, it is the visual discourse which serves as the guarantee of truth for the reader: 'the spectator can do no other than identify with the camera'.[3] In filmic discourse the relationship between the viewer and reality – the film – is one of pure specularity, in which the look of the spectator is denied, locking the spectator into a particular sense of identity. Ultimately, classic Hollywood cinema is always in the third person – it is always objective – unless subjectivity is marked in the image itself (e.g., the blurred image of Gutman in *The Maltese Falcon*).[4] The narrative of events at the level of the visible provides the knowledge of how things really are and constitutes the dominant narrating instance.

In *Double Indemnity* the process of articulation between the narrating discourses at play is foregrounded by the 'novelesque' aspect of the genre itself, providing a complex interplay of convergence/divergence – a conflict at the level of the knowledges which the film provides for the viewer, setting in motion its own enigma. As the film progresses the narrator loses control of the narrative to the point where he himself comes under scrutiny. Keyes, the company claims investigator, the 'you' of Neff's first person narration, begins to investigate the case and Neff becomes a witness, subject to Keyes' investigation. It is the articulation of the 'I' and the 'you' of the first person narration (the relationship between the two men) with the narrative of events in the realm of the visible (the objective, third-person process of narrativisation) which situates a split relationship to knowledge for the viewer and, with it, the enigma. At the centre of the enigma is the Oedipal trajectory of the hero – the problem of the knowledge of sexual difference in a patriarchal order.

The title sequence sets the film under the mark of castration: the silhouette of a male figure in a hat and overcoat looms towards the camera on crutches. In the next sequence we see Walter Neff, injured and bleeding, enter the offices of his insurance company and begin his 'confession' to Keyes on the dictaphone. 'I killed Dietrichson – me, Walter Neff – insurance salesman – thirty-five years old, no visible scars – till a while ago, that is. ... I killed him for money – and for a woman. ... It all began last May.'

It is to Keyes that Walter Neff's discourse, the 'I' of the voice-over, is addressed; a 'you' which is split between the Symbolic and the Imaginary[5] – a split that insists in the attempted overlapping of the functions of symbolic father and idealised father. Neff's opening 'confession' establishes Keyes as the representative of the Law – the symbolic father: 'you were right, but you got the wrong man'. As symbolic father, Keyes' unshakeable access to the truth, to knowledge, resides in his phallic attribute, his 'little man' which, by a process necessitated by censoring mechanisms, 'ties knots in his stomach', enabling him to spot a phoney claim instantly. His knowledge of the laws of mathematical probability, epitomised in his very name, enables him to chart the social excesses of the world and ensure the stability of property relations in the name of the insurance business. In the first scene in the claims office we see him interrogate a man with a phoney claim and render him an 'honest man' again. He describes his function within the institution as 'doctor', 'bloodhound', 'cop' and 'father confessor'.

As signifier of the patriarchal order, Keyes represents for Neff what it means to be capable of saying 'I am who I am', to be the one who knows; he is transcendent. In order to resolve the positive Oedipus and gain access to the Symbolic, the boy has to accept the threat of castration from the father. As Lacan has indicated, 'Law and repressed desire are one and the same thing'.[6] The Oedipus complex allows access to desire only through repression: it is through lack that desire is instituted. As Keyes says of Neff: 'you're not smarter, you're just taller'. Neff's belief in Keyes' knowledge is absolute: 'you were right'. At the same time the Law always offers itself for transgression: the desire to 'con the system', to devise a scheme so 'perfect' that it can challenge the father's phallic function, his knowledge, and thus reduplicate the perfection of the system once more. But the symbolic father can only be imperfectly incarnate in the real father. As Neff's symbolic father, Keyes is marked by a lack, a blind spot. In the voice-over in the first scene in the claims office, Neff says (in retrospect) that he 'knew he had a heart as big as a house' – the reason why he 'got the wrong man'. It is the repressed, maternal side of Keyes which constitutes a blind spot for the patriarchal order, and it is this blind spot which for Neff sets in motion the desire for transgression which the son may always attempt against the father: to take his place.

Keyes also represents the idealised father for Neff: the ideal ego founded on narcissistic identifications constitutive of the realm of the Imaginary. As Freud indicated,[7] identifications in the pre-Oedipal phase are associated primarily with one's sexual like. The repressed homosexual desire of Neff for the idealised father rests on narcissistic identification, to 'think with your brains, Keyes', to possess his knowledge. In the all-male universe of the insurance business, women are seen as untrustworthy: as Keyes comments, they 'should be investigated' before any relationship is embarked on. Women represent the possibility of social excess which the insurance business seeks to contain – they 'drink from the bottle' (Keyes). The repressed, homosexual desire between the two men, the negative Oedipus, is symbolised by the visual rhyme, running throughout the film, of Neff's ritual lighting of Keyes' cigar as Keyes fumbles each time for a match. This signifier is underpinned in the first scene in the claims office by Neff's words 'I love you, too' as Keyes jokingly threatens to throw his desk at him. Neff's pre-Oedipal, narcissistic identification with Keyes implies a disavowal rather than an acceptance of castration. Thus the film traces the precariousness of the patriarchal order and its internal contradictions precisely in this split between Symbolic and Imaginary symbolised in the place and function of Keyes in the fiction, and the inscription of castration for men within that order. Neff must both assume castration in a process of testing the Law so that he can take the place of the symbolic father, while, at the same time, disavowing castration in his narcissistic identifications with a father-figure – the idealised father.

As an example of the film noir, *Double Indemnity* poses a social reality constructed in the split, the interface, between the Symbolic and the Imaginary of a particular social order – that of the male universe of the insurance business – an order which activates/reactivates the trouble of castration for the male in patriarchy. It is in relation to the women in the film, to Phyllis Dietrichson/Barbara Stanwyck and her stepdaughter Lola, that the internal contradictions of the patriarchal order (the Oedipal trajectory of male desire focused in Neff) are to be played out. The 'woman' is thus produced as the signifier of the lack, of heterogeneity – the 'fault' inherent in patriarchy as an order.

As Laura Mulvey has elaborated,[8] it is the contemplation of the female form which evokes castration anxiety for the male: the original trauma being the discovery that the mother is, in fact, not phallic, but castrated. As locus of lack/castration, as the site where radical difference is marked negatively, 'woman' is the pivot around which the circulation of male desire is played out in the text, and it is this process of circulation of desire which fixes the representation of women in the text. Phyllis Dietrichson/Barbara Stanwyck, celebrated female star and *femme fatale*, represents Neff's attempt to disavow castration in his repressed homosexuality and to test the Law, while Lola functions as the term in relation to which an acceptance of castration and the Symbolic Order is inscribed. As the narrative progresses, Phyllis Dietrichson/Barbara Stanwyck gives way to Lola and the contradictions of the patriarchal order opened up by the film are contained for the next generation. It is Neff's paternal function in relation to Lola which restores her as good object within familial relations. The enigma of the problem of the knowledge of sexual differences is thus resolved by the Law *for* patriarchy.

In the scene immediately following Neff's 'confession' to Keyes, both Phyllis Dietrichson/Barbara Stanwyck and Lola are introduced into the narrative, as Neff goes to renew an insurance policy at the house. His voice-over fixes them as memory, *as already known*, in the 'I' and 'you' discourse between the two men. In a dusty, semi-darkened room Phyllis Dietrichson/Barbara Stanwyck, covered in a bath towel, stands at the top of the stairs offered to and held in the mastery of Neff's gaze. Neff jokes that she might not be 'fully covered' by the insurance policy on the car: the hint of social excess. At the same time the voice-over draws our attention to the photograph on the piano of Dietrichson and his daughter by his first marriage, Lola. Visually, the women resemble each other in age and general appearance in a striking way. 'Mother' and 'daughter' are nevertheless, from the beginning, established as inhabiting a different space in the diegesis, Phyllis Dietrichson/Barbara Stanwyck frozen as fetish object in Neff's look, already outside the space of familial relations, and Lola frozen in the family photograph from which Phyllis is excluded.

The initial shots of Neff's encounter with Phyllis Dietrichson/Barbara Stanwyck are marked by a fetishistic fascination: simultaneously the dangerous site of castration and the pleasurable appearance – the object of the look – she is the source of reassuring pleasure in the face of castration anxiety. The 'I' of the voice-over talks of this fascination, converging with the 'I' of the look: the viewer is thus drawn into a fetishistic split between belief and knowledge. As she begins to come down the stairs of the California-style Spanish house, we see a close-up of her legs and her golden anklet. The camera follows Neff and catches his image in the mirror as he watches her finish buttoning up her dress and putting on her lipstick. She

turns from the mirror, leaving him still fixed in his gaze, and moves over to the other side of the room.

His privileged look at her exhibitionism in the mirror shot, a moment of pure specularity, marks a disjunction between his look and that of the viewer: imprisoned in his narcissistic identifications, the identity of Neff and viewer is simultaneously doubled, split and recomposed – his gaze becomes uneasy. He must investigate the woman further and discover her guilty secret in his desire to test the Law. The possibility of social excess which she represents, her incongruity as suburban housewife, suggests her as a vehicle for his Oedipal transgression. She asks him about accident insurance for her husband and he flirts with her, continuing the driving metaphor around the car insurance, to discover more. She says he's 'going too fast'. He leaves, making an appointment to call the next day.

The following scene of his visit to the house the next day is dominated by shots of Neff watching her as he tries to discover her guilty secret. We see her descend the stairs to open the door as the voice-over recalls her anklet: the mastery of his gaze is re-presented as a memory image. He asks her to call him Walter and offers to run the vacuum cleaner. As he watches, she tells him about the boredom of her married life and asks him about taking out accident insurance on her husband's life. He interrogates her and asks her why she married her husband. The camera remains on his face as she asks how she could take out the accident insurance without either her husband or the company knowing. He tells her how it could be done and says, as he leaves, she 'can't get away with it'. In the voice-over Neff says, 'I knew I had hold of a red hot poker and it was time to drop it before it burned my hand off'. The images confirm his complicity for the viewer, his sadistic play with the woman.

As Laura Mulvey notes,[9] the disavowal of castration for the male in its fascination and the desire to know her guilty secret is fundamentally sadistic – it must also involve her punishment. Phyllis Dietrichson/Barbara Stanwyck, entombed in the domesticity of the Spanish house, represents the possibility of a libidinal satisfaction which cannot be contained within the Symbolic Order and the structure of familial relations. For the patriarchal order founded on castration, she is a trouble which can be spoken about but not acted upon. As such, she encapsulates the concerns of the film noir itself – that (as Neff says in the voice-over) 'murder can sometimes smell like honeysuckle'. In her very impossibility, she offers herself as a vehicle for Neff to test the Law, but the erotic drives she represents must finally, in the film noir, become subject to the Law – she must be found guilty and punished. These drives can only be destructive and lead to death, in that she represents, pre-

cisely, the heterogeneity which must form the outside of the Symbolic Order, the excluded that allows the order to exist as an order.[10]

The love scene necessitates the confession of her guilty secret – that which troubles the order and which will have to be worked through in and by the text: 'it was only the beginning ...' (Neff). The bell rings and she stands in a pool of light, offered to the gaze of Neff and viewer, in the doorway of Neff's darkened apartment. The voice-over suggests an appointment which the image denies: 'it would be eight and she would be there'. She is holding his hat and is returning it. Later they embrace on the sofa and he draws her into confessing her guilty secret – that she would like her husband dead. As they embrace, their love-making is elided by the camera tracking out of the apartment room and, in the next shot, into Neff's office as he tells Keyes on the dictaphone that he always wanted to 'con the system'. The camera then tracks back out of the office and back into the apartment room to find them again on the sofa. Sexual knowledge of the woman and Neff's Oedipal trajectory, *vis-à-vis* Keyes, to test the Law, are held and relocated diegetically for the viewer in this relocation of sex with Phyllis into the verbal interchange with Keyes. As she begins to leave, Neff agrees to help her to get her husband to sign the insurance papers. As we hear the car drive away, Neff's voice-over says 'the machinery had started to move'; he would have to 'think with your brains, Keyes', assume mastery of the Symbolic Order, the system, in order to explore its interstices.

At this point the sexual drives opened up by the woman and the need for narcissistic identification with the father come into contradiction. We return to Neff's office and the 'confession' to Keyes on the dictaphone, as Neff tells him he 'didn't like the witness' to Dietrichson's signature, how he felt 'queer in the belly'. There is a fade to Lola's image sitting in mid-shot playing Chinese chequers. The transition emphasises Lola's

position on the side of mastery within the order which Neff is testing for gaps – in this sense, Lola is on the side of Keyes. As witness she represents the social order encapsulated in the persona of Keyes: the containment of social excess and the regulation of property relations. The camera tracks out from Lola to reveal the family scene, and as Dietrichson signs the documents, her image remains central in the frame. Neff's eyes follow her as she goes upstairs.

The threat to Neff which Lola represents is precisely her centrality within the family, her role of daughter, subject to the Law of the Father. As witness, she functions as a reference to, a sign of, the Symbolic Order which he seeks to transgress – she's a 'nice kid'. He leaves the house, and arrives at his car to find her sitting in the front seat. At this point there is a disturbance in the point-of-view structure in the text. She asks him to give her a lift into town, and confides in him that she is secretly going to see her boyfriend, Nino. Neff's attitude is paternal. As he drops her off in town the voice-over comments: 'the father was a dead pigeon'.

In order to stimulate Dietrichson's death from a moving train and claim the double indemnity on his life, Neff has to take his place. In so doing he not only becomes Phyllis's 'husband', but Lola's 'father'. In destroying the family unit, in testing the Law, Neff has entered an impossible family, a family explicitly based on a sacrificial murder, and thus socially censored. After murdering Dietrichson and taking his place on the train his desire vanishes: having successfully achieved a replica of the family, he is now in the position of the master in an *other* symbolic order, one that exists alongside and in the face of the social order represented by Keyes. The car fails to start: he and Phyllis part on a reluctant embrace. On the way to the drug store, after establishing his alibi, Neff's voice-over says: 'I couldn't hear my own footsteps ... it was the walk of a dead man'. The impossible family is a nightmare. Neff exists in a no-man's land.

In committing the 'perfect' crime, he and Phyllis now exist outside the certitude of the Symbolic Order represented in the legality of the insurance contract signed by Dietrichson. They can no longer meet at the house, and have to meet at the supermarket. The libidinal drives which Phyllis represents can only lead to her death: she is guilty and will be punished. Keyes's 'little man' will tell him something is wrong. But Neff can rely on Keyes's blind spot, his maternal side, the 'fault' in the Symbolic Order. Neff knows he has a 'heart as big as a house'. Outside the symbolic, Neff remains, nevertheless, subject to the Law: Keyes's relentless scrutiny of the insurance claim and the look of the camera, this time on Neff, as the investigation proceeds.

At this point in the film, the balance in which Phyllis and Lola are held in relation to Neff begins to change in terms of spatial relationships at the level of the visible. Keyes comes to Neff's apartment to tell him that he suspects Phyllis and that he intends to 'put her through the wringer'. Phyllis has come to see Neff and is hiding behind the door as Keyes leaves to get something to ease his stomach. Before he gets to the elevator, he takes out a cigar and turns to Neff for his ritual light. The shot encapsulates a change in the direction of Neff's Oedipal trajectory, with Phyllis foregrounded behind the door in darkness and the men in the light of the hallway on the other side of the door. When Keyes leaves, Phyllis complains that Neff is 'going off her'. They embrace and there is a fade and transition (for the first time without the voice-over to signal it) which completes this change in direction, revealing Lola waiting outside Neff's office: 'Do you remember me, Mr Neff? ... Look at me, Mr Neff.' The camera underpins his look at the witness.

Lola says she knows Phyllis is guilty and is going 'to tell': she threatens to interrupt Neff's confessional voice-over to Keyes. She will become the narrator and break the imaginary duality of the Neff/Keyes relationship. She says she has moved out of the house and is living alone: the scene ends on a close-up of her tearful face. As 'father', Neff must return the 'daughter' to the safety of familial relations. As the voice-over tells us how he has decided to take her out to 'keep her quiet', we see a series of two-shots, idyllic images of happiness, as they eat in candlelight at a restaurant and go driving in the countryside. At the discursive level, the voice-over no longer provides the truth with which to read the image. In the transition from Phyllis to Lola, unmarked by Neff's voice-over and visible in terms of spatial relationships, Phyllis gives way to Lola, and the Symbolic Order which she represents returns, threatening from within the replica of the family which has been constructed.

From now on the metaphor of the car is replaced by that of the 'trolley ride'. Having established Phyllis's guilt, Keyes is now looking for her accomplice – the 'other person'. As Keyes says: 'they are on a trolley ride together and the last stop is the cemetery'. Desire which cannot be contained within the Symbolic Order (the trouble represented by Phyllis) can only lead to death, in that it represents the outside of that order, that which must be repressed or contained if that order is to continue to exist. As Keyes says, 'they are digging their own graves'. In the supermarket scene, Phyllis continues Keyes's metaphor: 'It's straight down the line for both of us, remember?'

The inexorable link between desire and death is relocated diegetically for the viewer as we return to Neff's office and the dictaphone: 'It was the first time I thought of Phyllis that way – dead, I mean, and how it would be if she were dead.' Continuing, he says how at that moment he thought of Lola, and there is a transition to a series of shots of their trip to the Hollywood Bowl. As they sit in two-shot, Lola's back is to the camera and, in the darkness, the physical resemblance to Phyllis is striking. Phyllis, already as good as dead, is replaced by Lola, restoring 'woman' as good object for the patriarchal order: the trouble is contained in its rightful place.

Having acknowledged the impossibility of his Oedipal trajectory, the narrator loses control of the narrative. The voice-over can no longer hold the narrative of events, and becomes questioning and uncertain. Keyes's investigation, inaugurating a counter-discourse to the narrative discourse of Neff's 'I', structured around the enigma of 'that somebody else', comes to hold the process of narrativisation for the viewer. This resituating of the 'I' and the 'you' of the narrative discourse is underpinned in the scene where Neff, thinking Keyes is double-crossing him, goes to Keyes's office and listens on the dictaphone to Keyes's confidential memo on his investigation of him, to discover that Keyes 'personally vouches for him'. The rhyme of the dictaphone asserts the 'you' at the level of the visible, at the same time confirming Keyes's blind spot: he doesn't see Neff's culpability. Having come to occupy the place of the father against the Symbolic Order, and discovered its impossibility, Neff must 'get rid of the whole mess' – Phyllis. 'Woman', locus of castration, of anxiety, the source of the 'whole mess', must be punished: he must 'get off the trolley car' before its logical end.

The rhyme of Phyllis's legs descending the stairs, now no longer caught in the mastery of his gaze, introduces the final flashback scene at the house. We see her descend, holding a gun wrapped in a chiffon scarf, unlock the door and put the gun under a cushion. She pursues her function in relation to the order whose excess she is and reaffirms her guilt still further. She says she is 'rotten to the heart' and that she is trying to persuade Lola's boyfriend, Nino, to 'take care of Lola'. Neff circles round her as she speaks. He walks to the window to shut it and she shoots him. He staggers towards her telling her to try again. The camera is held on her as she drops the gun and moves into a close-up as they embrace. She confesses that she never loved him but that she couldn't fire the second shot. As they remain locked in their embrace, he shoots her: she looks surprised. The eroticisation of death in the final scene of the flashback confirms a universe where access to desire is only through repression: the impossibility of a radical heterogeneity represented by the feminine.

Mortally wounded, Neff leaves the house; he meets Nino and gives him a nickel to ring Lola and make it up with her, restoring, symbolically, the *status quo ante*. The flashback ends and we return to Neff's office and the dictaphone. He ends his message to Keyes by asking him to take care of Lola and Nino. The 'father' restores the 'daughter' to the Symbolic Order and familial relations. 'Woman' as good object is reinstated for the next generation. The patriarchal order is now reaffirmed, and with it the internal contradictions for the male universe of the insurance business. The trouble of castration for the male in patriarchy as it insists in the disjunction between the Symbolic and the Imaginary fathers is reactivated. As Neff finishes his message to Keyes, the camera angle suggests a subjective look. It is the look of the 'you' to whom the 'I' has been addressed. Neff turns and acknowledges Keyes's presence. When asked why he couldn't 'figure it out', Keyes acknowledges his blind spot: 'You can't figure them all, Walter.' Neff asks for four hours' grace to cross 'the border'. Keyes replies that he won't even reach the elevator: he's 'all washed up'.

The split between the Symbolic and the Imaginary which structures the text insists in Keyes's overlapping function as symbolic and idealised father, driving the film towards resolution and closure. As symbolic father Keyes must represent the Law and hand Neff over to the police. As idealised father there remains the problem of narcissistic identification, and with it, repressed homosexuality – 'the border'.

The camera holds the two men in frame and follows Neff as he staggers towards the glass doors of his office while Keyes, now out of frame, speaks on the telephone: 'It's a police job.' Keyes then walks into frame as Neff lies slumped against the door and kneels beside him. Neff says: 'I know why you couldn't figure this one ... because the guy you were looking for was too close ... right across the desk from you.' Keyes replies: 'Closer than that, Walter', to which Neff gives his customary ironic reply: 'I love you, too.' As Neff lies dying he gets out a cigarette and the rhyme completes the mutual confession: Keyes returns Neff's ritual gesture and lights the cigarette. Having handed over his function as symbolic father to the police, Keyes can now acknowledge and return Neff's love in the signifier of repressed desire. The challenge to the patriarchal order eliminated and the internal contradictions of that order contained, a sublimated homosexuality between the men can now be signified. But there can be no more words – only 'The End'.

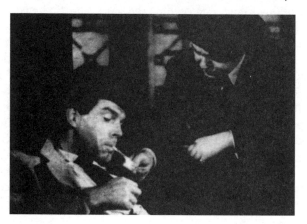

Notes

1. Tzvetan Todorov, *The Poetics of Prose* (Oxford: Blackwell, 1977), pp. 42–52.
2. Christian Metz, 'Current Problems of Film Theory', *Screen*, vol. 14, nos. 1/2, Spring/Summer 1973, p. 69.
3. Christian Metz, 'History/Discourse: Note on Two Voyeurisms', *Edinburgh '76 Magazine*, p. 23.
4. Stephen Heath, 'Narrative Space', *Screen*, vol. 17, no. 2, Autumn 1976, p. 93.
5. For an account of the psychoanalytic framework to which these terms belong, see Rosalind Coward, 'Lacan and Signification: An Introduction', *Edinburgh '76 Magazine*.
6. Jacques Lacan, *Écrits* (Paris: Editions du Seuil, 1966), p. 782; Jacques Lacan (trs. from the French by Alan Sheridan), *Écrits: a selection* (London: Tavistock Publications, 1977).
7. 'Instincts and their Vicissitudes', *Collected Papers* (London: Hogarth Press, 1951), p. 65.
8. 'Visual Pleasure and Narrative Cinema', *Screen*, vol. 16, no. 3, Autumn 1975, p. 13.
9. Ibid., p. 14.
10. See Julia Kristeva, 'Signifying Practice and Mode of Production', *Edinburgh '76 Magazine*.
11. Ibid.

7
Klute 2: Feminism and *Klute*
Christine Gledhill

What is at stake for feminist analysis in examining *Klute* in terms of film noir? For instance, a persuasive account of the film is given by Diane Giddis in which she not only makes Bree the central figure of the film, but converts the two male characters into symbolic extensions of the heroine's divided self: 'The film functions on both levels, as a straight suspense story and as a dramatisation of intense inner conflict, but it is from the second level that it derives its power.'[1] In other words, she is prepared to ignore the conventions of film noir, as *mere* conventions which simply carry a deeper revelation of one of the 'greatest contemporary female concerns: the conflict between the claims of love and the claims of autonomy' (p. 57). But from the discussions of the location of women within film noir in this volume, I hope it is clear that conventions have at least a structuring role, placing constraints on the production of the female image. An analysis which observes these conventions reappropriated in the name of contemporary exploration, and assimilated to the stylistic needs of modern cinema, enables us to bring into sharper focus the strategies and conventions of that cinema, often less discernible for their modernity, and so perhaps to become a little clearer about the operation of patriarchal ideology in current film-making.

This is all the more vital a need in the case of *Klute* which puts Jane Fonda – the star famous for her change of image from sex object to 'serious' politicised roles under pressure from her growing political consciousness – in the role occupied by the *femme fatale* or evil woman in the 40s film noir. This role is now defined in more upfront sexual terms as the prostitute – although a prostitute with ambitions to become an actress. In other words, the film is trying to articulate, within the ambience of the thriller, a modern version of the independent woman, conceived of as the sexually liberated, unattached, hip woman and so without mentioning feminism or women's liberation arguably trying to cash in on these concerns to enhance the modernity of the type. At the same time the film locates the heroine's dilemma within a contemporary moral and sexual malaise, articulated in the archetypal opposition of country/city but dressed in updated terms – attacking the libertarian, hippie counter-culture of the 60s as decadent, morally corrupt and psychically alienated.

In fact, as I hope to show, the ideological project surrounding this version of the independent woman stereotype is the same as when it emerged in the 1890s under the guise of the 'New Woman', namely to show that, however fascinating, different and admirable the would-be emancipated woman is – struggling to assert her own identity in a male world, and professing a new, non-repressive and sexual morality – in the end she is actually neurotic, fragile, lonely and unhappy. I would argue that *Klute*'s production of the stereotype is no different in its ultimate effect, and that the film operates in a profoundly anti-feminist way, perhaps even more so than the 40s thrillers from which it derives.

To begin to substantiate this proposition we need to examine how it is that, in Diane Giddis's words, the 'greatest contemporary female concerns' are articulated within the thriller and what happens to them in the process. I would argue that Pakula's ambition to explore contemporary issues within the framework of the genre, together with his modernisation of the genre, works on those conventions to wrest them out of their formulaic nature and turn them into conscious metaphors for the 'human condition' assimilable to contemporary concerns.

For this reason it is perfectly feasible for Diane Giddis to discover within the functioning of the thriller a story about female problems which evokes a powerful sense of recognition, and part of my ultimate disagreement with her analysis of the film is an ideological one with her estimation of what she recognises.

However, such an evaluation is made more likely by the critical tradition she draws on, which, by demanding that the critic reconstitute the film's meaning as a coherent expression of a world-view, allows her to read all the film's operations in terms of the heroine's subjectivity as the unifying principle. The terms of this unification are then provided by the metaphors of the human condition with which the European cinematic tradition abounds.

The point is that to constitute all the items of filmic production as metaphors for a meaning in an overarching discourse – the exploration of the human condition etc. – leads away from their particular ideological effects within the organisation of the text to a system of values constituted outside the film, which may not actually speak for the critic's ostensible interest.

This is not to suggest that a 'correct reading' is to be discovered only 'inside' the film. Any reading, whether thematic or what I'd loosely call 'structural', is bound to be carried out from a particular reading position, and both Diane Giddis and I work from within a feminist perspective. But the issue is how such a perspective is to be articulated in terms of critical practice.

Diane Giddis's feminism leads her straight to the heroine's subjectivity, which, without considering the twists and turns of plot, character, formal device etc., she takes the rest of the film as expressing. This then puts on her the onus of reconstructing the psychology of 'The Divided Woman' which in turn diverts her from the feminist proposition that the problems for women of entering personal relationships are as much to do with the forms those relations have to take in a patriarchal, capitalist society, as with the seemingly eternal psychological differences between the sexes – the tenet of the tradition she is using. This then leads her to a conclusion, the implications of which are at odds with feminism, namely, that women must put more of their identity and independence at risk in personal, hctcrosexual relationships than men.

On the other hand, to focus on textual operations means both bearing in mind the kind of reading the film invites us to make according to traditional critical values and refusing their elaboration; instead, the critic looks at the structural relations between different aspects of the text which cannot be turned directly into a 'meaning' but which affect or produce implications for the placing of woman in the film – 'woman' being understood here not as an individualised character, but as a cultural and social category which in its turn has a structuring effect on the place actual, concrete women find themselves in within patriarchal society. A key notion for this argument is point of view. Diane Giddis asserts that: '*Klute* is told from a highly subjective viewpoint and the other characters, while "real", can be seen as projections of the heroine's psyche' (p. 57).

The critical methodology by which Giddis goes straight to the film's immanent meaning means that she does not have to ask how point of view is constructed in the cinema or within specific genres. But in my discussion of point of view in film noir I have suggested that the structural location of women within the film text may have very different implications from the meanings derived by interpreting the film in terms of a character. Point of view is an effect structured into the text by a number of different operations and is not simply the result of thematic emphasis. Perhaps this seems a little unfair to Diane Giddis's argument, for she does follow this observation with a convincing account of the parallelism between Klute and Cable of which she says:

> In fact, that threat, Bree's potential killer, can be seen as the incarnation of the emotional danger presented by Klute. From the beginning the two men are almost always shown in juxtaposition. The morning after Bree receives a 'breather' call from her tormentor, Klute makes his first appearance in her life. (p. 57)

But while within Diane Giddis's terms this reading makes thematic sense, it is difficult to see how this relation between the two men is established in the filmic operation of the text as the expression of Bree's subjectivity. Rather, if we trace the play of noir conventions within this Europeanised production it seems more feasible to say that Bree is the object in a struggle between two different male constructions on female sexuality and that the discourse of woman is severely restricted.

Again, what is at stake for feminist film criticism in stating this disagreement? It is not merely a question of posing a 'correct' reading against a less complete one, for although analysis of textual operations produces implications for meaning, it is not concerned to come out with a coherent interpretation, a reconstitution of the text in terms of an overall meaning. As far as *Klute* is concerned *textual analysis* requires in the first place *not* following the film's invitation to separate the level of 'serious issues' from the level of the detective story, seen simply as metaphoric support of a world-view. Rather, we are required to reconstitute sets of textual operations: first, the specific determinations on the female image carried out by the conventions and devices of the noir thriller, and second, the fictional and stylistic conventions emanating from the European art movie as genre, which make the presence of 'serious issues' available to recognition and the work they perform on the female image. It may then be possible to show how the articulation together of the two traditions – the noir thriller and the European art movie – produces a structure in which the problem posed by Women's Liberation is displaced on to the 'trouble' the female image constitutes for the former – the film noir – only to be recuperated and resolved in terms of the moral perspectives of the latter – the European tradition.

The result of this process is that the disturbances, inconsistencies and dislocations of the noir thriller are diminished, if not harmonised and the place of the woman is relocated in far less threatening terms, her image reduced and brought under control at far less cost to the male psyche than happens in the noir thriller.

An analysis of the place of woman in *Klute*

As we have noted, *Klute* recasts some of the traditions of the noir thriller and seeks to assimilate them within an exploration of the contemporary condition. Pakula aims both for stylisation, the dramatic potential of the genre, and the revelation of a certain truth. In this respect he has more self-conscious, more seriously 'artistic' ambitions than did the genre workers who produced the noir thrillers of the 40s and 50s. He doesn't want simply to reproduce the genre but to rework it to his own ends. What does Pakula take from film noir? How does he assimilate what he takes to contemporary conventions? What consequences do these choices have for the location of women?

Narrative structure

To begin with those features of film noir which I have suggested are crucial to its ambiguous location of women, its particular investigative narrative structure and consequent thematic organisation.

First, the *investigative structure*: the *family* and the *heroine* form a set of relations that resemble aspects of the noir plot and at the same time exhibit striking differences. These relations are initiated in the pre-credit opening sequence of the film. The investigation starts out from an Edenic and pastoral image of the family: husband and wife in intimate rapport among a gathering of friends joining together in an open-air meal. A leap in time, an empty chair, the father is missing, and illicit sex appears to have broken the family up. The only evidence of Tom Gruneman's whereabouts is a foul letter he has written to a prostitute, whom he is supposed to have beaten up.

The wife's loyal denials of the suggestion that her husband is 'a very sick man' are juxtaposed to the mystery shot of a tape recorder which opened the film – now playing back the voice of Bree Daniel, the film's prostitute heroine, calmly recommending her client unashamedly to act out his desires: 'Don't be ashamed, nothing is wrong, let it all hang out.' Thus the image of the family is dislodged by the voice of a woman activating sex, and will only be evoked for three more brief moments: by the pimp Frank Ligourin's parodic reference to his 'family' of whores; by John Klute's enquiry to Cable about the people back home; and by Bree's final ironic dismissal of domesticity. So John Klute, an old family friend and ex-policeman who has undertaken to search for Tom Gruneman, will have to travel from the Tuscororan countryside to New York and start his investigation by seeking out the prostitute who may or may not have led the missing man astray. From there he will go on to uncover the moral decadence and sexual alienation of city life.

Thus sexuality is central to the ex-policeman's investigation, and the dominant images of the criminal ambience and investigation in *Klute* – the tape recorder, the telephone, phone-calls from 'breathers', bugging – suggest a prying search into areas of private life and its personal secrets, rather than the plottings of criminal organisations. The psycho-sexual dimension of this privacy is further emphasised by the vertical camerawork,[2] sudden plummeting downward zooms, or ascensions in liftshafts, and by an imagery of netting, wire mesh, and claustrophobic rooms made vulnerable by skylights, and suggesting insecurity, sudden submersion, imprisonment.

But already crucial differences stand out indicating the way in which noir traditions are being rearticulated to mesh in with contemporary cinematic conventions and ideological emphases. A major change in the relation of the investigator/hero to his task of uncovering events. For a start, he does not have to reflect on his own actions. Secondly, the process of detection remains important in plot terms in that the criminal activity is still proceeding into the future and there is still a possibility of Gruneman's being discovered alive and well. Consequently there is a much more straightforward linear drive to the narration of events, more chance of the hero's gaining control over them, with none of the circularity, reversals and gaps of the typical 40s noir plot.

How then does this more mainstream detective construction accommodate the investigation of sexuality which seems central to film noir? To begin with, the place of the woman in the criminal complex is different. She is not the instrument of Tom Gruneman's fate but rather a clue on the way to its discovery. Thus, the structural relation of the detective to the heroine is very different from what is usually the case in a classic film noir. Thus, although the relation Klute establishes with the prostitute supersedes solution of the crime in importance – indeed, the identity of the murderer is given away very early in the film to facilitate this – it is not itself at the centre of the criminal problem. Rather, the development of the relationship takes a parallel course to the process of detection, which, rather than being submerged in the sexual relations set up by the plot as in classic film noir, retains a distinct if skeletal outline. This disengagement of the criminal problem (albeit a sexual one) from the relationship between the detective and heroine means that this relationship is freed of the psychopathic quality it has in the 40s thriller, so that Pakula, in the tradition of the European art movie, is able to use it as a means of exploring the serious contemporary issues he wants to accommodate within the thriller.

Of greater interest to us, however, is a shift in sexual emphases between the plot's various roles. In the 40s thriller the great issue in question is the reliability or otherwise of the woman, the degree of fidelity or treachery inherent in her sexuality. In *Klute* the myth of woman as sexual instigator or predator is very quickly undermined, in the early scenes that document her life, scenes I shall discuss in detail later. Here, however, John Klute's mission is in the first instance to establish his friend's honour, the sexual integrity of the man. And in the course of using the prostitute to help him gain access to the city's sexual haunts, he develops a protective attitude towards her too, and far from seeking to expose the evil of her sexuality, his desire is to save her. But before we go further into this reinflected characterisation of the detective/hero, we need, as a necessary context, to look more closely at the investigative structure of *Klute*.

Patterns of investigation in *Klute*

There are at least four variations on the investigatory/confessional patterns in *Klute*, which can be schematised as follows:

1.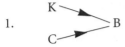

Klute and Cable are both spying on Bree Daniel, the prostitute. Cable, because it was his encounter with Bree and her permissive counter-culture philosophy – 'nothing is wrong, let it all hang out' – which first led him to locate all the evils of the world and male backsliding with women. Armed with a tape recorder, he compiles a morbid dossier on the moral decadence into which he sees Bree and her associates leading men, and is conducting a private campaign of terror against the women which culminates in the ultimate punishment, murder. Klute is spying on Bree first as a detective, because it is only through Bree's work as a prostitute that he can hope to trace the client, known for beating up call-girls, who is reputed to be Tom Gruneman; later, however, he keeps watch as a protector, wanting to save Bree from unknown intruders.

2.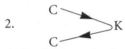

A circular investigation, in which Cable employs Klute, a friend of the Gruneman family, to search for its head whom he himself has murdered; in other words he initiates an investigation into himself, an investigation which forces him to hasten the completion of his work, his final confrontation with Bree, in which he makes his confessional accusations against her, laying his three murders at her door, and claiming that, as he is not an evil man, the blame must be hers.

3.

This confessionally oriented investigation represents the noir investigation of female sexuality but divorced from the male hero and instigated by the woman herself. Bree recognises her sexual activity as a prostitute as a kind of sickness, wishes to find its origins and effect a cure. This structure dominates the interpretative field of the film. If there is any sense of dislocation between the different discourses of the film, it is between the ongoing dialogue of prostitute and psychotherapist in juxtaposition with the detective story. But the effect of such dislocation is to draw attention to the psychotherapeutic discourse as the key to the other investigatory structures, demanding they be read in psycho-spiritual terms. This does not mean, however, that the psychotherapist takes over from the detective in providing the answers, as I shall try to show later, but that the metaphoric power of noir *conventions* is brought into more conscious play, enabling the film to do the work of a 'serious exploration of contemporary life' rather than generic entertainment. Above all it is a structure that rearticulates the *femme fatale* stereotype of film noir to bring it in line with contemporary female stereotypes and in so doing, I would argue, contributes to the neutralisation of the female threat to patriarchy.

4. The final investigative structure cannot be schematised as neatly as the preceding ones and does not concern characters, but rather represents the picaresque elements in a certain kind of detective story, developed more recently in the police movie (*Dirty Harry, Magnum Force, Coogan's Bluff*, TV police serials) in which the lone investigating hero's pursuit of the criminal leads him into a descent into the underside of city life, reminiscent of Bunyan's Vanity Fair where each door that is opened displays a tableau representing one further aspect of the city's decadence and corruption – e.g., the hippies, pot-smoking in the basement of Bree's apartment building; the visit to the high-class madam, and then the downbeat Mama Reese's; the two desperate junkies, awaiting their connection; the disco-dive, where Bree puts herself once more under the protection of her ex-pimp, Frank Ligourin; the pimp's flat where he poses as a high-class photographer, living off the earnings of his ersatz family etc. It is a city located not in a socio-economic system but in a moral sphere, and condemned for its abandonment to desperate hedonism, material acquisition, indulgent self-expression, perverted pleasures.

John Klute: detective hero

If we look at the way these patterns of investigation relate to each other we can see a change in the organisation of the classic noir plot in that the hero's role of investigating and evaluating female sexuality is split, first between Klute and Cable and second between Klute and the psychotherapist. The effect of this, as I have already suggested, is to facilitate a separation of the plot motives of detection and passion. Because of where the heroine is placed in the criminal investigation, the detective is relieved of the burden of judgment on her, which now lies with the criminal himself, whose role, consequently, assumes much larger proportions in the plot. The articulation together of the two patterns of investigation associated with Klute and Cable means that at the point where the detective is becoming involved with the heroine, she is cleared of direct involvement in the crime (Klute hands Bree back her tapes) and in fact she comes to the hero's aid. Thus the fatal passion of film noir, relieved of criminality, can be humanised into a love story, which is helped into being by the psychotherapist. At the same time the heroine's guilt is redefined as Cable's investigation bears more heavily on her life and the detective hero is able to take up the role of saviour. The roles of the psychotherapist and Cable I shall deal with in more detail later. Here I want to look at how the narrative reorganisation of the role of the noir hero effects a rearticulation of his stereotype and characterisation, and the consequent placing of the heroine in relation to him.

Two features dominate this characterisation, both of which serve to distinguish Klute from his forerunners: silence, and a puritanical, almost virginal sexuality. Like the 40s noir investigator, Klute is a loner, an outsider and a stern moralist; however, the origins of his moral rectitude are different. Rather than deriving from cynicism built on an embittered and disillusioned experience of the world, Klute's power stems from his innocence – a country boy, with his illusions and morals intact; his qualification for the task of searching for Gruneman is that 'he's interested, he cares'. Indeed, the plot goes out of its way to disqualify him in police terms, for he has no experience of 'missing persons work'. Klute's innocent puritanism also distinguishes him sexually from his predecessors in the noir thriller. While the 40s private eye moralised against the *femme fatale*, he was too cynical not to take what she offered and through this she could exercise some power. Klute, however, is markedly virginal, bluntly refusing Bree's offer of her body in exchange for the tapes he has made of her phone calls and withholding sex on other occasions where the 40s private eye might be expected to take advantage of the availability of the heroine; for instance, the night an intruder appears above the skylight, he sits up all night in a chair by her bedside and later, when she goes to his basement flat afraid, he offers her his bed while he sleeps on a spare mattress.

Thus a further structural change takes place in the relation of hero and heroine in the noir thriller. Rather than the hero reluctantly succumbing to the heroine's first sexual initiatives, Klute's puritanism undermines Bree's confident sexual assertiveness, and she has to wait until he is asleep before seducing him. Bree and Klute first make love after she has gone frightened and waif-like during the night to his basement room to ask for his company and comfort. This is a scene very uncharacteristic of sexual encounter in film noir: the eroticism is played down with Bree dressed in an old mac and men's pyjamas; yet this scene is sandwiched between scenes of 'aberrant' sexuality that have incurred Klute's stern, disapproving gaze – first their visits to Bree's former mentor, the high-class madam who offers her a home any time she is in need, and to the disco where Bree meets some apparently lesbian friends in search of Jane McKenna; following this scene, they make a visit to Mama Reese's, where they find prostitutes draped over fat middle-aged businessmen. Thus the force of Klute's moral rectitude, which places these city-life tableaux, and others like them, as decadent, is characterised as something totally other, different from the values of the world he scrutinises, and not founded on disillusioned experience of this world as is the morality of the 40s noir hero. This is reinforced by a further difference: whereas the hard-boiled investigators of the 40s thrillers are remarkable for their cynical, wise-cracking repartee and commentary on events – something the voice-over technique indulges – Klute is characterised by an inscrutable silence. Such silence is facilitated by the picaresque, tableau-like structure to the detective strands of the plot, but marks even scenes of personal relationship where dialogue might be expected. More will be said about Klute's silence later.

In place of the brutalism of the 40s hard-boiled hero, Klute's moral disgust at the sexual permissiveness and general decadence of the city is tempered by mothering qualities which respond not to Bree's sexuality but to the lost child in her. He protects her when she is frightened, puts her to bed when she is freaked out, tidies up her flat, chooses her the best fruit in the market. But Klute's gentleness in no way undermines his masculinity. In case this might be in doubt after his refusal of Bree's sexual advances in her flat, he is immediately given the opportunity to demonstrate his male authority, through his command of the situation when he hears somebody above the skylight of Bree's flat, and in the course of a rooftop to basement pursuit pulls his gun – something which he doesn't then have to do till the final confrontation with Cable at the end of the film. Klute's gentleness is accompanied by strong paternalistic traits. Twice his protectiveness towards Bree makes him sit her down and bow her head, and in one of the closing shots of the film she is sitting at his feet.

John Klute and Peter Cable

But the crucial placing of Klute's paternalism is in his structural relation to Cable. Diane Giddis and others have noted their close juxtaposition in the development of the narrative and the similarity of their actions in relation to Bree. Both watch her from the shadows, both follow her on her assignations, Klute taps her phone, Cable tapes her sessions with her clients, both are associated visually with lift-shafts, plummeting depths, screens of wire netting, shadows. Both bear towards her an intense and ambiguous staring gaze. Where the difference occurs is in their respective estimations of and judgments on the prostitute, Bree Daniel. For if the innocent Klute is something of a latter-day knightly crusader among the cesspools of contemporary decadence, and can regard the fallen Bree with a paternalist compassion, Cable, steeped in deadly experience, exhibits a distillation of the noir private eye's cynicism and moral contempt for female sexuality. The two sides of the 40s private eye stereotype's attitude to women – romantic idealisation, and embittered accusatory disgust – have been split here between two characters, representing complementary faces of patriarchy faced with the problem of female sexuality. Whereas Cable seeks to punish and destroy, representing the nineteenth-century, Victorian ethic, Klute, a modern humanitarian spirit, seeks to save. But in either case an active female sexuality, seeking sexual control for the woman's own ends, is no good, and least of all, it turns out, for the woman herself. But before we go further into what constitutes the threat of female sexuality and the contest between these two characters, it would be useful to consider the characterisation of the woman in the case.

Bree Daniel – from *femme fatale* to prostitute

The change of role in Bree Daniel's characterisation, as heroine in a thriller, from *femme fatale* to prostitute has a number of implications, and consequences. Bree Daniel has to fill the place of the film noir heroine in an investigation of female sexuality. At the same time Pakula wants to use the genre's conventions to explore issues of contemporary life. Thus the stereotype, as the centre of the film's investigative plot, must make some reference to contemporary life, must relate to more recognisable contemporary stereotypes than the rather passé *femme fatale* of 'classic' Hollywood, and must conform more closely to the needs of psychologically realistic characterisation. The ultimate effect of these modifications on the noir heroine, as I have suggested, is the relocation of woman in a place less threatening to patriarchy.

The role of prostitute as construed in this film does two things. First, it has journalistic appeal as a topic made acceptable for public discussion at the time of the film's making and therefore can be used to evoke references to the everyday world of contemporary reality, while at the same time the idea of prostitution has the metaphoric power to refer to deeper issues of morality and personal relationships: here it represents alienated sexuality which in turn represents the alienation at the heart of our society.

As a woman, attempting to survive independently in the city, any work open to Bree Daniel depends on the marketability of the female sexual image. We first see her, totally objectified in a model line-up, where the selectors discuss the details of the female applicants' appearance as if they were so much cattle. The would-be models sit under huge mask-like empty female faces, whose features are hidden behind netted veils. Bree is next seen trying the theatre, first with a trendy director who makes it clear that bed is a condition of his helping her, then in a harshly competitive audition for the part of St Joan. For all this, however, what *Klute* exposes in its exploration of contemporary times is not the socio-economic and related ideological structures that define women in terms of their sexual and reproductive role and create a marginal place for them within the labour market, but rather a moral, existential alienation of the psyche which is to be resolved in personal relationships, if at all.

Second, the prostitute, as an independent woman, working with other women to make a living out of men, offers a figure – especially when played by Jane Fonda, known for her supposed 'liberation' – which can accrue to itself some of the trendy modernity of the bachelor-girl stereotype and some of the more popularised aspects of the image of the liberated woman without having to stray too far from territory familiar to audiences and actually broach feminism. At the same time, however, the prostitute, whose definition is based on an independent and manipulative sexuality, can fill the place of the 40s noir heroine. But a reduction in the female image has taken place, for, by definition, the *femme fatale* is a stereotype designating the mysterious and unknowable power of women, whereas the role of prostitute represents a more defined sexual role, amenable to social control, and shorn of the earlier stereotype's fatality.

In part it is this social control that the psychotherapy sessions represent, for Bree Daniel/Jane Fonda is a special kind of prostitute, regarding her prostitution as a kind of sickness and seeking a cure. The *femme fatale* stereotype is brought further under control by the naturalisation of her temperament through psychological motivation. Bree Daniel shows many aspects of the noir heroine's temperament, approachable and loving one minute, cold and rejecting the next, but this changeability is no longer part of the grand manner of the *femme fatale*, it is simply neurotic. Her changes in mood are not incomprehensible, but motivated by a consistent psychology explained as a response to the alienating demands of modern society.

Thus some of the danger represented by the film noir heroine is mitigated by the systems of controls set up in her modern counterpart's representation: the cinéma vérité-style recording of the life of a prostitute; the confessional psychotherapy sessions; psychological motivation. And in this context it is highly significant that it is largely in these psychotherapy sessions that Bree Daniel, unlike the 40s *femmes fatales* who preceded her, is given an inner consciousness – the subjectivity that Diane Giddis sees as the centre of the film. I would argue, however, that it is a very circumscribed subjectivity, and in any case the power of the generic conventions accruing to the male, even in their modified form, means that a convincingly realised female subjectivity does not necessarily dominate the production of meaning in the text, and that to understand its operation in *Klute* we need to examine the relation of the psychotherapy sessions to the other investigatory structures in the film.

Woman's voice and the male gaze

So far we have not broached the question of one of the dominant devices of film noir – the voice-over. As we have already seen, the hero of *Klute*, although naming the film, is marked by his silence. On the other hand, an effect of voice-over is given to the heroine, in the tapes of her conversations with her clients, and in her discourse with the psychotherapist which sometimes takes off from its image and appears over the scenes in her life to which she is referring. Thus it might seem that the woman is given power again by virtue of being given a voice. However, I would argue that it is part of the film's ideological project both to entertain the female voice and then to undermine it.

This happens in several ways. For a start, except for the deliberately mystifying introduction of her taped voice in the opening sequences of the film, Bree's voice-over is motivated and thus naturalised within the narrative. Combined with the absence of flashback structure, this means her voice has little of the controlling distance often made possible in the noir use of voice-over. Then Bree's voice has been stolen from her by her aggressor, Cable, and turned against her. Words uttered in one context are in another turned into indices of the evil which female sexuality incites in men, and are played back to her over the phone and during her final confrontation with her judge.

Third, the female voice that speaks of a struggle for control, for independence, for refusal of involvement and its ensuing roles of dependency and domesticity – a voice that falteringly speaks some of the themes of feminism – is undermined and contradicted by the image. This happens twice very explicitly, when Fonda's voice to the psychotherapist declares her anger at Klute's intrusion into her life and her consequent manipulation of him. What the image shows is Bree melting under the power of his gaze and touch, and subdued by her emotion, kissing his hand. Again, at the end of the film her voice declares:

> I know enough about myself. We're so different. Whatever lies in store, it's not going to be setting up housekeeping in Tuscorora and darning socks. I'd just go out of my mind

– while in the image Fonda is sitting at Klute's feet. In these instances the voice is shown to be mistaken. Bree does not know what's right for her, or what's happening to her. Our belief in the image rather than the voice rests on a number of factors: first, the powerful stereotype of romantic love inevitably takes precedence over these half-articulations of the problems of would-be independent women; second, the ideology of the eye and the camera as offering first-hand evidence of reality may support the image against the voice, and moreover Pakula's candid camera introduction to Bree in her opening scenes has reinforced the status of the image against whatever her conscious voice might say to us.

This last point raises the issue of Pakula's style in these early scenes which establish Bree Daniel/Jane Fonda in the role of prostitute/liberated woman. A key question is whether in these scenes she is subject or object. I would argue that, while the camera style here suggests the creation of a subject, the character is in fact objectified. These sequences begin as social documentary, in which Bree is the silent object in a policeman's rundown on a call-girl's life. We then pass into a controlled candid camera observation of a typical scene between the prostitute and her client, in which we are invited to share the prostitute's view of events, and finally we are taken voyeuristically into the intimacy of her home, where we are offered the spectacle of how the bachelor-girl/prostitute spends an evening alone after her day's work.

In the course of this progression we are encouraged to feel that we have come closer and closer to the heroine's subjectivity, while at the same time the moral structures of the film are being set up to leave little room for a female point of view. So the scene between Bree and her client shows us the cool, controlled professional on the job, but the moment when our adherence to her point of view is clinched – when, groaning out a fake orgasm, she looks at her watch over her client's shoulder – is also the moment which encapsulates, however humorously, the grounds for her judgment and need of redemption. The scene which follows closely after, in which she spends the evening at home, continues to prepare this ground, offering, in contrast, insight into what the 'real' woman is like. Within the conventions of candid camera shooting, the fact of her being alone authenticates her behaviour as natural, unlike the role we saw her playing with her client – an authenticity reinforced by Fonda's improvisatory style of acting. We are shown details of the bachelor-girl's attic apartment and lifestyle – her trendy gear, hip décor, dim lighting, incense, dope – the conventional shorthand for the modern 'liberated woman'. At the same time the treatment of Fonda in this setting suggests fascination with this unaccustomed image of a woman alone, an image which evokes a certain asexuality in the sense that there is no man to perform for, and which goes some way towards defining the woman as constituted for *herself*. Nevertheless, this scene is also placed by the dominant discourse which tells us what such independence 'really' means – loneliness, insecurity, vulnerability to the male outside world and, above all, fear of men and sex.

I am not suggesting that these contradictions are not real entailments of women's struggle for independence and that the details of this scene are not sensitively observed and very recognisable, but that within the context of this film they lose their force as contradictions for female consciousness in order to be accommodated within a male fantasy of desire and fear of women. The scenes that follow simply emphasise the vulnerability, the lost child behind Bree's mask of modernity and independence. We are shown Bree's independence at the same time that it is undermined, set up as phoney, thus preparing for the psychotherapy that follows.

But there is another structure in the film reinforcing the truth of these scenes against what the woman says, the opposition words/silence in which Klute is a pivotal figure. As I have already suggested, Klute is distinguished from his noir predecessors by his silence. But silence is also his source of power, for words are shown in this film to be deceptive, not adequate to the truth, and eventually dangerous. If Klute disdains words, he is given control within the image. The most characteristic shot of Klute is a close-up of his face, a solemn gaze assessing and ultimately controlling the scene he surveys. Within this gaze there are a number of expressions – disgust, affront, hurt, compassion – but all bearing a paternal authority. Under its power Bree gradually moves towards her redemption. Within this opposition – words/silence: woman's voice/male gaze – the authenticity of Bree's early scenes is further reinforced. Not only is she alone, but she is silent, and although Klute's gaze is absent, she is under scrutiny of the camera and, by extension, the gaze of the audience.

Finally, we need to consider how the psychotherapy sessions relate to the opposition of words/silence. It is significant that Bree's confessions are given to a woman, a woman who according to her profession remains also almost silent. But within the structures of this film the psychotherapist's silence has little real power. Through the series of city-life tableaux to which Bree introduces Klute, Pakula offers a critical view of urban sensibility and culture, particularly its permissive counter-culture manifestations, and the scenes with Frank Ligourin show how city life has helped to mystify Bree about her true role as a woman. Thus the need for psychotherapy is a product of the city's falseness and it is under Klute's paternal gaze that Bree unfolds.[3] He takes on the true priestly role – the psychotherapist merely presides, maternal, over this return of Bree to the male.

Struggle for control over the female image

I have suggested that the dynamic of the plot of *Klute* springs from the splitting of the 40s noir investigator hero into two complementary opposites who are then engaged in contest. In some ways this contest recalls the struggle in film noir between different characters for control of the story. But whereas the struggle in the 40s thrillers was more often a fight to the death between hero and heroine, here the splitting of the hero means that the definition of female sexuality is contested between two male protagonists. It is now possible to flesh out this proposition. The antagonism between Klute and Cable rests in their different constructions of female sexuality which are yet two sides of the same thing. The basic threat to patriarchy which the film deals with is the possibility of women asserting their sexuality independently of men, using it to their own ends and deserting their succouring role to the male in order to gain control over him. Bree's enactment of a typical session with a 'john' demonstrates one end of the spectrum within which this threat appears; Cable's 'hell-fire' sermon at the close of the film describes the other. The scene with the 'john' shows us Bree in full sexual command of the situation, offering for payment a professional servicing of the male sexual ego. But while she offers her body and fakes orgasm, her mind is elsewhere, she is not involved. At the same time she reduces the man to a childlike dependency that is an affront to patriarchy. In this respect Klute's silent struggle for the definition of Bree is to return her to the condition of the dependent child – the natural woman, who looks lingeringly after a father carrying his child in the market, who tags happily on to Klute's coat-tails, and ends sitting at his feet, a cat in her lap, like any Gainsborough Miss.

Cable offers a more Victorian and biblical construction on female sexuality and its ills in a rehearsal of the Edenic myth. The prostitute's attempt to control her sexuality, her claim to wield the normally male prerogative of words, leads her to actively engage with male sexual fantasy, instead of passively being its object. In offering the male knowledge of his own sexuality, instead of helping him maintain a veil of secrecy over it, she releases all the repression on which patriarchal civilisation is popularly based and for this she must be punished and destroyed. So Cable is able to lay the blame for all three of his murders at Bree Daniel's door; thus she comes symbolically to fill the place of the noir heroine, responsible for murder even if she has not actually sought to harm anyone. Cable's denunciation of Bree recalls Adam's excuse for eating the forbidden fruit and not a little the disappointed Victorian romantic Ruskin's outrage at the failure of women to live up to his ideas and save civilisation from the barbarity perpetrated by men:

> And whether consciously or not, you must be, in many a heart, enthroned: there is no putting by that crown; queens you must always be: queens to your lovers; queens to your husbands and your sons; queens of higher mystery to the world beyond, which bows itself, and will forever bow, before the myrtle crown and the stainless sceptre of womanhood. But, alas! you are too often idle and careless queens, grasping at majesty in the least things, while you abdicate it in the greatest; and leaving misrule and violence to work their will among men, in defiance of the power which, holding straight in gift from the Prince of all Peace, the wicked among you betray, and the good forget. There is not a way in the world, no, nor an injustice, but you women are answerable for it; not in that you have provoked, but in that you have not hindered. Men, by their nature, are prone to fight; they will fight for any cause, or for none. It is for you to choose their cause for them, and to forbid them when there is no cause. There is no suffering, no injustice, no misery, in the earth, but the guilt of it lies with you. Men can bear the sight of it, but you should not be able to bear it. Men may tread it down without sympathy in their own struggle, but men are feeble in sympathy, and contracted in hope; it is you only who can feel the depths of pain, and conceive the way of its healing.[4] (Ruskin, 1960, p. 136)

The virulence of this judgment, however, is modified and assimilated to a more contemporary view of female sexuality through the reorganisation of noir narrative structure and recasting of roles. The effect of this is to redefine the woman's guilt. Male vengeance, now relocated in the criminal, is punished, but at the same time the discourse of psychotherapy that weaves through the film, together with the redefinition of the hero's role as saviour, shows the heroine's sexual philosophy to be wrong and indirectly responsible for the man's sexual crimes.

This relocation of the heroine between figures representing two sides of the noir hero is facilitated by the fact that she combines two stereotypes normally opposed in the noir thriller: victim and predator. This reorganisation of the balance of forces within the noir plot then paves the way to a rearticulation of its ending and consequent relocation of woman, and reduction of her threat by assimilation. At the beginning of the film Bree's words intrude on a family scene just as it is being destroyed through the agency of perverted sexuality. She, like any noir heroine, exists outside the family and earns an independent living from her sexuality. By the end of the film a change unprecedented in film noir has occurred in that the possibility of a fulfilled heterosexual relationship and of domesticity is posed, as Bree, despite her ironic comments about darning socks for a lifetime, goes off with Klute to the country. But by this time her *voice* has been thoroughly exposed. What we have *seen*, however, is Klute's systematic invasion of her apartment, first tidying it up, then gaining a key, and finally changing its whole style and colour scheme, from the sombre, brooding reds and purples of Bree's bachelor existence, to the cooler subdued blues and greys of domestic life. When she leaves, as some feminists have ironically noted, her room is stripped bare, but for the telephone, which no voice will answer. What Klute appears to have achieved is a rearticulation of the ending of *Double Indemnity*, arriving at the same conclusion – the heroine's realisation of the meaning of love and the return of her sexuality to its proper place – but positively rather than negatively, with less of a struggle from the woman and so with results less destructive to the male ego.

What does such a turnabout in the genre signify? In one sense the film can be seen as offering a dialogue within patriarchy between two opposing strategies in relation to the problem of female sexuality. Faced with the problem of women appearing to compete for masculine roles – here sexual assertion, the power of words, arbitration of morality, dispensation of knowledge – the male protagonist splits, reviving a primitive type of hero, who brings a New World innocence to bear on the exhaustion of our latter-day fascistic moral guardians represented by Cable. This hero is wiser than the serpent and the woman, keeping his counsel to himself. By not committing himself to words, he doesn't run the risk of dividing against himself and so splitting and losing his identity; he retains the power of inner integrity. And in his purity he doesn't need women sexually and so is free of their power. In these respects, the hero maintains his masculine control, while appearing to take up traditionally feminine positions – silence, virginity – and eventually reconciling the wayward woman and saving her sexuality for himself. Meanwhile, Cable, the representative of the old order, is driven to self-destruction, engaging Klute in a circular investigation which leads to his own exposure and defeat. Within this structure, indicative perhaps of an ideological struggle within patriarchy to maintain control over female sexuality and its new, would-be liberating manifestations, are enmeshed fragments that refer forcefully to the images and problems of a struggling feminism.

Notes

1. Diane Giddis, 'The Divided Woman: Bree Daniel in *Klute*', *Women and Film*, vol. 1, nos. 3/4, 1973, pp. 57–60.
2. '*So in Klute we don't see the countryside the detective comes from*. Exactly the opposite and quite deliberately so. At the beginning you see the missing man's family and the different society, which one won't see again. Klute carries the country with him wherever he goes. From the visual point of view, I wanted *Klute* to be a vertical film. And with Gordon Willis, the director of photography, I tried to go against the horizontal format of Panavision, by seeking out verticals. Horizontals open out, create a pastoral feeling, and I wanted tension. Bree's apartment should have been seen as if at the end of a long tunnel. I framed a lot of shots with the back of another character in front, to mask a part of the screen, or made use of other sombre surfaces as masks, in order to create this feeling of claustrophobia which reflects the life of this girl [sic],' from 'Entretien avec Alan J. Pakula', by Michel Ciment in *Positif*, no. 36, March 1972, p. 36.

3. A link between the way urban culture mystifies women about their role and the problem for patriarchy of the 'woman's voice' – her attempt to gain a position from which to speak and be heard – can perhaps be construed in Bree's choice to read for the audition the claim of St Joan to hear holy voices which she must convey to the people. Bree fails the audition, while Klute looks on.
4. John Ruskin, 'Of Queens Gardens', in *Sesame and Lilies* (London: George Allen & Unwin, 1960), pp. 136.

8
Resistance Through Charisma: Rita Hayworth and *Gilda*
Richard Dyer

The argument of this article is that in *Gilda* it is possible to read the generic construction of Gilda as *femme fatale* as being in some measure overturned and exposed, partly by certain features of *mise en scène*, partly by the casting of Rita Hayworth in the role. The argument is based on three assumptions: about film noir, about stars, and about critical reading.

Film noir

Apart from certain broadly generic features (e.g., labyrinthine narrative structures, 'expressionist' lighting and composition, an iconography of hard-boiled heroes, *femmes fatales* and decadence, etc.), film noir is characterised by a certain anxiety over the existence and definition of masculinity and normality. This anxiety is seldom directly expressed and yet may be taken to constitute the films' 'problematic', that set of issues and questions which the films seek to come to terms with without ever actually articulating. (To articulate them would already be to confront masculinity and normality as problems, whereas ideology functions on the assumption that they can be taken for granted.) This problematic can be observed in, on the one hand, the films' difficulty in constructing a positive image of masculinity and normality, which would constitute a direct assertion of their existence and definition, and, on the other hand, the films' use of images of that which is *not* masculine and normal – i.e., that which is feminine and deviant – to mark off the parameters of the categories that they are unable actually to show.

To illustrate this. The heroes of film noir are for the most part either colourless characterisations (cf. the parade of anodyne performers in the central roles – Dana Andrews, Glenn Ford, Farley Granger) and/or characters conspicuously lacking in the virtues of the 'normal' man (e.g., John Garfield, immigrant, loner, a Red; Fred MacMurray as a weak insurance salesman in *Double Indemnity*; Ralph Meeker, plain nasty and unattractive). The exceptions are the characters played by Humphrey Bogart and Robert Mitchum, and it would be interesting to analyse whether it is these characters as written or only as played that makes them seem to be positive assertions of masculine norms. The fact that most film noir heroes are rootless and unmarried, and the implication of quasi-gay relationships in certain instances (*Dead Reckoning*, *The Big Combo*, *Double Indemnity*, *Gilda*, *inter alia*), all serve to rob them, as they are substantially constructed, of the attributes of masculinity and normality. Consequently, the burden for assuring us of the continued validity of these traditional notions falls to other elements of character and milieu construction in the films.

There are two aspects to this. First, film noir abounds in colourful representations of decadence, perversion, aberration, etc. Such characters and milieux vividly evoke that which is not normal, through connotations (including of femininity, homosexuality and art) of that which is not masculine. By inference the hero, questing his way through these characters and milieux, is normal and masculine.

Second, women in film noir are above all else unknowable. It is not so much their evil as their unknowability (and attractiveness) that makes them fatal for the hero. To the degree that culture is defined by men, what is, and is known, is male. Film noir thus starkly divides the world into that which is unknown and unknowable (female) and, again by inference only, that which is known (male).

In this context, any film noir that allows us to 'know' the *femme fatale*, not in the way the hero comes to know her (i.e., by having knowledge of her, finally controlling her), but in the way we 'know' all major characters in novelistic fiction, is making trouble for itself. Once the woman is not the eternal unknowable, the hitherto concealed inadequacy of the hero is liable to become evident. This is what happens in *Gilda*.

Stars

One of the central themes of Molly Haskell's *From Reverence to Rape* is the capacity of the great women stars to 'resist' the demeaning roles to which they were assigned. Haskell theorises this is terms of certain stars' 'sheer will and talent and determination'.[1] While not wishing to diminish the real struggles over representation of such women as Mae West, Greta Garbo, Bette Davis and Marilyn Monroe, it might be more useful to think of this in terms of the signifying function of a star's image within a film. A star's image is constructed both from her or his film appearances (typical roles, modes of presentation, performance and dress styles, etc.) and publicity (including promotion, advertising, fan magazines and gossip). In any particular film, this image is an already signifying complex of meaning and affect. The problem then arises of the 'fit' between this complex and the character the star plays as written and otherwise constructed (e.g., through dress, *mise en scène*, etc.). In the case of *Gilda*, certain elements in Rita Hayworth's image do fit the generic *femme fatale*, but others do not, and this 'misfit' is sufficient to foreground the functions of the *femme fatale* in relation to the problematic adequacy of the hero.

Critical reading

In the analysis of *Gilda* that follows, I am not aiming to produce a definitive reading, nor yet a 'counter-reading' in the spirit of 'semiotic guerrilla warfare'.[2] Rather, I am interested in indicating some of the readings that the film makes possible. In this case, the readings are in certain respects mutually contradictory, and this suggests something of the terrain of ideological struggle within which the film is situated. In this respect these readings need to be returned to the specificities of the film's audiences (e.g., its contemporary cinema audiences, old-movies-on-television audiences, readers-of-articles-like-this audiences, etc.) – something we have not yet learnt how to do.

Gilda

Johnny

Through the decisive device of the voice-over, *Gilda* is very much signalled as being Johnny/Glenn Ford's film. It is his story, his point of view, his destiny that is to concern us. He has the double quest of the film noir – to solve the mystery of the villain and of the woman – and his voice-over guides us through it. Within this, we are repeatedly told what to think of Gilda, to side with him in his denunciation of her, to rejoice in his final possession of her.

Equally, there is no question but that Gilda/Hayworth is set up as another *femme fatale* in the film noir tradition. She is the object of desire in a type of film in which the object of desire is unknowable and treacherous. Hayworth's successful previous roles in dramas (as opposed to her roles in musicals) were as the 'other woman' (*Only Angels Have Wings, Strawberry Blonde*) and most vividly as an archetypal evil seductress in *Blood and Sand*, roles that made it easy to read Gilda in *femme fatale* terms. She is moreover dressed in the film with that combination of artifice and sensuality characteristic of the noir woman (cf. especially the use of long hair, coiffed to appear naturally 'unreally' lustrous and flowing, and of tactile fabrics such as velvet and satin made into dresses that make obvious use of bones to distort the figure).

Yet compelling as these conventions are (the voice-over, the film type, the star image), it is not so easy either to identify with Johnny as the hero or to assent to his view of Gilda. This is partly because he is oddly placed in the film in relation to her and the other main character, Ballin, and partly because Gilda is Hayworth.

The problematic of masculinity and normality is particularly keen in *Gilda* by virtue of the implications of gayness that are built into the relationship between Johnny and Ballin. Apart from evidence external to the film,[3] the manner of Ballin's picking up Johnny, the exchanges of glances and the innuendoes of the dialogue between the two of them, all point to this dimension of their relationship.[4] More importantly, for the concerns of this article, Johnny, the hero of the film, is placed in the position of the woman within the relationship. (As is characteristic of filmic treatment of gays, the Ballin–Johnny relationship not only assumes such relationships are sick, decadent etc., but also assumes that they are structured according to the male–female norms of heterosexual relationships.) This is suggested from the very first scene in which Ballin picks him up. (He rescues him from a fight with some dice players and, taking a fancy to him, invites him to his casino where he becomes his right-hand man.) It becomes more explicit when Gilda arrives on the scene.

By a series of parallels, the significance of which Gilda, but not Johnny, is shown to be fully aware, the film shows Johnny to be placed in the same position *vis-à-*

vis Ballin as Gilda is. They are both his pick-ups. Both say that they have no past, living only from the moment they met Ballin: 'I was down and out – he put me on my feet,' says Johnny, to which Gilda replies, 'What a coincidence.' All this is explicable, if you follow the extremely elliptical dialogue very closely, in terms of Johnny and Gilda desiring to bury the past that contains their relationship to each other. This is, however, never clearly stated and what is said is also meant to be about their present common relationship to Ballin. Hayworth's glamour, a given of using her in the film at all, is complemented by a definite glamorisation of Ford. Where his previous appearances (mainly in Westerns and other action films) use harsh lighting, close-cropped hair and rough costuming, in *Gilda* he is softly lit (with his weakly sensual mouth in particular highlighted), his hair is brilliantined (thus rendered an interesting visual surface) and he is fastidiously dressed. In these respects then Ford-as-hero is none the less structurally placed and to a degree visually constructed as an object of desire.

If Johnny and Gilda are both objects of desire for Ballin and the camera, they are also objects of desire for each other. It is Gilda's traditional noir woman's function to be this, as well as Hayworth's. What is surprising about the film is the degree to which Johnny/Ford is in turn established as an object of her desire. In their first meeting in the film there is an exact reciprocity in the exchange of looks between Johnny and Gilda. From the moment we first see Gilda in this scene, cut in on a movement tossing her hair back and looking straight to where Johnny is standing, each shot of her looking at him is complemented by a shot of him looking at her. Each shot is of equal length; a shot over his shoulder matches a shot over hers, and so on; the sensuous play of light is identical. This establishment of him as an object of desire – which at the verbal level is also signalled as a desire she does not welcome – is maintained, though less forcibly, throughout the film: in the way he is photographed and in her repeated remarks on how 'pretty' he is.

In these ways, Johnny/Ford, despite his voice-over and status as protagonist, is placed in the position of the woman (in patriarchy), looking but also to be looked at. Once this is established, however, it seriously questions his authority as narrator, and in particular the degree to which we perceive Gilda through his judgment of her in voice-over. We are told that she is superstitious, that she is frightened, that she is promiscuous, but we see only the slenderest evidence of it (even accepting that conventions concerning promiscuity in 1946 were different from today). After their marriage, when she comes to beg him to be a husband to her, we are told by him (voice-over) that it is 'wonderful' – but by this stage in the film, it is questionable whether we are going to share this response to her evident humiliation. There is an increasing disjunction between Johnny as the signalled narrator and the actual narration of the plot and of Gilda.

Gilda

Although placed (by the role in this film type, by Hayworth's image, by the film's publicity) as the dangerous and unknowable function of the hero's destiny, this traditional placing of Gilda has been put at risk by the exceptional placing of Johnny/Ford in the film. This gives the character of Gilda the kind of illusion of 'autonomy' and 'being there for her own sake' (and not just for the sake of the hero) usually reserved for men in film. This is further achieved through giving

Gilda a 'private' moment and through other elements in the Hayworth image.

Private moments, in the rhetoric of Hollywood character construction, are moments of truth. What they tell us about the character is privileged over what the character says (and even does) in public. The moment in question in *Gilda* is her first rendition of 'Put the Blame on Mame'. This is not strictly private. She sings it to the men's room attendant. However, his presence if anything reinforces the privileged quality of this moment, for he is signalled throughout the film as the wise man, down to earth, of the people, who 'understands' Gilda. Their relationship is constructed such that it assumes a transparency between them. Nor is the scene totally unobserved (within the film) – Johnny does come in on the end of it. However, it is sung in large part without his presence as observer, and the use of close-ups in the song powerfully asserts the truth of Gilda's expression at this moment. (Close-ups are one of the central mechanisms for the construction of the private.)

All this signalling as a moment of privileged access to Gilda's character is devoted to a song which points to how men always blame natural disasters on Mame – that is, women. The song states the case against the way film noir characteristically constructs women. The content of the song, together with its privileging *mise en scène*, points to the illegitimacy of men blaming women, where film noir generally is concerned to assert just that. (In *The Lady from Shanghai*, this rhetoric of the private is used to generate a certain pity for the Hayworth character, as it is here, but only all the more bitterly to expose by the end of the film this very appeal for pity as the *femme fatale*'s most damnable wile of all.)

This moment of truth informs the rest of the film. We are likely to use it to read Gilda's collapse at Johnny's feet (when the phoney lawyer brings her back to him from Buenos Aires) not with sadistic delight (as the voice-over urges us) but with pity of identification. The second, public rendition of 'Put the Blame on Mame' becomes a song of defiance, not just of a trapped wife against her husband, but of a woman against the male system.

The casting of Hayworth as Gilda gives the character a positive charge (where *femmes fatales* are usually negative, in the sense of being absent in terms of personality, mere functions or the eternal unknowable). This is, to begin with, partly due to the sheer status of Hayworth as a star. As one might expect from films that were usually low-budget productions, the *femmes fatales* of film noir were not usually played by major stars. (Crawford as Mildred Pierce belongs to the 'woman's film' emphasis of that film; only Barbara Stanwyck in *Double Indemnity* and Lana Turner in *The Postman Always Rings Twice* compare with Hayworth as major stars playing *femmes fatales*.) Hayworth was already established as a star with a known image and biography. In this sense, she has charisma. This is not in fact a 'magic presence', but it is constructed and experienced in this way. It is difficult for a *femme fatale* to be unknowable and 'absent', when incarnated by someone so known and present as Rita Hayworth. (Only by the most implacable destruction of Hayworth's image, including, crucially, cropping her hair and changing its colour, was Orson Welles able to do this in *The Lady from Shanghai*.)

It is not just her star status that gives Hayworth her presence in the film. It is also her position as an identification figure, and her dancing. Both of these relate to the issue of Hayworth as a sex object for the male viewer. The first raises the question of the female viewer, the second that of the processes of objectification.

Hayworth was primarily a 'love goddess', and as such very much a star for heterosexual men. However, by the time of *Gilda*, elements were accruing to the Hayworth image that would, in traditional terms, make her an identification figure for heterosexual women. These were partly her role as partner (rather than menace) in musicals, and partly details of her life surrounding marriage – married to a businessman in 1937, divorced 1942, married to Orson Welles 1943, bearing a daughter 1945 (just before shooting *Gilda*). What Gilda/Hayworth does can thus be read not only as a projection of male fantasy but also as an identification of female life concerns. (This is complicated. We do not know what audience members, female or male, do with films, in general or in specific instances, and women may identify with the most exotic of male projections. More importantly, the life concerns of marriage-and-family are very much to do with where women are placed within a male-dominated society. To say that women might identify with a star/character by virtue of the latter's involvement in marriage-and-family is only to acknowledge that many women are interested in the place to which they have been assigned.)

No other *femme fatale* dances. Undoubtedly, the numbers in *Gilda* are there because Hayworth was known as a dancer, rather than for any necessity of the Gilda character. However, once there, they introduce a new element into the construction of the character as a sexual object – namely, movement.

It is worth noting, first, that Hayworth dances in a manner different in certain respects from that of previous leading women dancers in Hollywood. Unlike Ginger Rogers, Hayworth did not require a partner for her dancing; and unlike Eleanor Powell, who did do solo numbers, Hayworth's style is not mechanical and virtuoso. (Powell is technically the most brilliant tap-dancer film star, but she does not use tap expressively.) The use of dance as 'self-expression' as instanced by Fred Astaire was also available to and used by Hayworth (though always in a less developed form than Astaire's). Although 'self-expression' is a problematic concept in relation to the arts, as a notion informing artistic practices, and especially dance, it is extremely important, and especially in the context of a character who is generically constructed as having no knowable self.

The comparison with Rogers and Powell is also important in terms of style. The former is identified principally with social dance (the Astaire–Rogers *pas de deux* are elaborations on the waltz, foxtrot, etc.), and iconographically with social dance in the upper echelons of society. Powell, on the other hand, was billed as 'The World's Greatest Tap Dancer', a dance form associated principally in this period with the white appropriation of (black) tap dance in vaudeville. Hayworth, by contrast, dances in a Latin American style, and even if this were not recognisable from the dancing, it was known through her image (her parents were Spanish and she started work as a member of their Spanish dance troupe; Spain is not Latin America, but the popularity of Latin American dances in the 40s made the slippage from one to the other easy, and *Gilda* compounds it by being set in South America). The appropriation of Latin American dances into North American social dance is a characteristic example of the latter taking over a dance from a culture it considers primitive (e.g., European peasantry, American blacks) in terms of that culture's more 'authentic' erotic expressivity. Identifying Hayworth with the style in the solo numbers in *Gilda* makes it possible to read her dancing in terms of eroticism for herself as well as for the spectator.

This reading is also made possible by the more general fact of Hayworth/Gilda's sexuality being importantly constructed in terms of movement. In her essay 'Visual Pleasure and Narrative Cinema',[5] Laura Mulvey suggests an opposition between stasis and movement in relation to sexual objectification. The former fixes or controls the object of desire for the pleasurable gaze of the spectator, whereas the latter 'escapes' this control. Mulvey discusses this in terms of spectacle and narrative respectively, but one can also speak within the purely spectacular of sexual construction through stasis and movement. Significantly, by far the greater part of the history of women as sex objects in the cinema has been in terms of stasis – through the back-up industry of the pin-up (in this context, a most revealing term), through the isolation of specific fragments of the female body (Grable's legs, Lake's hair, Mansfield's breasts, etc.), through glamour photography that depends for its moulding and modulating effects on the stillness of the subject (cf. especially close-ups of the 'loved' one), and through 'choreographic' traditions that minimise movement (e.g., Busby Berkeley's patterned chorines, the slow, haughty parade adopted from Ziegfeld, the use of the fashion show). In all these ways, the woman as sex object is fixed, held in place, controlled. Hayworth, on the other hand, is first seen cut in on a movement (tossing her hair back), a particularly dynamic effect, and her dance numbers are important moments in which the film dwells on her sexuality. In terms of the narrative, they are also moments of escape (borrowing generically from the musical), the first away from Johnny in Buenos Aires, the second defiantly and finally against him in his nightclub.

The fact of movement, the particular kind of movement, the association with it of Hayworth's image, its narrative placing, all make it possible to read Hayworth-as-Gilda either in Marjorie Rosen's terms: 'for the first time a heroine seemed to say, "This is my body. It's lovely and gives me pleasure. I rejoice in it just as you do"',[6] or else in terms of male heterosexual enjoyment of the character – of surrender rather than control. (There is after all no reason why heterosexual men should not enjoy in the cinema a sexual position – of passivity – that they are not supposed to enjoy, or be capable of, in actual heterosexual relations.)

Once we have pushed this far, however, we are close to suggesting that the film is far from placing Gilda/Hayworth as the unknowable against which to set Johnny/Ford as the known, and therefore as the validated masculine norm. On the contrary, according to this reasoning, it is Gilda/Hayworth who is known and normal, and Johnny who is unknown and deviant.

It is doubtful that most of us would come away with quite that conclusion. Generic conventions are very powerful as are more overarching conventions, such as the happy heterosexual ending, in certain senses signalling Gilda/Hayworth's capitulation, and the fact that, after all, Johnny/Ford is a man, already signifying masculinity and normality, just as Gilda/Hayworth as a woman already signifies femininity and deviance. As emerges from the discussions of the topic by Elizabeth Cowie and Griselda Pollock,[7] representations of women and men already powerfully signify the social place of women and men even before a film does anything with them.

Yet signification is never that fixed, and the narrative and star image procedures of *Gilda* do do some mischief with these normative conventions. There is a danger when making such a case of wanting to claim that we can therefore 'rescue' *Gilda* as a 'progressive' film. Perhaps we can, but it is worth noting at what price *Gilda* effects, in so far as it does, this construction of the female as normal over against the film noir hero. It is by suggesting that Johnny/Ford is not a 'real man', that he is in the position of the woman *vis-à-vis* Ballin, the camera and Gilda, and that he is in some sense homosexual, that the construction of Hayworth-as-Gilda gains real force. The implication that Johnny is inadequate (also suggested by the overtones of sadomasochism in his relations with Ballin and Gilda) involves a criterion of adequacy. This can in part mean being like Gilda, but in this society it will still be notions of what real men are and should be like that allow the film to place Johnny as inadequate. In other words, the film does in some measure expose its own problematic, while still holding on, at one further remove, to traditional notions of masculinity and normality.

Notes

1. Molly Haskell, *From Reverence to Rape* (New York: Holt, Rinehart & Winston, 1974, p. 8, and Baltimore: Penguin, 1974). For a critique of this position, see Claire Johnston, 'Feminist Politics and Film History', *Screen*, vol. 16, no. 2, pp. 115–124.
2. Umberto Eco, 'Towards a Semiotic Enquiry into the Television Message', *Working Papers in Cultural Studies*, no. 3, Autumn 1972, p. 121.
3. 'According to Ford, the homosexual angle was obvious to them at the time: they could see the implications in the relationship between the men in the early part of the film – nothing stated, just mood', John Kobal: 'The Time, the Place and the Girl: Rita Hayworth', *Focus on Film*, no. 10, p. 17.
4. I have discussed this aspect of the film in an article, 'Homosexuality and Film Noir', *Jump Cut*, no. 16, pp. 18–21.
5. Laura Mulvey, 'Visual Pleasure and Narrative Cinema', *Screen*, vol. 16, no. 3, pp. 6–18.
6. Marjorie Rosen, *Popcorn Venus* (New York: Avon Books, 1974), p. 226.
7. Elizabeth Cowie, 'Women, Representation and the Image', *Screen Education*, no. 23, pp. 15–23; Griselda Pollock, 'What's Wrong with Images of Women?', *Screen Education*, no. 24, pp. 25–33.

9
Postscript: Queers and Women in Film Noir
Richard Dyer

Gilda seems unusual among films noirs for having as its hero an ordinary guy who also has a homosexual relationship. The ordinariness of the film noir hero does not consist of the unspectacular decency most usually constructed by Hollywood as ordinariness; film noir heroes are weak (*Double Indemnity, Detour*), perplexed (*Dead Reckoning*), cynical (*Farewell My Lovely*), obsessive (*The Big Combo*), paranoid (*The Dark Corner*), sadistic (*In a Lonely Place, Kiss Me Deadly*) or just bland (*Laura*) – but they are not queers. Johnny in *Gilda* manages to have a touch of all the usual screwed-up film noir ordinariness and yet also to be willing to have an affair with Ballin. At the same time there is no lack of queers (female and male) in film noir, most obviously in *Farewell My Lovely, In a Lonely Place, Laura, The Maltese Falcon, Strangers on a Train* and, on the edges of noir, *Rebecca, Rope* and *The Seventh Victim*. Yet these are unordinary characters, stereotypically marked and sometimes splendidly played as queer. Not so Johnny.

It takes two to tango. In focusing on the remarkableness of Johnny, it is easy to forget his partner, Ballin. And he turns out to have affinities with one of the great queens of film noir, Waldo Lydecker (Clifton Webb) in *Laura*, as well as Hardy Cathcart (Webb again) in *The Dark Corner*[1] (and their less evidently gay counterpart, 'Grandy' Grandison (Claude Rains) in *The Unsuspected*). Less witty and brilliant (more George Macready than Clifton Webb), Ballin is none the less, like Waldo and Hardy, fastidiously dressed and mockingly perverse (the standard signs of homosexuality in film noir),[2] as well as élitist, powerful and cruel. However, what makes them most alike, and most queer, is their relationship to women. It is this that I want to explore here, widening the discussion to consideration of the role of queers in the construction of women in film noir.

We know that Ballin is open to gay sex, but he marries Gilda. Equally, Waldo is a classically waspish, fussily dressed queen, with rococo and Orientalist tastes in the decorative arts (and played by the virtually 'out' Webb); yet he shows only contempt for men and is obsessed with Laura, even saying (in voice-over) that he is the only man who really knew her, while ducking detective McPherson's question as to whether he was in love with her. Hardy in *The Dark Corner* is in many ways a re-run of Waldo, an art dealer apparently most relaxed in the company of old women (whom he patronises) and a blond gigolo, Tony Jardine. The first scene in which he appears establishes his character in a series of *bons mots* at a party he is throwing: he greets one woman with 'Guten Abend, Frau Keller', then whispers to

Jardine in explanation that she is the 'wife of the Austrian critic – she always looks like she's been out in the rain, feeding poultry', a queer cocktail of snobbery, misogyny and unkindness masquerading as wit; his remark, 'I never confuse business with sentiment – unless it's extremely profitable, of course', is Wildean in its pacing, while his comment, 'As long as I'm amusing you'll forgive me', is surely the queer's credo. Yet the film pivots on his revenge for the infidelity of Mary, his wife, in the arms of Jardine. In other words, there is much to indicate that Waldo, Ballin and Hardy are queers and yet they have primary relationships with women. All, however, have the same relationship with women: they aestheticise, 'adore', them, without really desiring them sexually.

They see Gilda, Laura and Mary as beautiful creatures. Waldo moulds Laura into the ideal woman, elegant, gracious, cultivated and above all beautiful. Much of his flashback is his account to Mark McPherson (Dana Andrews) of the process by which he effected this transformation of a rather ordinary, if pushy, young woman into the epitome of high-class glamour, a woman worthy to be seen on his arm and to sit among his antiques, so much so that she became 'as well known as Waldo Lydecker's walking-stick and his white carnation' (Waldo's words). Hardy keeps a portrait by Raphael in his vault, recounting to a group of visitors how he worshipped it until one day he met Mary, its living embodiment. He tells the latter that he never wants her to grow old, a sort of transferral on to her of the crypto-queer desire to fix beauty recounted in *The Portrait of Dorian Gray*. Mary tells her lover Jardine that, though Hardy gives her 'everything a man can give a woman', yet 'still it isn't enough' – a fascinatingly ambiguous pronouncement which surely strongly suggests that Hardy does not give her the one thing that it is most commonly assumed men give women within marriage, sex. For Hardy, Mary is a work of art, adored to the point of sickness, providing a grim undertow to his quip to a party guest that 'the enjoyment of art is the only remaining ecstasy that is neither illegal nor immoral'; he kills not to have his work of art robbed. There is nothing as explicitly aestheticising with Ballin, but the way he introduces Gilda to Johnny (not, presumably, knowing that they have already met) sets up a similar version of a male–female relationship. Johnny comes to the house, letting himself in (one of the many small details indicating the nature of their relationship) and hears Gilda's voice. 'Quite a surprise to hear a woman singing in my house, eh Johnny?', says Ballin, pointedly, to which Johnny, equally suggestively, replies, 'Yes – quite a surprise', his voice tailing off in confusion. Then Ballin leads Johnny into the mansion, up a splendid staircase, through spacious corridors, to present him with his jewel – Gilda. Johnny's response to the marriage suggests that he assumes that it is a sexually expressed one, that Gilda has come between him and Ballin, yet there is never any sign of any marital intimacy between Ballin and Gilda, none of the touching and glances, the closeness in the frame and intense, unspeaking shot, reverse-shot patterns, the musical surges and chromaticism, which construct physical 'chemistry' in Hollywood cinema of the period. The absence of all of this and his parading of Gilda throughout the film suggest that his relationship to her is much like Waldo's to Laura and Hardy's to Mary.

This aestheticising tendency is of a piece with their villainy. Queers generally in film noir are not evil just because homosexuality is abnormal or wrong. Nor is it even only because they are 'like' women, something which is abhorrent either because they are like the sex they are not supposed to be like, or because, women being on the whole *fatales*, then so must be any man like them. Queers are also evil because the aesthetic gives them an access to women that excludes and threatens the normal male. On the one hand, the very feeling for the aesthetic is coded as feminine in the culture; on the other hand, its asexuality allows queers a closeness to women uncomplicated by heterosexual lust.

A clear instance of this is the character of Lindsay Marriott in both versions of *Farewell My Lovely* (1944 and 1976).[3] The first, of necessity more discrete, conveys Lindsay's sexuality through his dealing in jewellery, the ring on his little finger, the softness of his large overcoat, the almost blowsy quality of his white cravat which he primps up during his conversation with Marlowe and, especially, his perfume, the very fact of being perfumed. A gag is made out of this: the lift man tells Marlowe he has a visitor and Marlowe assumes it's his hulking client, Moose Malloy; he asks if he's sober and the lift man says yes, adding in a sardonic voice, 'he smells real nice'; when Marlowe reaches his office, he discovers Marriott, smelling of perfume. The whole thing is laid on with a trowel in the remake, with Marlowe remarking repeatedly to Marriott on the smell, and a character later commenting that all the *fatale* Mrs Grayle's male friends are 'like that'. Perfume links Marriott (in the 1944 version) with another queer, Jules Amthor, when Marlowe takes a carnation from Amthor's corpse and sniffs it,[4] and also with Joel Cairo in *The Maltese Falcon*, whom, like Marriott, we are first introduced to via his perfume ('Gardenia', says Sam Spade's secretary Effie archly, handing him Cairo's calling card). Perfume is not only feminine, it is insidious: it gets in everywhere, can't be seen or touched or, therefore, controlled, it's a typically female piece of in-direction, of a piece with seduction, manipulation, deceit and the other strategies of fatality.

The effeminate aestheticism of queers is an exaggeration or parody of feminin-ity, in effect a foregrounded performance of it. They both adore, inflate, the fem-ininity of already highly feminine women and, by association, also suggest its artifice. This femininity contrasts with the nice and supposedly 'natural' wife/sweetheart mode of femininity (and thus destabilises the dénouements of *Gilda* and *Laura*, where it is hard to believe that Johnny and Gilda or Laura and McPherson are really set for marriages made in heaven). Though present and cen-tral throughout *The Dark Corner* in Lucille Ball's Kathleen, warm and domesti-cated femininity more often appears, if at all, on the edges of films noirs (*Out of the Past, The Big Heat, Kiss of Death*), and much of the angst of the genre derives from the sense of a world without wives and sweethearts.[5] That world is also one of male and female queers, by definition outside of the safe, understood spheres of heterosexual relations, namely, home and courtship. Womanhood in film noir most often – or, certainly, memorably – figures as over-elaborate or sheened coif-fure, strikingly perfected couture, sophisticated mannerisms – in short, the prod-uct of the queenly arts.

What the heroes' screwed-up ordinariness has to contend with, then, is not just powerful gangsters and henchmen and vividly alluring and generally deceptive women, but a whole miasma of femininity spun around them by queers. The lat-ter both keep the hero from the woman, in a sickly bonding over the faintly eroti-cised arts of fashion, jewellery, *savoir-faire* and scents, and are part of the confusion, uncertainty, deeply untrustworthy character of the appearances of this world.

Female queers figure differently in relation to the central female figure. Not so much Mrs Danvers in *Rebecca*, perhaps, if one counts this as part of film noir. Her relation to the dead Rebecca is one of adoration, of an enrapture with scents and silks that she herself does not wear. Like other film noir lesbians, however, she has a closer physical intimacy with a woman than do the male queers. The latter may keep the guys from the women, but they have no sexual interest in the women. Not so the dykes. In *In a Lonely Place*, Laurel's masseuse Martha has, of course, the most intimate and erotically suggestive of jobs, fondling her mistress's body, all the while calling her 'angel' (to which Laurel shows no objection). Similarly, Frances Amthor in the 1976 *Farewell My Lovely* has half-naked 'girls' clustered around her in her brothel: 'there she was – in the flesh', says Marlowe in voice-over. Both women have scraped back hair, that is mannish especially by comparison with the coiffure of other women in the films – no queen has been at these dykes' hair. They are thickset; their large bosoms give them bulk, but are covered by plain, unfussy blouses that de-emphasise them as signs of womanliness.

These heavy hints of butchness and the tactile intimacy of their relations with women make them seem formidable rivals to men. Literally, they do threaten the male protagonists. The shots of Laurel and Martha are taken from a low angle, so that Martha looms powerfully over Laurel; the latter has the three-point lighting that eliminates shadow and gives a glow, whereas Martha has a shadow across the face which brings out the malevolent hardness in her features. Massaging her all the while, she reminds Laurel that 'they've still not found that check-room girl', last seen in the company of Dix, and tells her what Dix did ('beat her up, broke her nose') to Frances Randolph whom she, Martha, 'used to take care of'. She wants to turn Laurel against Dix and take her away from him. Frances threatens Marlowe more directly: she stands over him and slaps him about the face, injects him in the neck, putting him out for hours, and then laughs at him when he comes round and, still woozy, points a gun at her.

Yet the dykes' threat must also be shown to be dealt with summarily and even brutally. Laurel dismisses Martha angrily, and she is never seen again in the film (though, as V. F. Perkins (in Cameron (ed.), 1992: 228) suggests, her parting words – 'I'll get out, angel. But you'll beg me to come back when you're in trouble. You will, angel, because you don't have anybody else' – may not be so wide of the mark). Frances suffers a worse fate, for though she is shown as tough and violent, she is also shown as easy to defeat. When she slaps Marlowe repeatedly, it has little effect, he makes no sound and it is all shown within one take; one punch from him, however, sends her reeling back and draws blood, she gulps/moans and there is a reverse angle cut emphasising the impact (we see over her shoulder as he punches her and cut to a frontal shot of her staggering back holding her mouth). She is interrupted in her laughter at Marlowe by one of the girls coming in and telling her that one of her favourites, Doris, is in bed with one of her henchmen; she lumbers off and bursts in on them, only to be at once shot dead by the man. She's ungainly and she waddles, she has none of the tough guy's elegance, and she bounces when she collapses dead on the bed. In both cases, the lesbian is estab-lished as no match for the hero on two counts – first, the desired woman does not desire the dyke (Laurel rejects Martha, Doris would rather go with a man than with Frances) and second, in trying to be tough and aggressive, film noir dykes are readily portrayed as trying to be like men and, poor things, inevitably failing.

Yet this very despatchability of the butch lesbian (so different from the lipstick menace of *Basic Instinct*) also relates to the construction of femininity as threat in film noir. The gay man bonds insidiously with the *fatale* woman through the feminine, whereas the lesbian is weakened and defeated by her mannish alienation from femininity. In short, queers of both sexes, but in different ways, emphasise excessive, undomesticated femininity as a problem and source of anxiety for the hero.

All of this is in contrast with healthily homosocial relations. In general, film noir heroes trust no one, but if it's going to be anyone, it will be another man. *Dead Reckoning* is one of the clearest cases, with Rip (Humphrey Bogart) spending the whole film trying to find out what happened to his army buddy, Johnny. It would be possible to interpret this as a (repressed) homosexual relationship (just as others have tried to do with Neff and Keyes in *Double Indemnity*). The first scene has them sharing a railway sleeping compartment, with Johnny changing his clothes in front of him; he describes Johnny later, beautifully and hauntingly, as 'tough, laughing and lonesome', and at the end of the film tells Coral, the woman of the film, unequivocally that he 'loved [Johnny] more' than her. Yet one might more profitably think of this as homo-eroticism in Michael Hatt's sense of the term (in Benjamin (ed.), 1993: 8–21), that is, not as cleaned up/repressed homosexuality, but as the production of a sanctioned physically intimate male bonding that is not 'sexual'. The value of this formulation is that it allows us to acknowledge the intensity, physicality and variety of male–male relations (or indeed female–female ones) without having to understand this through privileging genitally expressed sexuality in the explanation of human relations. It also, in the present context, adds something further to our understanding of the threat of the *femme fatale* and her conspirator in femininity, the male queer. For it is sexuality, with all its urgency and irrationality, which makes femininity threatening. It is sexuality that makes people remember Gilda and Laura as *femmes fatales* when they are nothing of the sort. It is sexuality that may draw the hero into the web of the uncertainty of the world through his desire. What a relief to fall back on the bonds of loving homosociality.

It is femininity, sexualised, excessive femininity, that disturbs the masculine sense of security, selfhood and knowledge of the world in film noir. One might even say that it is effeminacy, whether of the kind bespeaking male queerness or of the performative, artificial kind so dependent on the queenly arts. Lesbians threaten the hero because they have physical access to women and knowledge of womanhood; as rivals with more going for them on these fronts than the heroes, they must be quickly despatched; but, in film noir, they don't threaten his hold on the world. It is femininity (including that of queers) which does this.

This presents us with a recurrent conundrum of feminism. If femininity is so dangerous, doesn't that give power to women? If it's the sexuality of femininity that is powerful, doesn't that make men vulnerable when prey to their desires? Isn't it the case that what we remember about so many films noirs are Gilda and Laura, Veronica Lake and Jane Greer, Phyllis Dietrichson's anklet and Barbara

Clifton Webb as Waldo Lydecker (top) in Laura *(1944) and as Hardy Cathcart in* The Dark Corner *(1946).*

Stanwyck's wig, Waldo and Cairo. ... Doesn't one often think that one would really rather spend time with a Gloria Grahame floozy or a Clifton Webb queen than with Mark Stevens, Dana Andrews or Cornel Wilde? Much of the continued fascination with film noir has lain precisely in the way it mobilises the fascination and power of the feminine. This is why Elizabeth Cowie (in Copjec (ed.), 1994: 135) can challenge 'the tendency to characterise film noir as always a masculine form', emphasising the way 'these films afforded women roles which are active, adventurous and driven by sexual desire'. It is part of what Joan Copjec (1994: 192–5) is getting at in her discussion of the *femme fatale* as the site of *jouissance*, that delicious but uncontrolled surrender to the libidinal which the hero both wants and can't cope with.

The reason why I suggest this is a conundrum, however, is that the feminine has also often been seen as a construction, projected on to women by men (including gay men, politally problematic players in all this). If it is powerful to be designated as feminine, still it cannot therefore be construed straightforwardly and unambiguously as a free choice. If (some) women and queers participate in the construction and performance of femininity, is that seizing the opportunity afforded by male desire or colluding in it, or do we need to revise the idea that the feminine is solely the product of uneffeminate male imaginings? Film noir is interesting not because it resolves this conundrum, but because it foregrounds it, and not least by the presence of its queers. Film noir queerness suggests that the feminine is not coterminous with womanhood – that there are different ways of being feminine, that some men can be feminine, that some women can be effeminate. And in doing all this, it may make us wonder what is so very masculine and straight about heterosexual male sexual desire for the feminine. In short, it takes us from the queers of pre-gay liberation to contemporary queer theory, unsettling the notion that there are, clearly and separably, queers and straights, winkling out the queerness of everything. I'm inclined to believe that most culture works to hold the line of sexual differentiation, but not film noir, or at any rate not always definitely.

Notes

1. As this film (directed by Henry Hathaway at 20th Century-Fox in 1946) is much less known than *Gilda* and *Laura*, and I shall discuss it in a little detail, a brief account of it may be helpful here. The central character is Brad Galt (Mark Stevens), a private eye who believes his ex-partner Tony Jardine (Kurt Kreuger) is trying to kill him. Hardy Cathcart (Clifton Webb) is a wealthy art dealer with a beautiful, much younger wife Mary (Cathy Downs), who is in love with Jardine. Out of jealousy, Cathcart arranges to have Jardine killed, pinning the blame on Brad. The latter finally works out what has happened with the help of his loving secretary Kathleen (Lucille Ball).
2. Cf. Richard Dyer, 1993.
3. The original US title of the first version is *Murder My Sweet*.
4. See Jonathan Buchsbaum (1992: 96).
5. Cf. Sylvia Harvey's essay in this book.

129

10

Female Spectator, Lesbian Spectre:
The Haunting
Patricia White

Feminism has shaped contemporary film studies in a fundamental fashion. Nevertheless, it has become increasingly apparent that discussions of critical issues such as desire, identification, and visual and narrative pleasure do not automatically encompass the lesbian subject. The dominance of the heterosexual concept of 'sexual difference' as term and telos of feminist enquiry has impoverished not only the study of specific film texts, but also the very theorisation of female subjectivity. In this essay I attempt to trace the ghostly presence of lesbianism in classical Hollywood cinema on the one hand, and in feminist film theory on the other, through the reading of two texts in which a defence against homosexuality can be detected.

Genre and deviance

What have been considered the very best of 'serious' Hollywood ghost movies – *The Curse of the Cat People* (1944), *The Uninvited* (1944), *The Innocents* (1961), and Robert Wise's 1963 horror classic, *The Haunting*, to name a few, are also, by some uncanny coincidence, films with eerie lesbian overtones. Masquerading as family romance, these films unleash an excess of female sexuality which cannot be contained without recourse to the supernatural. To be more explicit, in the case of *The Haunting*, female homosexuality is manifested in the character of Claire Bloom. Regrettably, though perhaps understandably, eclipsed by two films Wise directed just before and after *The Haunting*, namely *West Side Story* and *The Sound of Music,* the film will maintain its place in cinematic history for two reasons. First, it is one of the few Hollywood films that *has* a lesbian character. Claire Bloom appears as what is perhaps the least objectionable of Sapphic stereotypes – the beautiful, sophisticated, and above all predatory lesbian. Although not herself a fashion designer, her wardrobe is by Mary Quant; she has ESP, and she shares top billing with Julie Harris, a star who from her film début in *The Member of the Wedding* through her incongruous casting as James Dean's love interest in *East of Eden,* to her one woman show as Emily Dickinson, has insistently been coded 'eccentric'. The second reason for which *The Haunting* is remembered is its effectiveness as a horror film. Like its source, Shirley Jackson's *The Haunting of*

Hill House, the movie is adept in achieving in the spectator what Dorothy Parker on the book jacket calls 'quiet, cumulative shudders'. At least one reliable source pronounces *The Haunting* 'undoubtedly the scariest ghost movie ever made' (Weldon, 1988: 307). It is clear that reason number two is related to reason number one – for *The Haunting* is one of the screen's most spine-tingling representations of the disruptive force of lesbian desire.

Though the alliance of horror with lesbianism may leave one uneasy, it should be pointed out that the horror genre has been claimed by film criticism as a 'progressive' one on several grounds. Concerned with the problem of the normal, it activates the abnormal in the 'threat' or the figure of the monster. In 'When the Woman Looks,' Linda Williams has noted a potentially empowering affinity between the woman and the monster in classic horror films, without exploring the trope of the monster as lesbian. The omission of any mention of lesbian desire is all the more striking given her thesis: 'it is a truism of the horror genre that sexual interest resides most often in the monster and not the bland ostensible heroes' (Doane, Mellencamp, Williams (eds), 1984: 87). She continues, 'clearly the monster's power is one of sexual difference from the normal male'.[1] The horror genre manipulates codes specific to the cinema – camera angles that warp the legibility of the image and the object of the gaze; framing that evokes the terror of what lies beyond the frame; sound effects that are not diegetically motivated; unexplained point-of-view shots that align the spectator with the monster – for effect and affect.

In *The Haunting* the two female leads, both 'touched by the supernatural' (as it were), are invited to take part in a psychic experiment in a haunted New England mansion. As explicitly deviant women, they are asked to bear witness to another power, an alternative reality. They join their host, Dr Markway (Richard Johnson), the pompous anthropologist turned ghost-buster, and the wisecracking future heir to the house, Luke (Russ Tamblyn), who is sceptical of any unusual 'goings-on' (fig. 1).[2] A truly terrifying sojourn with the supernatural at Hill House leaves the Julie Harris character dead due to unnatural causes and the spectator thoroughly shaken.

Secret beyond theory's door

The lesbian spectre can also be said to haunt feminist film theory, in particular to stalk the female spectator as she is posited and contested in that discourse. The 'problem' of female spectatorship has taken on a dominant and in a sense quite puzzling position in feminist film theory, which in some instances has denied its very possibility. Laura Mulvey herself, revisiting her widely read 'Visual Pleasure and Narrative Cinema', in an essay called 'Afterthoughts on "Visual Pleasure and Narrative Cinema"', explains: 'At the time, I was interested in the relationship between the image of woman on the screen and the "masculinization" of the spectator position, regardless of the actual sex (or possible deviance) of any real live movie-goer' (1981: 12). This parenthetical qualifier, '(or possible deviance)', is one of the few references to sexual orientation in the body of psychoanalytic film theory. Yet within the binary stranglehold of sexual difference, lesbianism is so

Fig. 1. Claire Bloom, Russ Tamblyn, Julie Harris and Richard Johnson in The Haunting.

neatly assimilated to the 'masculinization of the spectator position' as to constitute an impossible deviance. In asserting the female spectator's narcissistic over-identification with the image, in describing her masculinisation by an active relation to the gaze, or in claiming that the fantasy of the film text allows the spectator to circulate effortlessly among identifications 'across' gender and sexuality, feminist film theory seems to enact what Freud poses as the very operation of paranoia: the defence against homosexuality.[3] Female spectatorship may well be a theoretical 'problem' only in so far as lesbian spectatorship is a real one.[4]

In *The Desire to Desire: The Woman's Film of the 1940s,* Mary Ann Doane addresses female spectatorship in relation to the film gothic, a (sub)genre which she aptly designates the 'paranoid woman's film'. Doane argues that the figuration of female subjectivity in the woman's film plays out the psychoanalytic description of femininity, characterised in particular by a deficiency in relation to the gaze, a metonymy for desire itself. Within this framework 'subjectivity can ... only be attributed to the woman with some difficulty' (p. 10), and 'female spectatorship ... can only be understood as the confounding of desire' (p. 13) – or at most as the desire to desire.

The gothic sub-genre has a privileged status within Doane's book, corresponding to its ambiguous position within the woman's film genre. Related to the 'male' genres of film noir and horror 'in [its] sustained investigation of the woman's relation to the gaze', the gothic is both an impure example of the woman's film and a 'meta-textual' commentary on it (pp. 125–26). The 'paranoid woman's film' is inadvertently privileged in another sense. For, via Freud's definition of paranoia, the spectre of homosexuality makes a rare appearance in the text. The process by which it is exorcised is intimately bound up with Doane's definition of female spectatorship.

Paranoia and homosexuality

Doane devotes to the gothic two chapters entitled: 'Paranoia and the Specular' and 'Female Spectatorship and Machines of Projection', offering a compelling analysis of the genre to which my reading of *The Haunting* is indebted. Yet despite a lengthy discussion of the psychoanalytic description of paranoia, she qualifies Freud's identification of paranoia with a defence against homosexuality as the 'technical' definition of the disorder (p. 129). Freud himself was 'driven by experience to attribute to the homosexual wish-phantasy an intimate (perhaps an invariable) relation to this particular form of disease' ('On the Mechanism of Paranoia'). The relevance of homosexuality to the discussion of paranoia and to the content of film gothics returns as the 'repressed' of Doane's argument: [5]

> Yet, there is a contradiction in Freud's formulation of the relationship between paranoia and homosexuality, because homosexuality presupposes a well-established and unquestionable subject/object relation. There is a sense in which the very idea of an object of desire is foreign to paranoia. (pp. 129–30)

Homosexuality, it appears, is foreign to the definition of paranoia that Doane wishes to appropriate to describe the gothic fantasy. 'Because Freud defines a passive homosexual current as feminine, paranoia, whether male or female, involves the adoption of a feminine position.' This assimilation of homosexuality to the feminine effectively forecloses the question of the difference of lesbianism when Doane later turns to Freud's 'Case of Paranoia Running Counter to the Psychoanalytical Theory of the Disease'. In this case, which is said to run 'counter' to psychoanalytic theory on the point of homosexual desire, the fantasy which Freud ultimately uncovers as confirmation of his hypothesis (the homosexual wish betrayed by the discovery of a same-sexed persecutor) is read by Doane as the female patient's 'total assimilation to the place of the mother'. Desire is elided by identification. Doane writes that

> the invocation of the opposition between subject and object in connection with the paranoid mechanism of projection indicates a precise difficulty in any conceptualization of female paranoia – one which Freud does not mention. For in his short case history, what the woman projects, what she throws away, is her sexual pleasure, a part of her bodily image. (p. 168)

In forming a delusion as defence against a man's sexual advances and breaking off relations with him (whether this shields a defence against a homosexual wish is here immaterial), the woman is seen to be throwing away her pleasure.

For Doane homosexuality is too locked into the subject/object dichotomy to have much to do with paranoia. Femininity represents a default in relation to the paranoid mechanism of projection – 'what [the woman spectator] lacks ... is a "good throw"'[6] – precisely because the woman cannot achieve subject/object differentiation. The 'contradiction' between homosexuality and paranoia, and the 'precise difficulty' inherent in female paranoia are related by a series of slippages around a central unspoken term, lesbianism.

'Homosexuality' appears in Doane's text only furtively; female subjectivity is its central focus. Yet, remarkably, it is an account of 'lesbian' desire that is used to summarise Doane's position on female spectatorship:

> The woman's sexuality, as spectator, must undergo a constant process of transformation. She must look, as if she were a man with the phallic power of the gaze, at a woman who would attract that gaze, in order to be that woman. … The convolutions involved here are analogous to those described by Julia Kristeva as 'the double or triple twists of what we commonly call female homosexuality': 'I am looking, as a man would, for a woman'; or else, 'I submit myself, as if I were a man who thought he was a woman, to a woman who thinks she is a man' (p. 157).

Doane has recourse to what only Kristeva could call 'female homosexuality' to support a definition of female spectatorship that disallows homoeroticism completely – lesbianism and female spectatorship are abolished at one 'twist'. Female subjectivity is analogous to female homosexuality which *is* sexuality only in so far as it is analogous to male sexuality. The chain of comparisons ultimately slides into actual delusion: 'a woman who thinks she is a man'. In what seems to me a profoundly disempowering proposition, the very possibility of female desire as well as spectatorship is relinquished in the retreat from the ghost of lesbian desire. As we shall see, a similar path is traced in *The Haunting*.

A house is not her home

> An evil old house, the kind that some people call haunted, is like an undiscovered country waiting to be explored.

The male voice-over – Dr Markway's – with which *The Haunting* opens, will have, for some viewers, an uncanny resonance with a description of woman as 'the dark continent'. This connection between signifiers of femininity and the domicile is unsurprising; in cinema it appears in genres from the Western to the melodrama. Mary Ann Doane cites Norman Holland's and Leona Sherman's version of the gothic formula as, simply, 'the image of woman-plus-habitation' (cited in Doane, 1987: 124). It is the uncanny house that the heroine is forced to inhabit – and to explore.

Freud's essay on the uncanny draws on the literary gothic, particularly the work of E. T. A. Hoffman. In it he associates the sensation with the etymological overlap between the definitions of the uncanny, *das Unheimliche,* and its apparent opposite *das Heimliche* (literally, the homey, the familiar), ultimately identifying this convergence with 'the home of all humans', the womb. The woman provokes the uncanny; her experience of it remains a shadowy area.

In the threatening family mansions of the gothic, or in *The Haunting*'s evil old Hill House, a door, a staircase, a mirror, a portrait are never simply what they appear to be, as an image from Fritz Lang's 'paranoid woman's film' *Secret Beyond the Door* (fig. 2) illustrates. The title sums up the enigma of many of these films,

134

Fig. 2. Joan Bennett, publicity still for Secret Beyond the Door.

in which a question about the husband's motives becomes an investigation of the house (and of the secret of a woman who previously inhabited it). In *Secret Beyond the Door,* the husband is an architect whose hobby is 'collecting' rooms in which murders have occurred, one of which is the heroine's bedroom.

Hill House, too, reflects the obsessions of its builder, we are told. 'The man who built it was a misfit. ... He built his house to suit his mind. ... All the angles are slightly off; there isn't a square corner in the place.' Visitors become lost and disoriented, doors left ajar close unnoticed. The film's montage exploits this as well, disorienting the spectator with threatening details – a gargoyle, a door knob, a chandelier – and unexplained camera set-ups and trick shots. Yet as a house that is

Fig. 3. Advertisement for The Haunting.

'literally' haunted, Hill House poses another secret beyond its doors, one of which the architect himself is unaware. Hill House is 'uncanny' *for the woman;* it is a projection not only of the female body, but also of the female mind, a mind which, like the heavy oak doors, may or may not be unhinged. An advertisement for the film (fig. 3) uses the image of a female figure trapped in a maze. Architectural elements are integrated into the title design. Thus the aspect of the house, its gaze, are crucial in the film, as they were even for the novelist who, Shirley Jackson's biographer tells us, 'plowed through architecture books and magazines' for a picture of the perfect house before writing her tale, only to find out that her great-grandfather, an architect, had designed it (Oppenheimer, 1983: 226).

Robbers, burglars, and ghosts

The relationship between the representation of woman and the space of the house is not, Teresa de Lauretis tells us in her reading of Jurii Lotman's work on plot typology in *Alice Doesn't*, a coincidence or simply a generic requirement of the literary or film gothic. De Lauretis analyses Lotman's reduction of plot types to a mere two narrative functions: the male hero's 'entry into a closed space, and emergence from it'. Lotman concludes that

> inasmuch as closed space can be interpreted as 'a cave', 'the grave', 'a house', 'woman' …
> entry into it is interpreted on various levels as 'death', 'conception', 'return home' and so
> on; moreover all these acts are thought of as mutually identical. (quoted in de Lauretis,
> 1984: 118)

And de Lauretis sums up: 'the obstacle, whatever its personification, is morphologically female and indeed, simply, the womb' (p. 119). The sinister slippage in the chain of designations from grave to house to woman lends a narrative progression to Freud's uncanny. Given the collapse of 'woman' on to the space rather than the subject of narrative, and given the identification of heterosexuality *qua* conception with the very prototype of narrative progression, it is no wonder that the lesbian heroine (and her spectatorial counterpart) are so difficult to envision.

In so far as the cinema rewrites all stories according to an Oedipal plot, when the woman is the hero of a gothic such as *Rebecca* (1940), her story is told as the female Oedipus. Her conflicting desires for the mother and for the father are put into play only to be 'resolved' as the mirror image of man's desire. De Lauretis proposes that as the story unfolds the female spectator is asked to identify not only with the two poles of the axis of vision – feminist film theory's gaze and image – but with a second set of positions, what she calls the figure of narrative movement and the figure of narrative closure. Of this last, de Lauretis writes that

> The female position, produced as the end result of narrativization, is the figure of narrative closure, the narrative image in which the film, as [Stephen] Heath says, 'comes
> together'. (p. 140)[7]

We can recognise the 'narrative image' as fundamentally an image of heterosexual closure, or, in Lotman's equation, death.

It is in relation to the narrative work of classical cinema defined as the playing out of space (the house, the grave, the womb) as the very image of femininity that I wish to situate the story of *The Haunting*. It is an exceptional Hollywood film that would frustrate the hero's 'entry into a closed space' and stage a story of deviant female subjectivity, of the *woman's* return home as a struggle with the topos of the home. In figure 4, an odd, collage-like 'image of woman-plus-habitation' produced for *The Haunting* pictorially illustrates this difficulty.

The Haunting tells not the story of Theodora (Claire Bloom's character) but of Eleanor (Julie Harris' character), a woman whose sexuality – like that of the heroine of *Rebecca* – is latent, not necessarily, or at least not yet, lesbian. Her journey is articulated as female Oedipal drama almost against her will, and is resolved, with her death, as a victory of, exactly, the house and the grave (perhaps the

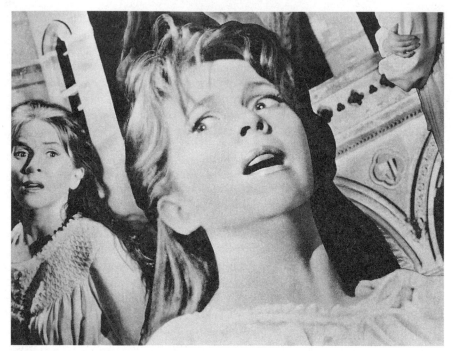

Fig. 4. Julie Harris, The Haunting.

womb). 'Now I know where I am going, I am disappearing inch by inch into this house,' she finally recognises. My reading of the film will attempt to trace the 'haunting' of Hill House as it shifts between homosexuality and homophobia.

The Haunting as ghost film dramatises not the lesbian's 'deficiency in relation to vision' as feminist film theory would characterise femininity, but a deficiency in relation to visibility or visualisation – in *The Haunting* we never see the ghost but we do see the lesbian. Which is not to say that we 'see' lesbian sexuality. *The Haunting* is 'not a film about lesbians'; it is (or pretends to be) about something else. I would consider 'something else' to be a useful working definition of lesbianism in classical cinema.[8] For it is precisely the fact that the 'haunting' is unseen, that there are no 'special effects', that renders *The Haunting* the 'ultimate' ghost film.

> Robbers, burglars and ghosts, of whom some people feel frightened before going to bed … all originate from one and the same class of infantile reminiscence. … In every case the robbers stood for the sleeper's father, whereas the ghosts corresponded to female figures in white nightgowns. (Freud, 1965: 439)

What is immediately striking in Freud's reading is the dissymmetry between the referents of the two dream symbols. Burglars and robbers stand quite definitively for the father; ghosts are a figure of – a figure. Not 'the mother', perhaps a governess, a nurse, or a sister.

'Scandal, murder, insanity, suicide'

Dr Markway's voice-over resumes after the opening credits of *The Haunting*. The story of Hill House as Dr Markway envisions it – literally en-visions it, for his narration is accompanied by a bizarre flashback/fantasy sequence – is the story of female death. The mansion, built by one Hugh Crain 'ninety-odd – very odd' years ago, is the site of the deaths of four women, which are enacted for us: his two wives, his daughter Abigail who lived to old age in the house, and her paid companion. This prologue sequence supplies us with a surplus of cinema's 'narrative image' – female scandal, suicide, murder, and insanity – *before* the drama even begins to unfold. It is as if all the visual power of cinema (surpassing even Dr Markway as narrator) is amassed to contain the threat that 'whatever' it is that haunts Hill House poses.

Dr Markway hides his interest in the supernatural under the guise of science; his true object of study, like that of Freud, another 'pseudo' scientist, is deviant femininity. He designates one room of the house the 'operating room' – 'that is, the center of operations', he reassures his female guests. Suave, paternalistic, Dr Markway is yet somehow lacking in relation to the law – or at least the laws of Hill House. (In contrast is Theodora's ESP, which affords her privileged knowledge of 'the haunting' and of Eleanor. She's thus a better analyst as well.) Dr Markway admits, when asked to reveal the laws of psychic occurrences, 'you'll never know until you break them'. His laughably inadequate readings of the goings-on in Hill House: 'I have my suspicions'; his lectures on the preternatural (that which will some day come to be accepted as natural); his efforts to measure the cold spot; become more and more readable as fumbling attempts to explore the 'undiscovered country' of female homosexuality. In this light his disclaimer on the supernatural, 'don't ask me to give a name to something which hasn't got a name', is also a disclaimer to knowledge of 'the love that dares not speak its name'. He rejects the word 'haunted' preferring 'diseased', 'sick' and 'deranged', pathologising, anthropomorphising and, I would argue, lesbianising the haunted house.

When his version of the story of Hill House includes the proclamation: 'It is with the young companion that the evil reputation of Hill House really begins,' we are prepared, indeed invited, to speculate what the scandal attached to the companion might be. It is on to the fates of the four female characters/ghosts, most crucially that of the companion who is extraneous (sub/ordinate) to the nuclear family, that Eleanor Lance maps her 'Oedipal' journey, her crisis of desire and identification.

As narrativity would demand, she starts out in the place of the daughter. Yet she is a grown-up daughter, a spinster, who leaves her family home – her mother has recently died, and as the maiden aunt she lives in her sister's living room – to return home to Hill House. Eleanor and Theodora are the remaining two of a select company of persons 'touched' by the supernatural who were invited by Dr Markway in the hope 'that the very presence of people like yourselves will help to stimulate the strange forces at work here'. The doctor's interest in Eleanor's case is sparked by her childhood 'poltergeist experience' – a shower of stones that fell on her house for three days. Eleanor at first denies – 'I wouldn't know' (about things like that) – what her brother-in-law calls the 'family skeleton', the secret of 'what

Fig. 5. Julie Harris and Claire Bloom, The Haunting – *'Like sisters?'*

[her] nerves can really do'. In the internal monologue accompanying her journey
to the house (a voice-over that recurs throughout the film, giving the spectator an
often terrifying access to her interiority) Eleanor refers to herself as 'homeless'. She
has never belonged within the patriarchal home and its family romance. Her
'dark, romantic secret' is her adult attachment to her mother, which she angrily
defines as 'eleven years walled up alive on a desert island'. Eleanor is thrilled at the
prospect of 'being expected' at her destination; for the first time something is happening to *her*. More is 'expected' of her than she dreams …

Things that go bump in the night

When Eleanor arrives at Hill House she is relieved to meet one of her companions. 'Theodora – just Theodora', Claire Bloom's character introduces herself to Eleanor, immediately adding, 'The affectionate term for Theodora is Theo.' 'We are going to be great friends, Theo,' responds Eleanor, whose affectionate name 'Nell' Theo has already deduced by keen powers of extrasensory perception which are exercised most frequently in reading Eleanor's mind.[9] 'Like sisters?' Theo responds sarcastically (fig. 5). Theo recommends that Eleanor put on something bright for dinner, sharing with her the impression that it is a good idea always to remain 'strictly visible' in Hill House. On their way downstairs, they encounter their first supernatural experience, with Eleanor shouting, 'Don't leave me, Theo,' and Theo observing, 'It wants you, Nell.' After they have joined the others Eleanor proposes a toast: 'I'd like to drink to companions.' Theo responds with obvious pleasure and the camera moves in to frame the two women. 'To my new companion,' replies Theo with inimitable, elegant lasciviousness. The toast, like their relationship, alas, remains unconsummated, for Eleanor continues – 'except I don't drink'.

Eleanor clearly is the 'main attraction' of both the house and Theo, each finding in her what Theo calls 'a kindred spirit'. The film, resisting the visualisation of desire between women, displaces that desire on to the level of the supernatural, Theo's seduction of Eleanor on to the 'haunting'.

The process whereby the apparition of lesbian desire is deferred to the manifestation of supernatural phenomena is well illustrated by a sequence depicting the events of the first night spent by the company in Hill House. Theo accompa-

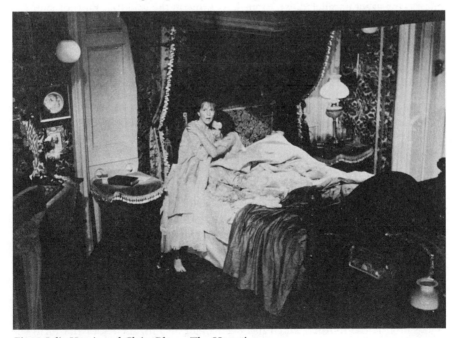

Fig. 6. Julie Harris and Claire Bloom, The Haunting.

nies Eleanor to the door of her bedroom, and invites herself in, under the pretext of arranging Eleanor's hair. Although Eleanor refuses Theo's advances, the women end up in bed together anyway, but not according to plan (fig. 6). Eleanor, realising with a mixture of relief and anxiety that she is alone, locks her door ('Against what?' she muses) and drifts off to sleep. A shot of the exterior of the house and a dissolve to a shot from the dark interior at the base of the main staircase are accompanied by a faint pounding which rises in volume. Eleanor stirs and, half-asleep, knocks in response on the wall above her bed: 'All right, mother, I'm coming.' When Theo calls out to her in fear, Eleanor realises her mistake and rushes into Theo's adjoining room. Huddled together in Theo's bed throughout the protracted scene, the women face off an unbearably loud knocking which eventually comes to the door of the bedroom. Finally the sound fades away, and Eleanor runs to the door when she hears Luke and the doctor in the hall. The men enter, explain they had been outside chasing what appeared to be a dog, and ask whether anything has happened. The women burst into laughter, and after catching their breath, sarcastically explain that something knocked on the door with a cannonball. Luke remarks that there isn't a scratch on the woodwork – 'or anywhere else', and the doctor soberly intones: 'When we are decoyed outside, and you two are bottled up inside, wouldn't you say that something is trying to separate us?' The sequence ends with ominous music and a close-up of Theo.

The knocking that terrorises the women takes up an element of the film's prologue – the invalid Abigail pounds with her cane on the wall to call the companion who fails to come, sparking malicious town gossip that she had somehow or other murdered her mistress. At this point in the film we are already aware that Eleanor harbours guilt about her own mother's death; what this scene makes explicit is the exact parallel, down to the knocking on the wall that Eleanor later admits she fears she may have heard and ignored on the fatal night, which puts Eleanor in the position of 'companion' *vis-à-vis* her own mother.

> When a wife loses her husband, or a daughter her mother, it not infrequently happens that the survivor is afflicted with tormenting scruples ... which raise the question whether she herself has not been guilty through carelessness or neglect of the death of the beloved person. No recalling of the care with which she nursed the invalid, no direct refutation of the asserted guilt can put an end to the torture. (Freud, 1946: 80)

Freud concludes in *Totem and Taboo* that a repressed component of hostility towards the deceased is the explanation for these reproaches, and similarly for the 'primitive' belief in the malignancy of spirits of dead loved ones: the *projection* of that hostility is feared aggression from the dead. Projection is also a technique of those suffering from paranoia who are 'struggling against an intensification of their homosexual trends'. In paranoia, Freud tells us, 'the persecutor is in reality the loved person, past or present' ('A Case of Paranoia', p. 99).

Eleanor's psychosexual history is similar to that of the subject of Freud's 'Case of Paranoia Running Counter to the Psychoanalytical Theory of the Disease'; a thirtyish woman living with her mother who forms a paranoic delusion to defend herself against the attentions of a man. In both cases, the loved person, then, the persecutor, is the mother. Much has been made in film theory of the form the patient's delusion took in this case: that of being photographed, sparked by an 'accidental knock or tick' which she hears while visiting the man in his apartment. The visual and the auditory, the camera and the click are the two registers of which the cinema is composed, rendering it analogous to paranoid projection, as Doane notes (1987: 123). The noteworthy point of Freud's case history is his reading of the instigating cause of the delusion: 'I do not believe that the clock ever ticked or that any noise was to be heard at all. The woman's situation justified a sensation of throbbing in the clitoris. ... There had been a "knocking" of the clitoris.' 'In her subsequent rejection of the man,' Freud concludes, 'lack of satisfaction undoubtedly played a part' (p. 109).

The knock recurs in this scene from *The Haunting* with the force of a cannonball (proportionate to the force of Eleanor's repression, manifested before in the violence of her 'poltergeist' experience) and intervenes precisely at the moment of a prohibition against homosexual desire. It is a knocking which on the manifest level can be read as the ghost of Abigail looking for a companion, or on a latent level as the persecution of Eleanor by her own mother in conjunction with her taking of a new lover. (That is, Theo. If we are reluctant to read this as a quasi-love scene I offer as anecdotal support the fact that, despite its centrality, it was cut from the version I saw on TV.) Like Freud, the men do not believe there had been any noise at all. Love between women is considered unspeakable; it is inaudible; and it doesn't leave a scratch. I do not contend that the laughter Theo and Eleanor share over the men's ignorance is subversive; indeed, the scene most literally transforms homosexuality into homophobia – replacing sexuality with fear. When the doctor pompously acknowledges that 'some thing' is separating the girls from the boys in Hill House, he resolves to take precautions. 'Against what?' Eleanor asks,

Fig. 7. Richard Johnson and Julie Harris, The Haunting. *Hysteria and heterosexuality.*

naively, for the second time in this sequence. For the camera tells us it is Theo, someone, not some thing, who separates the doctor and Eleanor.

The next morning Eleanor awakens a little too excited by her first experience of the 'supernatural'. Over breakfast, her hair arranged in a new style, she claims to be 'much more afraid of being abandoned or left behind than of things that go bump in the night'. This does not appear to be entirely true, for her feeling of excitement is accompanied by her turning away from Theo as potential love object and towards the doctor, whose paternalistic interest in her Theo calls unfair. When asked what she is afraid of, Theo responds, 'of knowing what I really want'. Her words make Eleanor uncomfortable on several levels. Eleanor misreads her own desire, as I suspect some feminist film critics would, as desire for the man, i.e., the father. Theo's attitude toward her demeaning rival is manifested with knowing sarcasm, telling Eleanor she 'hasn't the ghost of a chance'. A still image (fig. 7) freezes in a hysterical pose Eleanor's relationship to the doctor. Actually, he has just caught her as she is about to fall backwards over the railing. She had been staring up at the turret, and in a rapid zoom from the point of view of the tower window, she has been virtually pushed by the camera, the house itself, and the implied gaze of a (female) ghost. Eleanor's turning towards the father smacks indeed of a defence against a homosexual wish, and she literally begins to see Theo as a persecutor. The very forcefulness of this defence supports a reading of the night of knocking as a seduction scene.

More than meets the eye

The defence against homosexuality is mirrored on the level of the film's enunciation; when the supernatural events of the second night bring the women together, the cinematic apparatus emphatically separates them. The women are sleeping in beds pushed next to each other. Dr Markway (taking precautions) has advised the women to move in together. ('You're the doctor,' Theo responds.) When Eleanor wakes to mysterious sobbing noises she holds on tightly to Theo's hand. She finally manages to turn on the light and the camera pans rapidly to Theo on the opposite side of the room. Eleanor, horrified, realises that it was not Theo's hand she was holding but that of some ghostly companion. It is not the 'supernatural' alone that is responsible for this mean trick. The cinema itself renders the women's physical contact (albeit merely handholding) impossible. For we know that Theo's bed is not on the other side of the room. A cinematically specific code – and a disruptive one at that, the swish pan – intervenes to separate the two women from each other and to render the viewer complicit.

In a scene that encapsulates the 'Oedipal' drama of Hill House and thus the conflict over Eleanor's proper identification, the cinema works with the supernatural in allowing a lesbian reading. The four guests literally find their 'family portrait' in a massive group statue meant to represent St Francis curing the lepers, who are all female. The women notice that the statue seems to move when they look away, a classic 'uncanny' effect. Luke remarks that the configuration reminds him of a family portrait of the historical inhabitants of Hill House, Hugh Crain looming above his wives, his daughter, the companion, and a dog. Theo maps the

Fig. 8. Lois Maxwell as Mrs Markway with Julie Harris, The Haunting.

current group on to the statue and thus on to the original group, designating Eleanor as the companion, herself, tellingly, as the daughter 'grown up', the doctor as Hugh Crain, and Luke, the ostensible Oedipal hero, as the dog. Luke, startled, indicates with a glance at the women that he has finally caught on to Theo's sexual orientation, commenting that 'more than meets the eye' is going on in Hill House. This phrase, denoting lesbianism, applies equally to the supernatural events of *The Haunting*. Yet, immediately after the group leaves the room, 'more' meets the eye of the spectator – the camera zooms into two of the female figures, which seem to have moved so that one clutches the other's breasts. This privileged view is a cinematic flourish, and a key to a reading, implicating Eleanor in a lesbian embrace through the figure to which she corresponds, and suggesting that

145

the female forces of Hill House are beginning to close in on her.

'You're the monster of Hill House,' Eleanor finally shouts at Theo, several scenes later, coming closer to the truth than she knows. It is at the culmination of this scene: 'Life is full of inconsistencies, nature's mistakes – you, for instance,' that Mrs Markway, consistently, makes her entrance. Coming to persuade her husband to give up his nonsense, she embodies the missing element of the family portrait, marking the futility of Eleanor's attempt to identify herself with that position. In another still (fig. 8), the psychic importance of the mother to Eleanor is represented by her subordination to Mrs Markway.

The materialisation of the wife at this point in the film seems to be part of the process whereby cinema – like the house itself, which calls Eleanor home through ghostly writing on the wall – demands its tribute of the heroine. On this 'final' night of Eleanor's stay, she imagines she has killed off the wife/mother when Mrs Markway, because of her scepticism, becomes 'deranged' by Hill House, and disappears from her room – the nursery, Abigail's room, 'the cold, rotten heart of Hill House', that had remained locked until opening spontaneously on the night of her arrival. Mrs Markway then appears unexpectedly to scare Eleanor (ultimately to scare her to death) on two additional occasions.

First she interrupts Eleanor's intense identification with the place of the companion's suicide, the library. Eleanor's haunting by the wife is quite logically played out over the architecture of the house, which is fantasmatically inflected with Eleanor's own psychic history. Eleanor sums up her subjective crisis: 'So what if he does have a wife, I still have a place in this house. I belong.' As Eleanor runs through the house, she is frightened by her own reflection; we hear loud creaking and crashing, and the image rocks. She thinks, 'the house is destroying itself, it is coming down around me.' Eleanor had been unable to enter the library before, overpowered by a smell she associates with her mother, but tonight she seems to be called there; what is *unheimlich* is transformed into what is *heimlich*. Eleanor climbs the library's spiral staircase as if induced by the camera which makes the dreamlike ascent before her. The companion had hanged herself from the top of the staircase, and the camera had prefigured these later ascents in the prologue's enactment of this death: 'I've broken the spell of Hill House. I'm home, I'm home,' Eleanor senses. The doctor 'rescues' her when she reaches the top, yet just as she turns to descend, Mrs Markway's head pops into the frame through a trap door above. Eleanor faints, and the screen fades to black.

It is now that the doctor, futilely, decides to send Eleanor away from Hill House. For he misrecognises (as a hallucination) her recognition of the wife. Yet for once she has actually *seen* something that we, importantly, also see. She is terrorised, at the very moment of her identification with the companion, by the apparition of the heterosexual role model, the wife. Eleanor comprehends the displacement of her Oedipal drama (the substituting of herself for the mother) by the inverted drama of Hill House (the wife's substitution for Eleanor in relation to the house's desire). 'I'm the one who's supposed to stay. She's taken my place.' And Eleanor dies, ironically, literally in the wife's place.

For the 'narrative image' figured in the film's prologue – the death of Hugh Crain's first wife – her lifeless hand falling into the frame, after her horse rears, 'for no apparent reason' – is now offered as the 'narrative image' of the film. The shot is repeated exactly after Eleanor's car crashes into the very same tree, her hand falling into the frame. The first wife died before rounding the corner that would have given her the gothic heroine's first glimpse of the house; Eleanor cannot leave the gaze of Hill House.

She crashes, apparently, to avoid hitting Mrs Markway, who, for the second time, suddenly runs across her path. Mrs Markway appears as the agent of a deadly variant of heterosexual narrative closure. Eleanor is not allowed to live or die as the companion; incapable of living as the wife, she is tricked into dying in her place.

But, being a ghost film, *The Haunting* goes beyond the image of death. The final image is properly the house – the grave, woman? – accompanied by Eleanor's voice-over (or rather the voice of Eleanor's ghost) echoing the words from the opening narration: 'Whatever walked there, walked alone.' Prying the 'narrative image' from its Oedipal logic and usurping the authoritative male voice-over, Eleanor transforms the words: 'We who walk here, walk alone.' Eleanor finally belongs – to a 'we' that we know to be feminine and suspect might be lesbian, 'we who walk alone', and the house belongs to her. The 'haunting' exceeds the drive of cinema to closure, actually using the material codes of cinema, the soundtrack, to suggest 'something else'.

The Haunting exceeds the woman's story as female Oedipal drama enacted, Tania Modleski demonstrates, in a gothic like *Rebecca*.[10] In that genre the protagonist's search for the 'secret' of a dead woman is facilitated (or impeded) by a key figure, an older, sometimes sinister female character variously the 'housekeeper', the 'nurse', or in some other capacity a 'companion' to the dead woman. These roles are truly a gallery of the best of lesbian characters in classic cinematic history. Played by the likes of Judith Anderson (Mrs Danvers in *Rebecca*, fig. 9) or Cornelia Otis Skinner (*The Uninvited*, fig. 10) they are a compelling reason for the young woman, recently married and suspecting it might have been a mistake, to realise that it *was* one. I have discussed the centrality of the companion in the psychic history of Hill House and will venture that the companion function provides a mapping and an iconography of female homosexuality throughout the gothic genre. In *The Haunting* a crucial transformation has taken place with the manifest appearance of lesbianism. The representation of the dead woman, the object of the heroine's desire ('Rebecca' as precisely unrepresentable in that film), and the function of the companion, converge in the figure of Theodora, who is emphatically not the mother.

The canny lesbian

If the nameless heroine of *Rebecca* oscillates between the two poles of female Oedipal desire – desire for the mother and desire for the father – Mrs Danvers sets the house on fire and dies with it, joining the ghost of Rebecca which, as Modleski reads it, 'haunts' her (1982: 51).[11] And if Eleanor's trajectory sums up these two variants, Theo grows up – like Abigail, the daughter before her, and lives to tell of the terrors of Hill House. In developing a feminist film theory which would incorporate Theo, we might recall the model of spectatorship she offers in the film.

Fig. 9. Joan Fontaine and Judith Anderson, Rebecca.

Fig. 10. Ruth Hussey, Alan Napier, Ray Milland and Cornelia Otis Skinner, The Uninvited.

Telepathy, to lesbians and gay men as historical readers and viewers, has always been an alternative to our own mode of paranoic spectatorship: 'Is it really there?' The experience of this second sight involves the identification of and with Theo as a lesbian. As for *The Haunting*, it's a very scary movie, even a threatening one. As Leonard Maltin's TV movie guide recommends, 'See it with a friend' (Maltin, 1989: 444). Or, perhaps, a 'companion'.

Notes

1. The fact that the horror genre is not one which is traditionally associated with female audiences is nicely illustrated by Williams: 'Whenever the movie screen holds a particularly effective image of terror, little boys and grown men make it a point of honor to look, while little girls and grown women cover their eyes or hide behind the shoulder of their dates' (Doane et al., 1987: 83). The representation of the female gaze within the film, however, is a primary device of horror. As Mary Ann Doane reads Williams' argument in *The Desire to Desire*: 'Female scopophilia is a drive without an object ... what the woman actually sees, after a sustained and fearful process of looking, is a sign or representation of herself displaced to the level of the nonhuman' (1987: 141–42). Doane's remarks on the horror film are made within her discussion of the film gothic, a genre which does address a female spectator, and with which *The Haunting* shares an affiliation.

2. As one contemporary reviewer summarised the doctor's thesis: 'The occurrences, according to Markway, are "brought on by the people whom they affect", pointing to the similarity among theories of neurosis, homosexuality, and "haunting" which I will exploit later,' *Film Quarterly*, Winter 1963/4, pp. 44–46. The review focuses on the specifically filmic means by which Wise achieves the terrifying effects of *The Haunting*. The film's press book recounts how Wise was posed with the problem of how to film 'nothing', and how he devised an ingenious effect for filming a 'cold spot', thereby allying the director with the doctor scrutinising female sexuality.

3. 'In all these cases a defence against a homosexual wish was clearly recognisable at the very centre of the conflict which underlay the disease' (Freud, 'On the Mechanism of Paranoia' (1911); 1963: 29).

4. The appearance of the special issue of *Camera Obscura* on 'The Spectatrix' signals the continued vigour of these debates. National surveys and a host of individual responses to a series of questions on the theorisation and relevance of female spectatorship offer a great deal of information on scholars' research. However, the forum of the survey discouraged the participation of key figures in feminist film theory, most notably Teresa de Lauretis and Tania Modleski.

5. For instance, the important, lesbian-coded character of Mrs Danvers is barely mentioned in Doane's discussion of *Rebecca*.

6. Thus 'throwing away her pleasure' describes the process of female spectatorship:

   > [T]o possess the image through the gaze is to become it. And becoming the image, the woman can no longer have it. For the female spectator, the image is *too* close – it cannot be projected far enough. What she lacks, in other words, is a 'good throw' (Doane, 1987: 168–69).

7. The concept of 'narrative image' is a complex one to which the present discussion cannot do justice. Heath's introduction of the concept had only the suggestion of the overdetermined association with femininity that de Lauretis traces so convincingly. He defined the narrative image as 'a film's presence, how it can be talked about, what it can be sold and bought on ... in the production stills displayed outside a cinema, for example' (1981: 121). For instance, lesbian and gay supporting characters are evicted from the narrative image, from reviews, from plot summaries, from the images on posters. The production stills included in the present context are examples from a film whose narrative image is unrepresentable.

8. In *The Celluloid Closet*, Vito Russo notes the homophobic trope of claiming gay-themed movies are about 'something else' (1981: 126). Yet his implicit standard of 'coming out' – the search for the

overt, fully realised representation of homosexuality (particularly if the standard is arguably a masculine one) can lead to reductive readings of actual films, as is the case in Russo's discussion of *The Haunting*:

> Unconscious lesbianism is its own punishment … for Claire Bloom's neurotic Greenwich Village lesbian in *The Haunting* (1963). She gets her psychosexual jollies by hugging Julie Harris and blaming it on ghosts. But she is not predatory; she is just out of life's running. She professes no interest in actively seducing either Harris or *an attentive Russ Tamblyn*. The lesbianism is entirely mental, and her sterility leaves her at a dead end. Lesbianism is rendered invisible because it is purely psychological. *And since most lesbians were invisible even to themselves, their sexuality, ill-defined in general,* emerged onscreen as a wasted product of a closeted lifestyle. (p. 158; emphasis added)

I perceive the Bloom character as, on the contrary, very well adjusted, and I read the very 'invisibility' of lesbianism in the film as a strategy of representation. Parker Tyler describes the film with more *élan*: 'it might seem to both readers of the novel and viewers of the film … that lesbianism had a role in drawing these unusual ladies closer in the frightening, macabre situation to which they commit themselves and where they must 'cling' to each other.' (1972: 90)

9. The spectator/auditor is also able to 'read Eleanor's mind' through the voice-over device, although sometimes Theo seems to have even more privileged access – to Eleanor's unconscious thoughts and desires, as well as to effects of the 'haunting' signified to the spectator by other visual and auditory cues.

10. Tania Modleski, '"Never to be Thirty-Six Year's Old": *Rebecca* as Female Oedipal Drama' (1982: 34–41).

11. In the later version of her essay, Modleski makes explicit the lesbian element with the addition of this phrase, 'the heroine continually strives … to win the affections of Mrs Danvers *who seems herself to be possessed, haunted, by Rebecca and to have a sexual attachment to the dead woman*' [italics mine]. See Modleski's *The Women Who Knew Too Much: Hitchcock and Feminist Theory* (1988).

11

Femme Fatale or Lesbian Femme: *Bound* in Sexual *Différance*

Chris Straayer

In its black-and-white opening title sequence with stark lights and deep shadows, foreboding music, and a moving camera that weaves from extreme close-up obscurity to distanced readability (of the title), *Bound* (The Wachowski Brothers, 1996) immediately stirs memories and expectations of film noir. The film's first scene, however, poses a neo-noir twist. Trapped inside a clothes closet, the camera slowly descends from the ceiling, pointing downwards, alongside what appears to be the ceiling light's fixture, enlarging and distorting it to vulgar proportions and thus creating for the viewer a bulbous projection that suggests a sex toy as much as a ceiling light. Continuing downwards, the camera surveys a variety of hat boxes, evening dresses and spike heels and then careens the length of a woman's body lying on the floor: from her heavy boots and ankles tied with rope; past work pants, ribbed undershirt, and biceps displaying a labrys tattoo;[1] to her face slashed alongside one eye and her mouth gagged. In voice-over, two females (except for a single line spoken by a male) amplify the intrigue with remarks about sex and sexual merging, plans and choices, the 'business' and wanting out of it. In the following scene, presumably a flashback, the previously bound woman enters an elevator followed by a hetero-coded couple. The man stands up front, facing the door, while the two women exchange seductive glances behind his back. Both women wear black leather jackets despite their butch–femme contrast. Suddenly an overhead shot graphically articulates sexual triangulation. The man leaves the elevator, followed by the femme, whose legs are shot in classic film noir style except, in this instance, from the point of view of a (butchy) woman. As the man unlocks one door in the hallway, never acknowledging the femme who accompanies him, implications of prostitution arise. As the butchy woman enters the next-door apartment with a bucket of tools, it becomes clear that she is a handyman.

Bound revisits and revises film noir. The protagonist, here a dyke rather than the conventional male, is an ex-con who gets talked into a *femme fatale*'s proposition to steal from the mob. The film's flashback structure, which originates from midway in the story, is supplemented by a flash forward that liberates the narrative's conclusion from film noir destiny. Camera angles, plot twists, character types, and other motifs enlist film noir conventions for neo-noir purposes. This essay first locates the *femme fatale* figure in films noirs and neo-noirs as a site of gender and genre turbulence and then, more particularly, analyses the sexual *différance* instigated by a lesbian butch–femme couple in *Bound*.[2]

The *femme fatale* of contemporary film operates as an independent agent, always signalling but no longer contained by film noir. Today we watch women *from* film noir as often as *in* film noir. Perhaps the *femme fatale* always did transcend the film text if we recollect Janey Place's argument that viewers' memories privilege the *femme fatale*'s dangerously exciting incarnations over the defeats that most often awaited her in film noir conclusions.[3] Now the *femme fatale* is a metonym that travels among a variety of genres, summoning film noirness for atmospheric or hermeneutic effect.[4]

Ever since film noir's heyday in the 40s and 50s, high femme characters not only carry the mark of sexuality but also stand charged with deceit and potential violence.[5] And yet the *femme fatale* has multiplied in meanings and possibilities, not only as a result of socio-historical factors (for example, Alfred Kinsey's *Sexual Behavior in the Human Female* (1953); the feminist movement) but also due to an increase of explicit, on-screen sexual imagery[6] and proliferating media representations of fictional and non-fictional female killers. In the days of classic film noir, the depiction of women as killers was unusual compared with the more recent prevalence of violent women, whether crazed or justified, in horror movies, cop shows, gangster films, thrillers, action adventures, and reality television. *Femmes fatales* now circulate in a cultural milieu that has been sexually aroused by *Goldfinger* (1964) and sensitised to domestic violence by *The Burning Bed* (1984). Even the male buddy film has been invaded by *Thelma and Louise* (1991) which extends rape-revenge fight-back to other pervasive acts of sexism.

The generic problematic of classic film noir included the sense of economic hardship as a (remembered, existing, or possible) social condition. One might argue that ardent viewers simultaneously wanted to be untroubled poor Joes and to increase their buying power (whether to buy jewellery or women). Of course, one logical response to class inequality and material desires is theft. Certainly the male protagonist's susceptibility to stealing schemes, fuelled not only by the humdrum nature of his job, if he has one, but also by his otherwise unsuitability as the *femme fatale*'s mate, was sympathetically rendered, despite (and via) his fearful hesitations, practical concerns, and ethical anguish.[7] The sex-based underclass status of women, however, received little generic sympathy. That men remained women's primary conduit to economic status was overshadowed by the *femme fatale*'s criminal dealings; she answered sex-based inequity with sexual manipulation. In other words, the *femme fatale*'s greediness occasioned the (newly romantic) tough guy's responsibility, and his superego buckled under her clear thinking. Despite a façade of deference, the *femme fatale*'s take-charge decisiveness mobilised the narrative. Despite his masterminding attempts, the male protagonist was led to his destiny by the *femme fatale*. Ultimately, his psychological dimensionality yielded to her sexual dimension(s).

The radical intervention achieved by the original edition of *Women in Film Noir* two decades ago was its celebration of this male-imagined genre as a rare acknowledgment of female sexuality and power, i.e., of the *femme fatale* as an agent within the popular sexual economy. It is important to note, however, that the classic *femme fatale*'s lust was overwhelmingly for money rather than sexual pleasure.[8] Despite her sexualised image, economic ambition supplanted her libido and violence displaced sexual pleasure. The classic *femme fatale* was known for her trigger-happy killings, not her orgasms. Her sexuality *per se* was passive, limited to its allure. Although narratively she manoeuvred the male protagonist with her sexuality, the specifically sexual desire and pleasure it served belonged to the male.[9]

By contrast, the neo-noir *femme fatale* wants sexual pleasure as well as economic power. In *The Postman Always Rings Twice* (1946), platinum blond Cora (Lana Turner) trades in her older husband for the younger and more erotically appealing Frank (John Garfield), but in the film's remake (1981, with Jessica Lange) Cora not only gets off on rough sex but arouses herself manually while Frank (Jack Nicholson) is still getting into position – thus making her sexual goal explicit (to us as well as him). In *Double Indemnity* (1944), Phyllis (Barbara Stanwyck) teases Walter (Fred MacMurray) with double entendres, but in *Body Heat* (1981), black widow Matty (Kathleen Turner) entreats her lover-attorney Ned (William Hurt) – who thinks it was his idea to break through her door and have sex on the floor – 'Yes, yes, yes. Please do it.' The orgasmic *femme fatale* has become a staple of neo-noirs such as *Black Widow* (1986), *Fatal Attraction* (1987), *After Dark, My Sweet* (1990), *Basic Instinct* (1992), *Body of Evidence* (1992), *Romeo is Bleeding* (1994), *The Last Seduction* (1994), *Diabolique* (1996) and *Lost Highway* (1997).[10]

In classic film noir, the *femme fatale* propelled the action, but her narrative options were numbered: she either died, reformed, or turned out not to be a *femme fatale* after all.[11] Most adamantly, the *femme fatale* was denied romantic coupling. The implied author of film noir was morally superior to, yet sexually empathetic with, the male protagonist – an ambivalence that licensed the protagonist's confessional voice-over. The words of the unrepentant *femme fatale*, however, should not have been trusted in the first place. It is her duplicity that precludes romantic coupling in these films. Typically, after sharing in murder, the female-male partners-in-crime are destroyed by mutual, although dissimilar, distrust and disgust.[12] While the femme is clearly put off by the male protagonist's wimpishness more than the murder, it remains unclear whether the protagonist's guilty conscience or his realisation of her seductive deception (of him) is what turns him off. It appears likely that romantic union was impossible even before the unbearable (to him) crime occurred. In other words, the couple's downfall seems located in their individual characters rather than merely in their joint action. In classic film noir, the sexes do not complement and complete each other; instead, sexual attraction ignites a destructive combustion.

In fact, the male protagonist's desire for romantic coupling usually exceeded that of the *femme fatale*, who only deployed (false) promises of romantic permanence to secure his commitment to her crime. Furthermore, although the male protagonist was often portrayed initially as a loner, his generic goals eventually included coupling. Often, one of his primary dilemmas was whether to settle with the good woman or to follow the *femme fatale*.[13] The *femme fatale*'s coupling remained more problematic, presumably because she loved only herself. Perhaps it is our own commitment to romantic formulas that produces such speculations in the first place. But undoubtedly, the American dream of home, family, and 'security' is precisely the feminine fulfilment which the *femme fatale* intended to elude.[14]

Within 50s US culture (not to mention Hollywood's long-standing obsession with romance), the fact that the femme really never wanted to couple, by itself, warranted her a narrative disadvantage.

The implied author of neo-noirs of the 80s and 90s has tempered his self-righteousness and now, on occasion, even seems capable of switching sexual affiliation. With this new flexibility in governing attitude, it becomes possible for shared crime to strengthen the bond between partners and even fuel their sexuality. Of course, a male's attraction to a *femme fatale* still threatens his demise, as *Fatal Attraction* frantically emphasised. And, still, a male's nerve rarely matches that of the *femme fatale*: the willing vulnerability of Dan (Michael Douglas) during the final sex scene of *Basic Instinct* is a rare, and probably foolish, instance.

The reflexive remake *Gun Crazy* (1992)[15] dares to postulate that impotence underlies the cowardliness of many film noir male protagonists and, further, that such impotence might respond favourably to a concentrated dose of middle-class fantasy. In this film, a history of sexual abuse by her surrogate father and high school boyfriends makes Anita (Drew Barrymore) amenable to the sexual impotence of her ex-con boyfriend Howard (James LeGros). A rampage of violence stands in as surrogate consummation of their marriage (until the film's ending, when intercourse prepares the male protagonist for death). In other words, the displacement of sexuality on to violence, once primarily associated with the *femme fatale*, here accomplishes a phallic performance for the impotent male protagonist. Film noir's slippery signification between violence and sexuality extends its purview to the male protagonist, whose criminal involvement (or reservations) can be read as compensatory (or demonstrative) of sexual inadequacy. *Gun Crazy* further suggests that, just as the dream of upward mobility propels the *femme fatale*'s violence, so might it animate the male protagonist's sexuality. When Anita and Howard hide out in a middle-class home, dressing up in the owners' clothing to watch vacation slides of the 'legitimate' inhabitants, they at last succeed in having sex. The fantasy of class privilege makes them sexually functional. Immediately afterwards, however, the male protagonist offers his body for repetetive penetration by police bullets so that his now properly (de)sexualised wife might immortalise their short-lived romance via a (possible) teenage pregnancy.[16]

The most remarkable elaboration of the neo-noir *femme fatale* occurs in *The Last Seduction*. Bridgette (Linda Fiorentino), a hard-driving sales manager, has ambitions beyond corporate promotions. After getting her petty criminal husband to pull off a big drug deal, she steals the payoff. Hiding out in a small town, she uses a good-looking country guy for sexual pleasure and exploits his romanticism to trick him into killing her husband. Naturally, the plan backfires because, when the two men realise who connects them, they can only commiserate. As a result, Bridgette has to kill the husband herself and frame her country stud for the murder. By taunting him with ill-gained knowledge of his sexual naïveté (during an earlier try at city living, he unwittingly married a transvestite), she makes him so angry that he rapes her. At the same time, she methodically arranges the phone so that the rape as well as a macho but untrue murder confession are overheard by an emergency telephone operator. *The Last Seduction* offers a prime example of neo-noir's implied author switching his sympathy from the male protagonist to the *femme fatale*, or, to put it another way, allowing his superego to lighten up.

With resolute style, *The Last Seduction*'s *femme fatale* rejects romance, claims abundant sexual satisfaction, and walks away free with the money.

The gun that the classic *femme fatale* carried coded her as phallic, but her masculinity was also demonstrated by a ball-busting dominance over her male lover. This gender reversal (the combined result of each person's individual gender inversion) deconstructed yet maintained difference-based coupling and, decades later, now facilitates a displacement of binary sex by binary gender in certain neo-noir (same-sex, hetero-gender) couplings. As a result of its gender fluidity, classic film noir actually offered a variety of couples in addition to the phallic *femme fatale* and emasculated protagonist which I have focused on thus far. The coupling of a macho private eye and his secretary (for example, in *Kiss Me Deadly*, 1955) relied on more traditional gender roles. Like those that reflected gender reversal, this stereotypically gendered couple upheld gender difference as well as sexual difference.

Film noir also offered couples which undermined gender difference via a certain equality that existed between partners. In the mutually attracted Humphrey Bogart and Lauren Bacall characters of *Dark Passage* and *The Big Sleep*, one finds a same-gender coupling that advocates a pleasant sexiness in sexual equality. In *Gilda* (1946), Johnny (Glen Ford) and Gilda (Rita Hayworth) form a same-gender couple that attributes a hateful sexiness to sexual equality (until the film's ending). Because a sexually inclined but non-violent femme does not fit exactly into either masculinity or femininity, she makes a good match for a male protagonist who also steps out of gender. The Bogart characters mentioned above were actively flirtatious and sexy in their willingness to be caught, and Ford's Johnny was an erotic object himself. Rather than simply being entrapped by her otherness, these male protagonists shared some of the femme's qualities. Although the same-genders of these couplings differ (the first pair being more masculine than the second), both challenge the gender binary, for the better. The femme, as opposed to the phallic femme or the feminine woman, can be read, albeit inadequately, with or against either gender.

The obvious ability of gender to turn cartwheels on both male and female characters while upholding a sexual system of difference suggests that the notion of binary sex in the broader culture (which does assume parallel sex and gender binaries) depends on a tripartite structure obtained by doubling woman into whore and virgin, masculine and feminine. Only via contrast with the feminine good girl, however much she is relegated to the diegetic background, can film noir's male protagonist maintain his claim to masculine gender next to the *femme fatale*. Although permanent romantic coupling is forbidden to the gender inversion couple of classic film noir (and often is problematised in the other configurations), all of the various gender couplings outlined above remain heterosexual. In this way, film noir maintained difference-based coupling while deconstructing gender-sex alignment and allowing for gender inversion, gender trading, and same-gender coupling. Classic film noir set a scene of gender fluidity that now facilitates queer readings of and representations in neo-noir.[17]

Other scholars have deliberated on the same-sex configuration and its lesbian connotations in the neo-noir *Black Widow*, in which a data analyser turned investigator (Debra Winger) is read as masculine in her hypofeminine plainness next to the high femme spectacle of a black widow (Theresa Russell).[18] Because a (masculinised) woman holds the position of film noir's generic male protagonist in *Black Widow*, the film provides another instance of the phallic femme's gender versatility via a non-feminine contrast with masculinity.[19] In other words, here the *femme fatale* reads as the opposite of the masculine (woman) protagonist, although this opposition does not produce femininity *per se* in the *femme fatale*. Although *Black Widow* might seem the obvious precursor to *Bound*, the vigorous femme and humbled male in *A Rage in Harlem* (1991) also warrant a brief mention here.[20]

A Rage in Harlem's clean-cut male protagonist Jackson (Forest Whitaker) is drawn into a dangerous criminal world by the seductive Imabelle (Robin Givens). From the beginning, Jackson is feminised in a variety of ways that support the film's comic aspects without reinstating traditional (white) gender roles.[21] He is infantilised not only by his short pants and by a picture of his mama hanging over his bed, but also by his religious sincerity and sexual naïveté. Although the other characters (as well as film viewers) question Jackson's dedication to Imabelle, it is unfaltering. Despite being ill-equipped for the mission of saving Imabelle from her threatening mobster man, Jackson doesn't abandon her, he doesn't give up on her, and he doesn't read her as duplicitous. He is steadfast in being her partner. His vulnerability, in fact, favourably competes with the macho maleness around them. Although Imabelle has the sexual experience and initiates sex with Jackson, and although this sex is followed (generically) by danger and criminal involvement, her affection for him and presumably her sexual satisfaction are ultimately confirmed by the narrative. In what may seem the ultimate move away from mainstream masculine representation, the sex scene displays his face in orgasmic abandon rather than hers. Yet, in no way does this display of vulnerability imply sexual impotence on his part or sexual dissatisfaction on hers.

A neo-noir built on the romance and gangster genres, *Bound* pushes gender revisions still further. Femme and butch lesbians Violet and Corky (Jennifer Tilly and Gina Gershon) meet in an elevator at the film's beginning, and drive away together in a new red truck at its end. Between these romantic bookends, they steal $2,000,000 that Violet's mobster boyfriend Ceasar (Joe Pantoliano) is laundering (literally) for the mafia. They expect Ceasar to run when the evidence points towards him, thus freeing Violet from her position as a *kept* woman. Instead, Ceasar decides to fight it out in what he thinks is a duel of wits with the boss's son Johnnie.

Whether gangster or film noir protagonist, Ceasar is a parody of masculinity. He is absurdly gutsy, yet out of control. When he opens his briefcase and finds newspapers instead of the two million, the room spins around him. He talks frantically to himself while wrecking Johnnie's apartment in a vain search for the missing money. Later, after killing him, he shouts triumphantly into Johnnie's still face. Multiple plot twists tear Ceasar apart, yet he refuses to give up. Finally he discovers that Violet has crossed him, which leads to Corky's entrapment in the closet. He makes a final mistake, however, when he misjudges Violet. He refuses to believe that she is a *femme fatale*.

The primary enigma of *Bound* is its femme character. This is consistent with many films noirs and neo-noirs. From the point of view of Corky, who is both sus-

Violet (Jennifer Tilly) and Corky (Gina Gershon) in Bound.

picious of and attracted to Violet, the crucial question is whether Violet is a *femme fatale* or a lesbian femme. She certainly comes on to Corky with a sex kitten voice, but, if she's a *femme fatale*, she might seduce Corky into crime and then double-cross her. This is why Corky declares that, although having sex with a stranger is fine, to steal with someone requires considerably more knowledge about her. That said, Corky joins Violet in crime shortly after sleeping with her. By stating the risk and then taking it, Corky enlists viewers in a familiar film noir hermeneutic. In an important shift, however, Corky faces the enigma not by scrutinising Violet's criminality but rather by doubting her lesbian status.

In the femme-butch pairing of Violet and Corky, *Bound* puts pro-sex lesbian discourse and lesbian feminism into dialogue. The fact that Violet sleeps with men puts her lesbianism into question for Corky. Violet defines sex with men as work, but Corky sees duplicity. Violet claims to be a lesbian, but Corky can only see their difference. The implication is that, fatal or not, this femme is not trustworthy. Corky's lesbian feminism translates into a macho inclination to judge and delimit Violet's sexuality, until Violet proves that lesbian femmes are real lesbians too. She certifies this by shooting Ceasar.

Earlier in this essay I argued that classic film noir covered over women's sex-related economic disadvantage by portraying the *femme fatale* as greedy and crazy, as unexplainable. And yet there was in the femme's iconography the trace of a sex-specific economics. Because a sexualised woman, within a virgin–whore dichotomy, always hints at prostitution, the *femme fatale* contains an association with sex work. In *Bound* the connection between the *femme fatale* and sex work becomes tangible and, just as sex work can be made into crime, it can also motivate crime.

Corky and Violet are testing one another. Like Cora putting her life in Frank's hands by swimming as far as she can into the ocean with him in *The Postman Always Rings Twice*, Violet and Corky take part in a joint scheme that leaves each vulnerable to the other. Only at the end do they know for sure that they can trust each other. This knowledge is acquired through shared criminality but has larger implications. Violet is revealed to be *both femme fatale* and lesbian femme, duplicitous with men but not with Corky. And, in comparison with film noir's usual male protagonist, Corky offers a masculinity much more attractive to a femme. When Ceasar asks Violet, 'What'd she do to you?' Violet answers, 'Everything you couldn't.'

Swaggering with a difference, Corky is a masculine partner worthy of romantic coupling. Her plan is not perfect and she wrongly predicts Ceasar's reaction to the set-up, but she is calm-headed and steady in her support of Violet. Although Violet does the killing, Corky doesn't get squeamish on her. She is not fearful, naïve, or moralistic about crime. She accepts and shares Violet's need and desire for money. Most importantly, Corky finally admits that she and Violet are alike, something Violet has been telling her all along. In contrast to film noir's male protagonist, who is sucked in by female sexuality, Corky knows Violet's desire. Unlike the classic *femme fatale*, Violet is knowable after all.[22] And, all along she was knowing.

Corky is engulfed by Violet's world. As Corky renovates the apartment next door, she hears Violet having sex with Ceasar and, later, another man. Violet says that the thin wall makes it like they are in the same room, suggesting voyeurism on Corky's part. Violet's neighbourly displays of femininity – she brings coffee to Corky and requires her help after losing an earring down the sink – are transparent, even flagrant flirtations. Corky is wise to them but nevertheless willing, ready with her own double entendres. When retrieving Violet's earring, Corky is framed in medium close-up with Violet's legs behind her. Then in extreme close-up, we see water slowly seep from the pipe she is twisting. In no time at all Corky's hand is up Violet's dress. That Violet put it there is no small detail, nor is her sexual responsiveness. She's been thinking of Corky all day, she says, and her wetness confirms it.

In what seems a parodic homage to the wet streets of film noir, fluidity inundates *Bound*. The lesbian bar that Corky visits in a failed attempt to get laid is named 'The Watering Hole'. When Violet first visits her, Corky is snaking out a bathtub drain. The sounds of a vicious beating move with agonising clarity from Ceasar's toilet to Corky's. Sex and crime travel the same raunchy metaphor. In *Bound*, where there is no proper symbolic, action is restricted to a claustrophobic intersection of lesbian and mafia underworlds – just enough room for homosexuality to ruin a 'family'.[23]

One could produce a psychoanalytic reading of *Bound* by interpreting the sex that Corky overhears as a primal scene and her replacement of Ceasar as Violet's lover as an Oedipal overthrow.[24] What I think is more important to understanding the *différance* of *Bound*, however, is its impropriety, the anti-symbolic quality of its entire world. Corky's masculinity benefits from the lack of a symbolic father. Most notably, it appeals to femme sexuality. In addition to numerous tomboy poses complete with baggy pants and dirty face, Corky's body is repeatedly put on erotic display, for example, in an overhead shot of her lying on her bed in jockey shorts and a side view of her modelled statuesquely while painting the ceiling. Like Johnny in *Gilda*, the camera finds Corky beautiful.[25]

Gilda and *The Big Sleep* can be seen as forerunners for the neo-noir coupling in *Bound*. These films combine difference and sameness to spark sexual attraction and secure romantic coupling. Equality between partners eventually enhances rather than destroys sexuality. *Bound* also blends difference and sameness. While Violet and Corky's femme–butch iconography destines them for an attraction of opposites,[26] their shared voice-over foreshadows compatibility. In contrast to the most cynical films noirs, such as *Double Indemnity* and *D.O.A.* (1950), in which dying men narrate bad-luck stories in flashback, Violet and Corky author a series of flash forwards that puts a success story into motion.

Violet and Corky's criminal and romantic accomplishments derive from the exploitation of, rather than investment in, traditional sex roles. Even as she worries about Violet's trustworthiness, Corky urges her to manipulate Ceasar by crying and threatening to leave. Although Violet makes the threat and slaps Ceasar when he insinuates that Johnnie has bought her for two million dollars, she does not cry. Furthermore, Violet is not shown performing a housewife role in relation to Ceasar, nor does she help him wash and iron the bloodied money or clean up the living room after he slaughters Johnnie and his father. What she does do is stall the police, trick Ceasar, and sweet talk other mobsters to her advantage.

Bound combines the classic *femme fatale*'s predilection for gender disobedience with neo-noir's orgasmic female sexuality and then locates an equally evolved masculinity in the lesbian butch. During Violet and Corky's first conversation, Violet twice says, 'my pleasure'. For her, serving coffee is an aggressive move towards sexual pleasure. Although she does recruit Corky for a criminal partnership, she also 'wants to' seduce her. Interestingly, despite Violet's short skirts and low cut necklines, the breasts we finally see are Corky's. And, like Jackson's in *A Rage in Harlem*, Corky's openly displayed orgasm augments rather than disturbs a nouveau masculinity.

Bound deconstructs the sexual binary, not just through its queer coupling, but also through its complex rendering of feminist and lesbian discourse. Sexual difference theory, which many feminists and lesbians uphold, sees women and men as naturally different. As a consequence of this, an essential sameness is posited among women and another sameness among men. *Bound* ends on a statement that would support such an ideology. Butch Corky asks femme Violet, 'Do you know what the difference is between you and me?' Violet answers, 'No', to which Corky adds, 'Me neither.' The sameness embraced here celebrates their proven trust in one another. Through its narrative, *Bound* suggests that, in contrast to the heterosexual failings of classic film noir, women can trust one another. Because they are same sexed, lesbians make better partners in crime than heterosexual pairings. Moreover, this mutual trust allows for romantic coupling. But what prevents this sameness from desexualising into sisterhood?

At the same time that *Bound* reproduces a lesbian feminist discourse, it counters it with femme–butch difference as well as female violence. Corky's masculinity suggests a difference from other women. But Violet, too, is unfeminine. A popular tenet in the sexual difference school is that men are inherently violent and women non-violent. Violet's killing, then, fundamentally separates her from other women. Like *femmes fatales* before her, Violet is phallic. *Bound* complicates the binary of sameness versus difference, wrapping them around each other until there is only constantly varying relation. Violet and Corky's attraction rests on femme–butch difference; yet their sameness as women supports mutual trust. And, through this play of *différance*, to invoke a Derridian term, the film accomplishes a noir romance. In generic overkill, Violet plugs Ceasar with six bullets and leaves for a new world with Corky. Violet is *both* a *femme fatale* and a lesbian femme.

The classic *femme fatale* was a significant building block for the contemporary attack on binaries. This force should not be attributed solely to her phallic gun. Although her active sexuality was displaced on to violence, the *femme fatale*'s status as *femme* paved the way for neo-noir's orgasmic femme through its difference from and deferral of *both* femininity and masculinity. But *différance* doesn't produce freedom, just play. Similarly, genre relies simultaneously on both variation and repetition. So, *Bound* ends on a joke. No sooner are we freed by Violet and Corky's gender insurrection than stereotypes spring back to life with Tom Jones singing 'She's a Lady' over the ending credits. 'I can leave her on her own, knowing she's OK alone, and there's no messin.' 'Will they never learn?' the film seems to ask with this ironic reminder of masculine ego. 'She knows what I'm about; She can take what I dish out, and that's not easy.' But miscalculations can be fatal. 'Talkin' about the little lady.'

Notes

1. The labrys is a double-edged axe used by pre-patriarchal Amazon women that was adopted as an identity symbol by lesbian feminists in the 70s.
2. This essay will not engage in the continuing debates about the parameters of film noir and about whether film noir is a genre, cycle, or movement. I will use the term *genre* somewhat generally because I am concerned with how film noir functions *now* as a remembered fictional world with conventions and characteristic elements. Film noir's conspicuous lack of solidity as well as its tendency towards genre mixing can only serve my purpose here by suggesting a predisposition to the contemporary scatterings and fusions of neo-noir. My disinterest in defining film noir, then, does not curtail its discursive valence. My descriptions, at times necessarily generalising, will conjure associations of 'classic film noir', whatever that is or is not. Because *Bound* reflects a model associated with James M. Cain (a male protagonist becomes so sexually obsessed with a woman that he agrees to kill her rich husband and dies as a consequence), that model will no doubt be privileged in my references to 'classic' film noir. The majority of neo-noirs employ parody and postmodern pastiche in relation to film noir, although some attempt a continuation of the genre while others strive for a meta position. (The discussion of neo-noir's ability to incorporate that which would seem to be antithetical to film noir, i.e., comedy, must be deferred to a future article.) Many elements, stylistic and thematic, which are associated with film noir now signal the genre even when embedded in another environment. I am particularly concerned with this function of the *femme fatale*, whom film noir was unable to contain even in the 40s and 50s: *The Paradine Case* (1948) is an example of the black widow in a courtroom drama. It is my argument, nevertheless, that today her presence has the ability to contribute a noirish quality to any genre. Moreover, film noir's femme (sexualised woman) today always connotes deadliness until proven otherwise. Such is the lasting strength and timeliness of the *femme fatale*. On neo-noir, see Todd Erickson, 'Kill Me Again: Movement becomes Genre', in Alain Silver and James Ursini (eds), *Film Noir Reader* (NY: Limelight Editions, 1996), pp. 307–329; Leighton Grist, 'Moving Targets and Black Widows: Film Noir in Modern Hollywood', in Ian Cameron (ed.), *The Book of Film Noir* (NY: Continuum Publishing Company, 1995), pp. 267–85; and R. Barton Palmer, 'Conclusion', *Hollywood's Dark Cinema: The American Film Noir* (NY: Twayne Publishers, 1994), pp. 167–187.
3. Janey Place, 'Women in Film Noir', in this volume. The original edition of this anthology in 1978 quickly became a classic in the study of film noir. As is obvious from my notes, it provides many beginning arguments for what I say in this essay.
4. An unfortunate example of this occurs in *The Crying Game* (1992), where the murder of Jude (Miranda Richardson) is naturalised by her coding as a film noir spider woman. See Aspasia Kotsopoulos and Josephine Mills. '*The Crying Game*: Gender, Genre and "Postfeminism"', *Jump Cut*, no. 39, June 1994, pp. 15–24.
5. These associations are narratively powerful whether true or false. In *Body of Evidence* (1992), Madonna's casting as an S/M dominatrix charicatures the presumption that she is a black widow who killed her older love with a sexual overdose. In *Blood Simple* (1984), Ray (John Getz) automatically assumes that his lover Abby (Frances McDormand) is a killer because her husband (Dan Hedaya) earlier described her as duplicitous; instead of being a *femme fatale*, however, she experiences the film's diegesis as gothic.
6. Although classic film noir was praised for its erotic daring, Marc Vernet argues that it was at most a return to pre-Code standards. This is succinctly demonstrated by a photo from the 1931 version of *The Maltese Falcon*, which he captions, 'The *femme fatale*, as she will never be shown in the 1940s and 1950s: in the detective's bed.' Marc Vernet, '*Film Noir* on the Edge of Doom', in Joan Copjec (ed.), *Shades of Noir* (New York: Verso, 1993), p. 13.
7. On film noir's male protagonist, see Frank Krutnik, *In a Lonely Street: Film Noir, Genre, Masculinity* (London and New York: Routledge, 1991).
8. It is important to point out that only a portion of film noir's femmes were *femmes fatales*. See Michael Walker, 'Film Noir Introduction', in Ian Cameron (ed.), *The Book of Film Noir* (NY: Continuum Publishing Company, 1995), p. 12; and Angela Martin, 'Gilda Didn't Do Any of Those Things You've Been Losing Sleep Over!': The Central Women of 40s Films Noir', in this volume. At the same time, the sexuality of femmes separated them from the genre's domestic good girls. In a

virgin–whore dichotomy *femmes fatales* and femmes (sexual women) occupy the same endpoint. That we remember the *femme fatale* as a dominant generic character speaks to the believed danger of female sexuality. Thus, even when she is not murderous, the noir femme first and foremost triggers suspicion and fear.

9. A half-hearted twist to this paradigm occurs in *Detour* (1945), in which Vera (Ann Savage) blackmails Al (Tom Neal) rather than controls him sexually. In one scene she even acts disgruntled when he refuses to accompany her into the bedroom, but not nearly so disappointed as when she cannot buy a fur.

10. Many neo-noir *femmes fatales* are still traditional in that they use sex primarily to manipulate men, for example, in *Final Analysis* (1992). In such cases, I would argue that, although the films update the genre in other respects, their *femmes fatales* are more classic than neo. On the other hand, it should be noted that many neo-noir femmes who use their sexuality to manipulate men also actively gratify themselves in the process, for example, in *Red Rock West* (1992) and *Body Heat*.

11. In such films as *The Big Sleep* (1946) and *Dark Passage* (1947), the implication of Lauren Bacall's characters as *femmes fatales* was crucial to the audaciously sexy Bogart–Bacall star couple, yet eventually required denial to secure romantic coupling at the narratives' conclusions.

12. In *Red Rock West*, such a partnership precedes the film's beginning. Once viewers realise why a husband and wife want to knock each other off – for the money they earlier stole together – the generic partners-in-crime plot with all its sexual promise and final bitterness flashes into relevance. Because the original partnership and crime predates the film's beginning, *Red Rock West* reads like a sequel. This shorthand referencing, which immediately fleshes out the characters' motivations and frees the film's main protagonist from conventional plot obligations, provides another instance of metonymic play in neo-noir.

13. *Out of the Past* (1947) provides the ultimate example via the starkly contrasting *femme fatale* Kathie (Jane Greer) and the home-town girl and confidante Ann (Virginia Huston). In the film's pastoral beginning, Jeff (Robert Mitchum) is courting Ann; then his past reclaims him for *amour fou* with Kathy. *Raw Deal* (1948) foregrounds the element of choice but bends the formula. Joe (Dennis O'Keefe) is sprung from jail by his girlfriend Pat (Claire Trevor) but then falls for the good girl Ann (Marsha Hunt). Joe eventually dies in Ann's arms after turning her into a killer.

14. See Sylvia Harvey, 'Woman's Place: The Absent Family in Film Noir' in this volume.

15. *They Live by Night* (1949) seems to be the model for the 1992 *Gun Crazy*'s ending, which is considerably more sappy than that of the original *Gun Crazy* (1950).

16. One can contrast this with an equally absurd twist in *Fargo* (1996), a neo-noirish midwestern in which a small-town woman police officer kills nonchalantly as part of the job, all the while obviously pregnant.

17. Queer readings have also been performed on classic films noir. See, for example, Richard Dyer, 'Resistance Through Charisma: Rita Hayworth and *Gilda*', and Claire Johnston, '*Double Indemnity*', both in this volume; Jonathan Buchsbaum, 'Tame Wolves and Phoney Claims: Paranoia and Film Noir', in Ian Cameron (ed.), *The Book of Film Noir* (NY: Continuum Publishing Company, 1995), pp. 88–97; and Robert J. Corber, *Homosexuality in Cold War America: Resistance and the Crisis of Masculinity* (Durham, NC: Duke University Press, 1997).

18. See Christine Holmlund, 'A Decade of Deadly Dolls: Hollywood and the Woman Killer', in Helen Birch (ed.), *Moving Targets* (Berkeley: University of California Press, 1993), pp. 127–51; and Teresa de Lauretis, 'Guerrilla in the Midst: Women's Cinema in the 80s', *Screen* vol. 31, Spring 1990. *Jagged Edge* (1985) offers a further role reversal in that the woman lawyer (Glenn Close), with a past and lustful for sex, is attracted to male black widower (Jeff Bridges). In both *Black Widow* and *Jagged Edge* the conventionally male investigator's role is held by a woman whose sexual desire challenges her progress.

19. Again, femme is distinguished from feminine. Whereas the femme is defined as sexual, femininity requires its domestication. Elsewhere, I argue for an understanding of the femme (the actively sexual woman whether straight or lesbian) that differs significantly from the theorisation of femininity as masquerade, for example, by Mary Ann Doane, following Joan Riviere, in 'Film and the Masquerade: Theorising the Female Spectator', *Femmes Fatales: Feminism, Film Theory, Psychoanalysis* (NY: Routledge, 1991), pp. 17–32. See Chapter Five of my book, *Deviant Eyes, Deviant Bodies: Sexual Re-Orientations in Film and Video* (New York: Columbia University Press, 1996).

20. For a discussion of *A Rage in Harlem* (film and book) in relation to the differing functions of

blackness in formalist and content-oriented scholarship on film noir, see Manthia Diawara, '*Noir by Noirs*: Toward a New Realism in Black Cinema', in Joan Copjec (ed.), *Shades of Noir* (NY: Verso, 1993), pp. 261–78.

21. Chester Himes' novel, on which the film is based, contained a more elaborate complication of gender, but the film does retain some serious gender disordering. Although often slapstick, the film's comic aspects – which exceed gender issues – are not self-derogatory. To me, the film seems to celebrate a history of black comic performance without totally converting film noir into comedy.

22. On the (un)knowability of the woman in *Gilda*, which I posit as a precursor to *Bound*, see Mary Ann Doane, '*Gilda*: Epistemology as Striptease', *femmes fatales* (New York: Routledge, 1991), pp. 99–118 and Dyer, 'Resistance Through Charisma'. For Doane, Gilda demonstrates 'the difficulty posed by the woman as a threat to [phallocentric] epistemological systems' (p. 118). Doane compares the narrative's revelation of Gilda as a good girl after all to the striptease, which ultimately reveals the naturalness of woman's nakedness; and yet, Doane argues that this quest for knowledge fails because the film's ending lacks credibility and because Gilda is inseparable from her appearance/act (pp. 106–8). Also noting the phallocentric character of cultural knowledge, Dyer states: 'Any film that allows us to "know" the *femme fatale*, not in the way the hero comes to know her (i.e., by having knowledge of her, finally controlling her), but in the way we "know" all major characters in novelistic fiction, is making trouble for itself. Once the woman is not the eternal unknowable, the hitherto concealed inadequacy of the hero is liable to become evident. This is what happens in *Gilda*.' In *Bound*, Ceasar's death is the exact point between his misjudging and knowing Violet. It is also the point at which Corky (as well as film viewers) knows Violet as a *femme fatale*. This knowledge, however, does not impinge on Corky's adequacy as criminal or romantic partner, nor on Violet's qualification as a lesbian femme (if the stereotype of lesbians as man-haters still holds any valence).

23. See Harvey, 'Woman's Place' in this volume for a discussion of film noir's attack on 'dominant social values normally expressed through the representation of the family'. Here, of course, I'm punning on the mafia's description of itself as 'family.'

24. See Johnston, '*Double Indemnity*' and Doane, '*Gilda*'.

25. See Dyer, 'Resistance Through Charisma' for a discussion of the feminisation of Johnny in *Gilda*.

26. Providing an in-joke for many lesbians in the audience, Susie Bright, a high femme icon in her own right, is listed in the credits as technical adviser. This points us to the issue of authorship. Just as it was ironic that the collected authors of the first edition of *Women in Film Noir* discovered an image of powerful, sexual women in the male-imagined genre of film noir, my identification of lesbian discourse in male-directed neo-noir is ironic. Rather than ask if or how men might produce such a discourse, I prefer to take as my starting point a recognition that contemporary lesbian discourse has now entered the mainstream to the extent that it not only can serve as subject matter but also can contribute to a theatrical film's intertextual make-up.

12

The Postmodern Always Rings Twice: Constructing the *Femme Fatale* in 90s Cinema

Kate Stables

> As a tame beast writhes and wheedles,
> He fawns to be fed with wiles;
> You carve him a cross of needles,
> And whet them sharp as your smiles.
> (Algernon Charles Swinburne, *Satia Te Sanguine*)

It's a cinema made on Mars for me. I have no idea what is happening. New genres have been invented: there seems to be this Naked Jagged Edge Fatal genre, which has sexuality in it, like B-films of the 40s, but they are not as convincing, oddly enough. (Martin Scorsese, *Premiere UK*, July 1995)

Postmodern film, which pillages, adulterates and reconstitutes past cinemas with extraordinary facility, has an unslakeable appetite for film noir. Though this is frequently expressed as a sort of 'Noir-Lite', that's to say coating thriller scenarios in a thin dressing of 'expressionist lighting', 40s styling, and a saxophone soundtrack, the chief object of desire for recent mainstream film has been the *femme fatale*, transplanted wholesale from the thrillers of the 40s and 50s. The fatal woman has made a widespread return to popular cinema in the 90s, appearing in whole new strains as alike yet as diverse as the burgeoning sub-genres they inhabit. Monster villainesses mastermind *Basic Instinct* and *Malice*, unnatural mothers dominate *The Grifters* and *Mother's Boys*, and Madonna, postmodern sex toy *par excellence*, portrays a woman whose body is a deadly weapon in *Body of Evidence*. As well as a rush of deadly retro-noir housewives cut from the classic 40s pattern (*Red Rock West*, *Final Analysis*, *The Hot Spot*), psycho-femme killers prowl through such mainstream slasher hits as *Single White Female* or *The Hand that Rocks the Cradle*. *Disclosure* cast the *fatale* figure as bitch-goddess boss, and *The Last Seduction* gave us the first fully *fatale* protagonist.

To create a detailed study of the new *femme fatale* requires examination of the *sexually* fatal woman, 'the projection of those libidinous cravings, which, since they are forbidden, must always prove fatal'.[1] Pick-and-mix postmodernism in 90s cinema, and the ubiquity of horror genre elements, have created a plethora of *faux fatales*, in particular the proliferation of psycho-femmes in what might be termed the 'slasher-noir'.[2] These are, to invoke Barbara Creed's categories,[3] usually symbolically 'castrated women' (who murder in order to take possession of a child or husband which circumstances have denied them), rather than the 'phallic woman' recognisable from film noir. Sex is part of the psycho-femme armoury, but they are defined primarily by their psychosis – they may be women who are fatal to men, but they are not *femmes fatales*. The most fruitful examples of the startling new *femme fatale* can be found within a small group of mainstream 'erotic' thrillers, released in the first half of the 90s, which include *Body of Evidence, Jade, The Last Seduction,* and the mother of all 90s *fatale* movies, *Basic Instinct.*

Like her predecessors, exemplified in the 'spider woman' of classic noir, the new *fatale* represents and uniquely reflects current discourses around 'woman'. She is a timeless fantasy, a cross-cultural myth, but also a historical construct, whose ingredients vary according to the time and climate of her creation.[4] What marks out the contemporary *femme fatale*, and why is postmodern cinema so fond of her? Which contemporary cultural anxieties about women can be read and analysed through the *fatale* figure?

Key to the study of the contemporary *femme fatale* is an examination of the postmodern cinema in which she is situated, and which is a vital component of her make-up. Classical Hollywood cinema created homogeneous texts for an audience it assumed to be homogeneous. In the 90s, we have what Timothy Corrigan has called 'a cinema without walls', a postmodern cinema which has to reach a media-literate global audience, composed of wildly diverse cultural groupings.

We cannot apply the template of the classic movie *femme fatale* to her 90s counterpart and wonder at the ill-fitting result – the two figures inhabit film eras whose conditions of production, distribution, marketing and audience reception bear only the most basic resemblance to one another. Whereas the traditional noir *femme fatale* can be located with film noir within the classical Hollywood genres of the studio system, the 90s *femme fatale* inhabits a postmodern or post-classical cinema which has undergone a series of transformations. Hollywood itself has evolved from a 'vertically integrated' oligopoly producing large numbers of 'A' and 'B' pictures for an exclusively theatrical audience, to become a cluster of global multi-media corporations producing smaller amounts of film product. These are products which must work to maximum effect and straddle an ever-expanding series of distribution windows (theatrical release, pay-per-view TV, rental and sell-through video, satellite and cable pay movie channels) and global markets.

The 90s movie is exemplified by the 'high cost, high-tech, high stakes blockbusters',[5] a development rooted in the hit-driven decades of the 70s and 80s, when movies like *Jaws, Saturday Night Fever,* and later, the *Star Wars* and Spielberg *Über*-blockbusters established record-breaking global revenues. The blockbuster movie was in place as the standard form by the early 90s, when movies designed for success in all available markets became a necessity, brought about by the huge costs now involved in producing, marketing and distributing films.

Corrigan has suggested how these changes alter the fundamental nature of the film product, by forcing a wholesale reimagining of the conception of an audience.[6] In order to recoup massive production and marketing budgets, movies now have only one audience – the global audience – all of whose constituent audiences must be brought to see the film. This is a postmodern audience, however, relating to moving images in a completely different fashion from their forebears; an audience who are exposed to film and broadcast television, advertising and MTV in unparalleled amounts, and who control their image flows with the VCR and the remote control. Forced to address (and retain) the increasingly mobile interest of the global audience, Hollywood cinema in particular has developed an escalating dependence on high-concept projects, utilising spectacle and highly worked narrative, since these can be most easily marketed and consumed internationally. Tales of sexual obsession and violent death positioned as explicit in their depictions of both activities, translate speedily and effectively across a spread of markets. The complex characterisation which was a feature of post-war Hollywood films has also been succeeded in mainstream cinema by a preference for generic or archetypal characters, more broadly drawn than in previous eras – providing a powerful argument for the readoption of the *fatale* figure.

Weaving the new *femme fatale*

In addition to the changes in the industry and within the films themselves, there is a confluence of social and cultural discourses which conspire to make the *femme fatale* newly relevant, and to construct her in a manner similar to yet sharply different from previous versions. 'Our popular culture functions as myth for our society; it both expresses and reproduces the ideologies necessary to the existence of the social structure,' asserts Janey Place.[7] While postmodern cinema expresses and reproduces dominant ideologies, its polysemic nature allows films to accommodate and privilege radically opposing discourses at the same time. The postmodern film, rather than containing and masking the social contradictions structured into its narrative, is structured to utilise them for widely divergent interpretations of the same text. Thus *Basic Instinct* could be variously reviled as a misogynystic fantasy and celebrated as a feminist *tour de force*, condemned for blatant homophobia and celebrated as the ultimate cult lesbian movie. We may ask ourselves whether there is any longer a need to piece together a recuperative reading around the *femme fatale*, when the text can be experienced in these multiple fashions.

The discourses from which the postmodern film weaves the *femme fatale* are familiar and novel all at once. Chief among these is the profound threat to patriarchy posed by industrial, social and cultural changes at this point in time. Just as cultural anxiety about shifts in established gender roles lay under the eruptions of *fatales*-in-art in the late nineteenth century and post-World War II, today's deep crisis of masculinity is eminently visible in popular culture, and is nowhere more marked than around the *femme fatale*. Mass-market cinema has a unique ability to reflect insecurities in the male image, and the *fatale* figure which combines sadistic and masochistic male fantasies is a potent lightning rod for male anxieties. Such films as *Basic Instinct* and *Body of Evidence* make conspicuous display of male paranoia, which Amelia Jones illuminates in her 1991 discussion of 'new woman's films' as

> the fearful response of patriarchy to the loss of boundaries endemic to the condition of subjectivity in contemporary, so-called postmodern, American life. Their seemingly conventional narratives are, on closer look, distorted by projected anxieties provoked by

the postmodern collapse of traditional rules governing sexual difference. Male paranoia is a defence aimed at *rebuilding* the subject–object dichotomy that threatens to dissolve as more and more women (and men for that matter) take on both masculine and feminine roles.[8]

Jones sees this as working through a process of projection of sexual difference on to the phallically empowered woman. The *femme fatale*, the embodiment of both sexual threat and sexual difference, thus comes into focus as a

> woman only as seen through the man's fantasmic, paranoiac projections … [the film] takes up the explicitly gendered terms of the classic noir suspense narrative where the body of the woman (usually in the guise of the seductive *femme fatale*) constitutes the ambiguous center around which the investigation pivots.[9]

The other great change underlying the construction of the *femme fatale* is the proliferation of sexual discourse which dominates postmodern media, both in images of sexuality and debate about its import. While cinematic discourse on sex is as old as cinema itself, there has been a marked increase since the 80s in films which are very highly sexualised. The erotic thrillers discussed here have repeated and elaborate sex scenes which fundamentally alter the films' generic make-up, their narrative rhythm, their visual and stylistic codes, and above all our perception of the *femme fatale*.

Re-making the *femme fatale*

The postmodern fatal woman is a creature of excess and spectacle, like the films she decorates. For a polysemic, pick-and-mix cinema such as our current one, she is the perfect symbol, combining fear and nostalgia in equal amounts. But how does it construct her, and in what ways do these constructions vary from previous models? Using *Basic Instinct* as a primary text, we can unpick and identify the ways in which the traditional figure, current discourses, and the new cinema combine with unsettling results.

The *fatale* figure has been re-employed consciously because the fatal woman is a universal symbol for a global cinema that is forced to embrace archetypes. The *fatale* myth is common to all cultures[10] and her iconography is widely recognised as a result of a blanket of nineteenth-century European representations[11] as well as earlier cinema incarnations.[12] Woman = sex = death is an equation inscribed into mass consciousness around the world, common to the postmodern West and the pre-modern East. Commentators writing in the 70s, when the *fatale* figure seemed safely historical, made the assumption that western cultural movements such as feminism and 'sexual liberation' would render the idea of the *femme fatale* obsolete, reducing her to a quaint fantastical figure produced by repressed, male-dominated societies. In fact, the reverse has happened – in a movie-producing culture which abounds with mediated images of sex and proliferating sexual discourses, the sexually threatening woman comes to take centre stage. Though *Basic Instinct* can be summarised as the story of a cop looking for a homicidal maniac, it became a glossy vehicle for Sharon Stone's *Uber-fatale*, a fatal woman who not

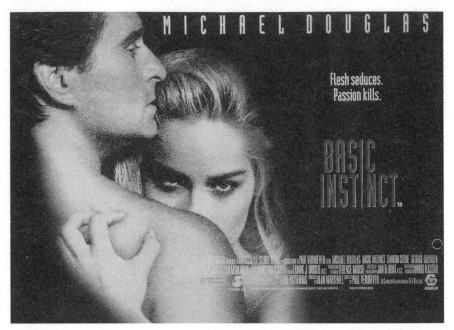

'Femme fatale' is an easily assimilated 'high concept' with which to attract global audiences.

only effortlessly outperfoms the hero in every way, but one who is actually controlling the narrative through the novel she writes throughout the film. *'Femme fatale'* is also an easily assimilated 'high concept' with which to attract audiences, the figure lending itself to global marketing in a highly competitive environment. 'Flesh seduces. Passion kills.' was the stark strap-line used internationally to market *Basic Instinct*; the words were placed over a naked midshot of Michael Douglas clawed by a feline Sharon Stone.

A later stage of the film's promotion centred on a key *fatale* factor, the promise of the sexually 'forbidden' to attract audiences. The 'forbidden' in this instance was the film's 'money shot', the much-touted few seconds of female crotch-flashing during the police interrogation scene, an idea designed to electrify audiences, already veterans of innumerable scenes of 'real' simulated sex, by introducing a note of soft-core pornography.

The *fatale* figure is subject to mutation, and even, in the case of *Basic Instinct*, complete transformation by the new cinema's knowing and eclectic combinations of genres and codes. In *Basic Instinct* the classic *fatale* figure is acted on by a host of influences, visual codes and references. There is a strong Hitchcockian influence, expressed through the *Vertigo* visual styling of Sharon Stone, and the close echo of the original plot and San Francisco location. A 1980s De Palma slasher aesthetic is also present, turning the implied castration threat of the *fatale* into an overt one, with the film opcning on a scene of transgressive sex, which becomes a convulsive fatal stabbing. The sex scenes employ the codes and choreography of soft-core pornography, which combine with the visceral horror of the initial killing to mesh the concepts and threats of sex and death very closely together.

Basic Instinct is also an example of the new genre combinations common in

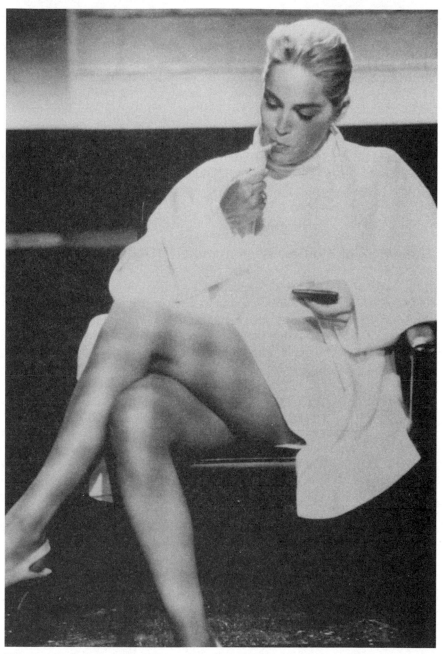

Preparing for the 'money shot'. Sharon Stone in Basic Instinct.

postmodern cinema, resulting in hybrid genres which are fertile spots for the *fatale* figure. Chief among these is the 'erotic thriller' which combines the basic elements of the thriller with sexual intrigue, and whose mainstream examples often draw heavily on film noir conventions and imagery.[13] These new generic hybrids involving the *fatale* are an instance of history repeating itself – where the original noir style was forged from several genres and had its origins in 'B' movies, the erotic thriller in popular 90s cinema is transplanted straight from the 80s video boom. Straight-to-video titles, produced rapidly to feed the market frenzy, were low-budget affairs, with a heavy male slant. Lacking in big name stars, they capitalised on market-crossing high-impact genres, which could be instantly recognised (horror, action adventure, martial arts, soft-porn thrillers) and which exhibited a marked preference for spectacle over narrative. Mainstream postmodern cinema has proven very permeable, absorbing these new forms alongside its rearticulation of classic film genres. A good example of this osmotic process can be found in Brian de Palma's 'erotic slashers' of the mid-80s, such as *Body Double* and *Dressed to Kill*, whose influence can also be seen strongly in *Basic Instinct*, and elsewhere in psycho-femme movies such as *The Hand that Rocks the Cradle, Single White Female, Poison Ivy* and *The Crush*.

The shock of the new *femme fatale*

If the *fatales* of the 40s and 50s were marked out from the vamp by their hunger for independence, their unfeminine ambition or unsettling sexuality, the threat they posed to cultural norms was merely that of the woman outside the conventional social structures. But in the 90s, the new freestanding *fatale* willingly inhabits the cultural margins; what motivates her is her enormous appetite for power, money and sex. When other motivations are introduced, they ring hollow (*Jade* destroys the credibility of its psychologist-hooker *fatale* instantly and inadvertently when she attributes her promiscuity to pain over her husband's infidelities). Always a supra-real projection of 'woman', the *fatale* begins to border on caricature in 90s cinema. (The ultimate example here is Catherine Trammel in *Basic Instinct*, constructed as an orphaned, homicidal maniac heiress who writes best-selling thrillers and flaunts her aggressively flexible sexuality.) A batch of new and varied features around the *femme fatale* underscore and contribute to this excess, adding to her extraordinary dominance within these texts. Long gone is the 'nurturing woman', representing a wholesome alternative in classic noir. Instead, the *fatale* is now surrounded by women who mirror and double her effects, as they too are discovered to be duplicitous sexual transgressors as the narrative unfolds.[14] Three of the four women in *Basic Instinct* are killers, linked by their unnatural blondeness (even brunette Beth is revealed to have been blonde during the period of her college obsession with Catherine) and their sexual or emotional relationships with one another. Their lesbianism is both a symbol of sexual outlawry, and an expression of Trammel's power over the hero, 'making her omnisexual as well as omniscient'.[15] Doubling also intensifies the film's underlying message about the true nature of woman since 'when we ask the film to tell us *who* did do it, the only answer it can give us is that the *women* did it, which is to say The Woman did it'.[16]

The *fatale* has also wrested *narrative control* in two of the examples explored here. Bridget, the *fatale* heroine of *The Last Seduction* gives us the *fatale*-as-protagonist, as she goes on the run with $750,000 of her husband's ill-gotten money, subsequently manipulating the dim lover she acquires into an elaborately scripted attempt on her husband's life.[17] Catherine Trammell has narrative control because she is the author of the novel whose events anticipate those of the film. This adds greatly to her power within the film – as Robert E. Wood observes: 'Catherine's narrative is central to the threat of death she poses. Catherine can make Nick cease to exist in three ways: she can kill him; she can cease to love him; and she can cease to imagine him.'[18]

Potentially the most fascinating new feature of the *femme fatale* is her ability to *avoid textual suppression*, to win on her own terms. If film noir *fatales* were almost inevitably destroyed (*Double Indemnity, Out of the Past*) or occasionally absorbed into marriage (like Gilda) in line with the dominant patriarchal discourse of the time, what are we to make of *fatales* who triumph? This seems to utterly subvert the classic noir procedure with the *fatale* in which the power of the strong sexual woman is first displayed, then destroyed, in order to demonstrate the necessity of its control. When Bridget escapes laughing into a limousine, or Catherine Trammel reclines with the hero in their bed, accessorised with a hidden ice pick, what is the film telling us? That the combination of polysemic narratives and the enigmatic figure of the *femme fatale* is producing films that cannot achieve closure? That ideology no longer requires the suppression of self-determining female sexuality?[19] Or that postmodern cinema works an ultimately dominant feminist discourse into its construction of the *femme fatale*? These endings are surely more ambiguous, suggesting that 'our notions of bad women and good, of normal and deviant, of male and female are crumbling'[20] and combining with a polysemic cinema to produce films which are simultaneously transparent and illegible.

Sluts and Sirens: the sexual suppression of the new *femme fatale*

I think she's the fuck of the century. (Nick Curran, on Catherine Trammell, *Basic Instinct*)

Basically it's like a black widow. … When the male starts to fuck the female he's very careful. Genetically he knows that's a dangerous thing, but he cannot resist so he fucks her anyhow. And then, slowly, he wants to pull back. He seems to succeed, but at the moment he seems out of reach she grabs him and sucks him to death, sucks all the blood out of him. That's basically the scene. That's the scene I wanted to make. (Paul Verhoeven on the inspiration for the opening scene of *Basic Instinct*)

As I've outlined, postmodern film employs the *fatale* figure as a universal archetype, as a marketing ploy, but most significantly as an anxiety pointer, a figure who processes and displays cultural concerns through popular film. Though the new cinema allows for a range of 'readings' around the figure, pulled together from the mass of cultural discourses which can be plaited or privileged within the film itself, there is a single overwhelming factor which determines every facet of the new *femme fatale*, and is ultimately the successful means of her suppression. All the formal, aesthetic and cultural strands which go to make up the new *fatale* figure are filtered through one mesh, to form a single overarching theme: that of *sexual performance*. As an observation, this may seem to border on the banal – the meaning of the *femme fatale* as sign has always been transgressive sexuality – but never before has the overt representation of sex been utilised in such a blanket fashion in her construction, and with such distorting results.

The wholesale use of heavily sexualised representation around the new *fatale* has the effect of reducing the female form to function, broadcasting what could only be hinted at in earlier incarnations. The new *fatale* uses the accumulated visual iconography of the *fatale* in art and film, but the introduction of three key areas: (1) repeated representations of sexual acts; (2) transparently sexual speech; (3) the open problematising of the *fatale*'s sexuality; has skewed the figure in a totally new way.

Narrative investigations of sexuality

Christine Gledhill, in her essays on Klute in this volume, outlines how classic noir worked thriller plots into narrative investigations of female sexuality. In the broad-strokes construction of the postmodern *fatale* this interest, once an underlying current, has become an explicit, literal obsession. Both *Basic Instinct* and *Body of Evidence* involve *fatale* figures literally or effectively on trial for untrammelled and transgressive sexuality – in the case of *Body of Evidence*, the *fatale becomes* the murder weapon, when she stands accused of using violent sex to murder an ailing tycoon. *Basic Instinct*'s central investigation is of Catherine Trammel's omnivorous and fatal sexuality, as well as the identity of the S&M killer. Her sexuality becomes a kind of virus, infecting not only the hero, but also discovered to have infected and inflected all the female characters in the film, who are revealed to have some kind of sexual history with her (Roxy, Beth and even the motherly Hazel Dobbs, have all slept with Catherine). The key to the identity of the killer in *Jade* is the secret of the legendary hooker the investigating hero suspects is hiding within his long-lost love. Sleazy anecdote ('she took it every way'), compromising pictures and blurry video footage of 'deviant' sexual practices are his clues, all brought together to create the 'truth' about the *fatale*. Within *Basic Instinct, Jade* and *Body of Evidence*, all three *fatales* are interrogated in detail by police over their sexual pasts, sexual preferences and sexual identities ('Would you describe yourself as a dominatrix? A sado-masochist?').[21] The final discovery of the killer's identity is, inevitably, anti-climactic within all these texts – the real central enigma is that of the *fatale*'s sexuality. 'Is it ultimately transgressive or recuperable?' is the central question these films ask.

The postmodern *fatale* utilises sex to deliver death. Trammel wields a weapon during sex; Carlson *is* the fatal weapon; Bridget brings about the death of the detective who threatens her by tricking him into sexual display ('I'll show you mine, if you'll show me yours'), and her lover's downfall by inciting him to violent rape, ensuring his capture by police. When the *fatale* is not a killer (as in *Jade*), her dangerous sexuality is still the explicit cause of several deaths – her husband kills repeatedly to suppress the truth about her activities, and to protect his good name, which she bears. Classic film noir sexualised its heroines through highly coded glamour, and an armoury of visual iconography arranged to signal sex and define her as a sexual *presence*. Put repeatedly on sexual display, the new *fatale* is rede-

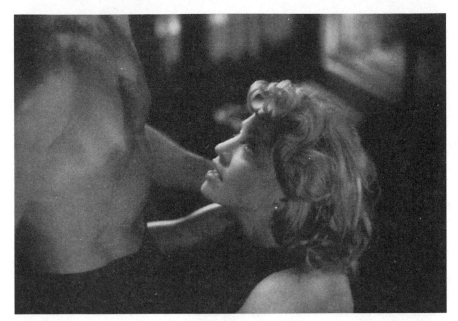

The new fatale *is redefined as a sexual performer, rather than a sexual presence. Madonna in* Body of Evidence.

fined as a sexual *performer* within a visual system which owes as much to soft-core pornography as it does to mainstream Hollywood.

Sequences of sexual performance involving the new *fatale* use the visual language of pornography tempered with the moderating codes of mainstream cinema. As Paul Verhoeven describes it:

> a lovemaking scene is softly lit, backlit mostly, moving bodies and fade-overs, dissolves. Basically you never really see people fuck, but that's how these scenes are normally done in American movies.[22]

The *fatale* is uniquely objectified in these sequences, which revolve around carefully posed, lit and choreographed depictions of female nudity and pleasure. They are distinguished by the active role the female takes, usually in initiating sexual practices perceived as deviant, marginal or transgressive by the dominant culture. Key among these in the early 90s was S&M, which features heavily in both *Basic Instinct* and *Body of Evidence*, and whose use of both props and ritual give an unwholesome, faintly religious and potentially or actively fatal cast to the sexual sequences. Sadomasochism is the prime sexual practice for the *femme fatale*, neatly combining sex and death in one package. Lashed to the bedpost (*Basic Instinct*) or restrained with his own belt (*Body of Evidence*), the hero is *acted upon* by the *femme fatale*, in patterns identical to those used earlier in the narrative on previous men who died in the pursuit of their transgressive desire. When 90s *fatales* claw or wound their male sexual partners (Rebecca Carlson, for example, scarring her lawyer lover with candle-wax burns and with broken glass), they leave behind visual clues as badges of their bearer's trip to the underworld. Patterns of submission and domination are very marked within sexual sequences involving the *fa-*

tale, even in those without intricate deviancy. There is often a compensatory sequence utilising sexual violence towards the *fatale* or a *fatale* substitute (Nick's displacement date rape of psychologist Beth, for example, in *Basic Instinct,* or Frank sodomising Rebecca Carlson in *Body of Evidence*), in an attempt to balance or satisfy both sadistic and masochistic male fantasies. Male protagonists in these films use sexual violence to punish the *fatale,* where classic noir males insulted or slapped recalcitrant women.

This (over)exposure of the *fatale* as the object of sexual spectacle is amplified by these films' propensity to include peeping Tom scenes (*Basic Instinct, Body of Evidence*) or video footage of the *fatale* at play (*Body of Evidence, Jade*), *within* the film itself, creating a bridging web of glances between the spectator and the male hero as he spies on the *fatale.* In the case of *Body of Evidence,* our first sight of the *fatale* is as a soft-porn video image, engaged in sex with the man whose death police are investigating. Exhibitionism is also a common *fatale* trait, with the *fatale* initiating sex in public places – alleys or cars (*The Last Seduction*) or lifts and parking lots (*Body of Evidence*) – where her lack of proper sexual shame threatens discovery and dishonour for her partner. Occasionally, an incident of sexual grandstanding will transmit this mixture of fear and desire directly to the audience – Catherine Trammel's brief genital display is designed to both titillate and terrify the spectator, with a glimpse inside Pandora's Box.

These series of sexual spectacles function as self-contained sections within the film's narrative, and have an accumulative effect in the overall construction of the *fatale.* Because of the amount and necessary variety of sexual 'numbers' within these films (which closely mimic the 'menu' of sexual acts in pornographic films)[23] they create a reductionist concept of the 90s *fatale* as a figure almost exclusively devoted to the practice of sex, whatever her notional career. Repeatedly staked out for the male gaze in sexual sequences, she is simultaneously objectified, 'consumed' by the male eye and deified. Film presents her as constantly erotically available, yet totally unavailable to the spectator, deviant yet desirable. Even where her sexual display is aggressive, such as Catherine Trammel's brazen show for a room of discomfited police, she is still the object of our, and their, hungry gaze.

'That's her pussy talking': constructing aural pleasure with the *femme fatale*[24]

'The spectator rather than the auditor dominates the parameters of sexual discourse,' observes Patricia Mellencamp. Analyses of the *fatale* have traditionally concentrated on the visual make-up of the figure, but I would assert that the structuring role of speech and language plays a large (and largely unappreciated) part in the construction and in the suppression of the new *fatale.* There is surely 'pleasurable listening' for an auditor (presumed male) woven into her composition, as much as 'pleasurable looking'. This new *fatale* produces sexualised speech and also sexual sounds – 'a whole gamut of pants and cries, to deal with the immense and catastrophic problem ... of the visibility or not of pleasure, to provide a vocal image to guarantee the accomplishment of pleasure'[25] during the performances described above.

She flouts the status quo through excess in language – her production of sound and speech now embrace the explicit and forbidden, rather than the subversive. The tone or pitch of her voice is exaggeratedly low, attractively textured (or in the case of *Body of Evidence*, disturbingly childlike). Her speech is open, her dialogue even transparent on occasion ('He falls for the wrong woman … she kills him' – Catherine Trammell) and unconfined by the male voice-over which arched over classic noirs inscribing a male 'author' above the *femme fatale*'s domination of the screen.

The classic noir *fatale* was distinguished by her verbal play and a refusal to utilise language as the law of the father. Her provocative speech ('If I was a ranch, they would have called me the Bar Nothing' – Gilda) was a verbal mirror of her visual come-on, her positions of speech as unstable as her characterisation, which gave her dialogue a slippery and unsettling power. There is little or no ambiguity in the new *fatale*'s candidly sexual outline of her existence – when Rebecca Carlson flatly informs her lover 'That's what I do – I fuck' she sums up the vocation of the 90s *femme fatale*. There is a blunt and naked quality to the new *fatale* conversation as it reduces human interaction and relationships to two-word sexual summaries, which refuses metaphor and strips speech until nothing more can be pared away. But like her elaborate and highly choreographed nudity, this speech is intricate in its candour, and complex in its effects.

Open and aggressively sexual female speech is a radical subversion of the usual order of language and seduction. In order to give an idea of the force of this change, compare and contrast the following two passages, separated by fifty years, both featuring first-meeting dialogue between *fatale* heroine and hero. The first is from *Double Indemnity* (1944):

PHYLLIS: There's a speed limit in this state Mr Neff, 45 mph.
WALTER: How fast was I going, Officer?
PHYLLIS: I'd say around 90.
WALTER: Suppose you get down off your motorcycle and give me a ticket?
PHYLLIS: Suppose I let you off with a warning this time?
WALTER: Suppose it doesn't take?
PHYLLIS: Suppose I have to whack you over the knuckles?
WALTER: Suppose I burst out crying and rest my head on your shoulder?
PHYLLIS: Suppose you try putting it on my husband's shoulder?
WALTER: That tears it.

The second is from *The Last Seduction* (1993)

MIKE: (bending to whisper) I'm hung like a horse. Think about it. (He walks away)
BRIDGET: Let's see …
MIKE: Excuse me?
BRIDGET: 'Mr Ed.' Let's see.
MIKE: I tried to be nice, but I can see that that's something …
BRIDGET: (interrupting but smiling) Now I'm trying … I can be very nice when I try. Sit down.
MIKE: (sitting) Maybe we just got off to a bad start. … (she unzips his fly) What are you doing? (Bewildered)
BRIDGET: I believe what we're looking for here is a certain horse-like quality. (She gropes in his fly)
MIKE: Are you serious?
BRIDGET: I never buy anything sight unseen.

The fatale *controls an open dialogue of frank sexual transaction. Linda Fiorentino in* The Last Seduction.

The *Double Indemnity* exchange is a consummate example of the male–female verbal tennis of classic noir, with the *femme fatale* putting the spin on the ball. Phyllis, as traffic cop, 'regulates' the speed of Neff's approaches, proposes to punish his transgression, and ends their exchange with a reminder of her status and that of her husband/'master' – an appeal to the law of the father. The sexual content of their conversation is entirely sub-textual, their conversation ritualised and strictly devoid of physical contact, with its effects achieved through double entendre.[26]

In *The Last Seduction,* the *fatale* controls an open dialogue of frank sexual transaction. Mike offers himself as a sexual object, and is shocked by Bridget's demand (and her physical search) for proof. Bridget upends the conventional male to female dynamics of the seduction scene, and then openly commodifies their exchange ('I never buy anything sight unseen') backing up her words with aggressive actions.

Where the classic *fatale* subverts language as power, 'sexuality exists in the interstices, gaps and double entendres of dialogue',[27] without exception the new *fatale* ignores conventional restrictions regarding 'forbidden' speech, to create areas of aural pleasure for the male spectator/auditor around her transgressive use of language. Language in which she frequently constructs and names herself as a form created solely for the purpose of sex: for example, 'I wasn't dating him, I was fucking him' (*Basic Instinct*); 'I fucked you, I fucked Andrew, I fucked Frank. That's what I do – I fuck' (*Body of Evidence*); 'I'm a total *fucking* bitch!' (*The Last Seduction*). Language which is also used to objectify her male partner – 'What are you? You are my designated fuck' (*The Last Seduction*); 'Fucking doesn't have to be anything more than fucking' (*The Last Seduction*).

The *fatale* signals her outlaw status through this forbidden language, but also

176

employs it so that speech about sex becomes another form of sexual performance – the narration of her past sexual experiences becomes a spectacle in itself. Conducted in police or courtroom interrogations, the *fatale*'s sexual tales are composed and delivered as foreplay and evidence all in one.

Q: Did you ever engage in sado-masochistic acts? (Policeman)
A: Johnny liked to use his hands too much for that. (Catherine Trammell)[28]

As the *fatale* seeks complicity with the hero/detective through the verbal styling and content of her confessions, her narrated speech also forges a bond with the male spectator. The incorporation of female 'evidence' concerning diverse erotic and dangerous scenarios creates a hallucinatory pocket of voyeurism for the male auditor within the *fatale*'s speech, filled with involuntary images. Her mode of expression and narration draws on the conventions of female speech traditionally used in pornographic prose ('She's seen me fuck plenty of guys,' for example, is how Catherine Trammell summarises her sexual arrangements). It consequently acquires the psychic function of this type of narration

which echoes the archaic, incestuous complicity between mother and child, a connection which pornography establishes more explicitly than other genes ..., a complicity which is sealed and gratified by the obscene utterance on the woman's part.[29]

The heavy presence of obscene speech, rather like the repetition of sexual spectacle, also presents the audience with several marked and novel areas of pleasure in their experience of the screen *fatale*. As she offers up obscenities like sweets, the terms gain an additional friction and pornographic quality from their context (since these are lower-class words enunciated by elegant upper-class females). Disarming the official language of legal questioning which elicits them, these are words which rub up against and unbalance the law of the father, and disturb and titillate the male auditor.[30]

A primary source of the pleasure the male auditor takes in the *fatale*'s enunciation of 'forbidden' speech lies in the hallucinatory force of the words she employs. Ariel Arango, in his survey of psychoanalytic insights into 'dirty words', identifies these words as 'obscene' (a corruption of the Latin 'scena' meaning 'out of scene') because they name what should not be mentioned in public – they reveal the truly sexual life.

Furthermore these words often carry a hallucinatory force. They arouse the picture of the sexual organ or scene in a most vivid way, and they also arouse strong licentious feelings. ... 'Dirty words' as well as dreams are a true way to the unconscious. They provide, like the old roads built by the government, wide and more perfect access to the hidden world.'[31]

The *fatale*, like the mythical Siren, evokes the irresistible promise of pleasure through her speech for the male auditor. When the *fatale* uses 'dirty' words, the effect is like that of a smutty joke: the image which arises for the auditor is the purpose of the exercise. This effect is reinforced by the cultural curiosity of hearing a woman employ the terms since their usage, as outlined by Freud, is a sexually aggressive act:

the off-colour saying is like undressing the person of the other sex to whom it is directed. With its obscene words it obliges the 'attacked' person to fancy the part of the body or action to which they correspond, making [her] see that which the attacker is now 'showing' them. Undoubtedly the pleasure of showing sexual parts totally unveiled is the primary motive of this type of saying.[32]

Perhaps most important in the construction of the *fatale* figure through speech is the claim that the obscene word makes to the function of *truth,* through its relation to primary or unconscious processes. Obscene language uttered by the *fatale* relates intimately to the body and its drives, which speaks to the deepest meanings of the *fatale* figure, and carves the inscription of sexual difference into her speech. Lucienne Frappier-Mazur notes how the obscene word unmasks sentimental discourse as euphemism, when it opposes the 'truth' of the demands of the body and its pleasure against the 'falsehood' of feelings.[33] This assumption of bodily honesty through speech has the effect of making the new *femme fatale* appear transparently sexual. She speaks the truth of the body, while all those around her lie:

> Rebecca: Have you ever seen animals make love, Frank? It's *intense.* It's violent. But they never really hurt each other.
> Frank: We're not animals.
> Rebecca: Yes, we are.
> (from *Body of Evidence*)

If, as Mary Anne Doane suggests,[34] the cinematic figure of the *femme fatale* betrays an unease about the limits of the visible, the sexual speech of the new *femme fatale* is designed to address this conundrum by revealing as much of her essential truth as possible through transparent speech and obscene language. If we cannot trust the image we can appeal to the voice, through which we may gauge her authentic internal essence. Like the sisters in the fairy story who each produced either toads or diamonds whenever they spoke, as unstoppable emissions which betrayed their fundamental natures, the new *femme fatale* gives forth sex ceaselessly when she speaks.[35] The search for the truth about the *femme fatale* is thus periodically displaced from the look to the voice and is rewarded by ample reductive evidence confirming sex as her animating characteristic. While the new *fatale* constructs and condemns herself out of her own mouth, her language opens up fresh areas of affective pleasure for the male auditor, to whom the sound of a woman speaking sex is a whole new route to objectifying women. 'Only words – but because they are about sex, the speaker as well as the subject spoken about is transformed into sex.'[36]

The lady is a trope

Postmodern cinema fashions the new *femme fatale*, like Swinburne's Faustine, as a 'love machine with clockwork joints of pure gold'. It constructs and constrains her with a set of codes imported from pornography, which neutralise or distort the strong and compelling visual presence inherited from classic film noir. While she is fabricated from (and speaks to) a set of current and often conflicting discourses around 'woman', she signals nothing but sex. The 90s *fatale* is a supreme cinematic symptom of what Fredric Jameson refers to as 'that reduction to the body everywhere present in the postmodern'.[37]

Made up of contradictory patterns, the new *fatale* is at once exhilarating and exasperating for the female spectator or critic, as her plethora of possible meanings jostle for attention. Each new feature which seems to break fresh ground – a *fatale* protagonist, triumphantly active and polymorphous sexuality, opportunities to escape textual suppression or control the narrative – is countered by a matching development which makes a mockery of critical claims for the equal-opportunity *fatale*. The strained status of patriachy and the polysemia of mainstream cinema allow for some of these discourses to speak to, and for women, but the dominant voice remains that of patriachy.

What kind of pleasures are there for female spectators within these texts? Julianne Pidduck, writing about the 90s 'fatal femme cycle' celebrates the possibility of identification with the *fatale*:

> Where in our everyday lives as women we are bombarded by the evidence of our increasing vulnerability, poverty and limited social power, the fatal femme's embodied social, sexual and physical powers offer an imagined point of contact, if not simply identification – an imagined momentum or venting of rage and revenge fantasies – the importance of which cannot be underestimated.[38]

Here, the *fatale* enacts a collective female fantasy of 'acting-out',[39] mistress of all she surveys as she mutilates the male body on our behalf. But while women salute and enjoy the *fatale* as she takes our revenge for us, the other messages she puts into circulation may be more detrimental. In these broad and illegible texts, the *femme fatale* has come to stand in for all women – once the figure of woman is comprehensively sexualised on screen, all females are reduced to form and (fucking) function. This mass objectification doesn't remove danger from desire – it simply serves to represent all women as dangerous.

With this addition of open eroticisation (woman-as-sexual-spectacle), to female glamour (woman-as-spectacle), 90s cinema rearticulates questions of knowledge and sexuality around the *fatale*. The profusion of sexual strands combined in her creation attempt to reveal the 'truth' about her – and by extension the truth about woman – by laying bare her body, her carnal activities and proclivities, and her speech. Perversely, through its elaborate artifices and excess cultural baggage this wholesale sexualisation serves to render the *fatale* more, rather than less, opaque. The new 'nude' *fatale* is in reality swathed (some might say disguised) by sex – the more she shows, the less we know.

Notes

1. Angela Carter, *Nothing Sacred* (London: Virago, 1978) p. 119
2. I would include in this category a slew of early 90s horror-thrillers such as *Poison Ivy, Single White Female, The Temp* and *The Hand that Rocks the Cradle*. While the women characters featured in

these films often have *fatale* elements, they are clearly coded as active obsessives – often objectivising the men or women they hound – rather than objects of desire.

3. Barbara Creed, *The Monstrous Feminine: Film, Feminism, Psychoanalysis* (London: Routledge, 1993). Creed identifies these women as symbolically castrated: 'This version of the female psychopath represents a more conventional view of female monstrosity in that woman transforms into a monster when she is sexually and emotionally unfulfilled. She seeks revenge on society, particularly the heterosexual nuclear family, because of her lack, her symbolic castration' (p. 122). By contrast, Creed types Catherine Trammell (*Basic Instinct*) as a *castrating* female psychotic, whose ice pick represents metaphorically her *vagina dentata,* rather than the 'phallic woman' (strong, sexual, gun-carrying) of film noir. 'The archetypes of the phallic and castrating woman are quite different and should not be confused : the former ultimately represents a comforting phantasy of sexual sameness, and the latter a terrifying phantasy of sexual difference' (p. 157).

I would suggest that one side-effect of the genre-mutability of postmodern film has been to render the new *fatale* almost exclusively 'castrating', rather than 'phallic', through its use of explicit body-horror and sexual imagery.

4. For the full background on the concept of the *femme fatale* as a construct woven from patterns of contemporary discourse, see Rebecca Stott, *The Fabrication of the Late Victorian Femme Fatale: The Kiss of Death* (Basingstoke: Macmillan Press, 1992). My analysis throughout this essay is indebted to Stott's model, which outlines the origins of the Victorian *fatale* in literature within nineteenth-century discourses around sex, disease, the 'woman question' and ethnicity.

5. Thomas Schatz, 'The New Hollywood' in Jim Collins, Hilary Radner and Ava Preacher Collins (eds), *Film Theory Goes to the Movies* (New York: Routledge, 1993).

6. Timothy Corrigan, *A Cinema Without Walls: Movies and Culture After Vietnam* (London: Routledge, 1992), pp. 20–2.

7. Janey Place, Women in Film Noir, intra.

8. Amelia Jones, '"She was Bad News": Male Paranoia and the Contemporary New Woman', *Camera Obscura,* 25–6. Jones uses the concept framed by feminist theorist Alice Jardine, who posits the inscription of 'the feminine' in nineteenth- and twentieth-century texts as an essential prophylactic against male paranoia. In *Gynesis* (Ithaca, NY and London: Cornell University Press, 1985).

9. Ibid., p. 297

10. For a detailed examination of the history and ubiquity of the *femme fatale* in art, myth and legend, see Mario Praz, *The Romantic Agony* (London: Oxford University Press, 1933; [2nd edition 1950]); and Camille Paglia, *Sexual Personae* (London: Penguin, 1990). Paglia sees the omnipresent *femme fatale* as a manifestation of the alienation of modernity from biology – 'The primary image is the *femme fatale*, the woman fatal to man. The more nature is beaten back in the west, the more the *femme fatale* reappears, as a return of the repressed' (p. 13).

11. Late nineteenth-century art and literature saw an extraordinary flowering of the image of woman as destroyer. Writers and painters of the Symbolist, Decadent, and Pre-Raphaelite movements, such as Wilde, Gaultier, Swinburne and Baudelaire, invoked the historical figure of the *femme fatale* ceaselessly as a subject of horrible fascination. Interestingly, the *fatales* of the 1890s and 1990s share some sensationalist characteristics common to sex-obsessed cultures, and absent from the classic film noir versions. The sexual cannibalism of Gautier's *Cleopatra* or Swinburne's *Faustine* finds an echo in the polymorphous and perverse sexual appetites of the heroines of *Jade, Basic Instinct,* or *Body of Evidence.* See Patrick Dale, *Femme Fatale: Images of Evil and Fascinating Woman* (London, Ash & Grant, 1979); or Mario Praz, *The Romantic Agony,* for a detailed overview of the nineteenth-century incarnations, and an analysis of the root cause of their eruption when, as Praz puts it 'the wellsprings of inspiration were troubled'. By the end of the century, the *fatale* had become a trope, firmly embedded in popular literature as well as high art – Stott analyses her appearance in the work of Thomas Hardy, H. Rider Haggard, Bram Stoker and others in *The Fabrication of the Late Victorian Femme Fatale* (see Note 4).

12. Prior to the appearance of the *femme fatale* in wartime cinema, the *fatale* made a first appearance in cinema as 'the vamp'. The 'vamp', who appears in early Hollywood cinema, is the last gasp of the cult of the *fatale*, which by the turn of the century had penetrated so far into the visual and live arts (decorating opera, stage melodrama, popular fiction and advertising) that it had become a commonplace. The vamp was incarnated on- and off-screen by such actresses as Pola Negri and Theda Bara, who starred in lurid screen adaptations from the *fatale* canon – *Carmen* (1915),

Cleopatra (1917), *Salome* (1917). Bara has a unique place in the history of sexual commodification – David Thomson notes that she was 'the first woman offered commercially in movies as an object of sexual fantasy'.

13. Linda R. Williams, in her examination of the absorption of the erotic thriller into the mainstream ('Erotic Thrillers and Rude Women', *Sight and Sound*, July 1993, pp. 12–14) points out the honest antecedents of the Hollywood versions. 'Sharon Stone as Catherine Trammell is only a more expensive version of erotic thriller video queen Delia Sheppard, who as Bridget the avenging lesbian of *Night Rhythms* at least sticks to her sexuality. Stealing the plots of their poor relations, cleansing them of any residual feminism and some of their raw "deviant" moments, what the blockbusters have done is to engage in a series of anodyne remakes, sanding down the revealing rough edges.'

14. Lynda Hart makes this point in the chapter she devotes to *Basic Instinct* in *Fatal Women: Lesbian Sexuality and the Mark of Aggression* (Princeton, NJ: Princeton University Press, 1994), pp. 124–34, as well as noting the autoerotic/narcissistic effect of the close resemblance of Catherine to her female lovers. Hart reads Catherine's lesbian relationships, however, as proof that 'Catherine reserves her *real* love for women'.

15. Karen Durbin, 'Psycho Femmes' in *Mirabella*, June 1992.

16. Lynda Hart, p. 130.

17. Bridget also extends her narrative control to other people's off-screen lives. She devises a scheme to root out unfaithful husbands via credit checks, and then pitches contract-killings to their wives.

18. Robert E. Wood, 'Somebody Has to Die: *Basic Instinct* as White Noir', *PostScript*, vol. 12, no.3.

19. 'The fantasy of a woman's dangerous sexuality is a feminine as well as a masculine fantasy, and its pleasures lie precisely in its forbiddenness.' Elizabeth Cowie has recently raised the interesting possibility that in classic film noir the wish to match active female sexuality with punishment is a fantasy for which one size fits all. 'To argue that it is only patriachy or the Production Code that requires its punishment is to misunderstand that it is the fantasy itself that demands the punishment, for in the punishment the reality of the forbidden wish is acknowledged' (in Joan Copjec (ed.), Shades of Noir [London: Verso, 1993], p. 136).

20. Karen Durbin, *Mirabella*, June 1992 p. 48.

21. Prosecutor questioning Rebecca Carlson during a police interview in *Body of Evidence*.

22. Paul Verhoeven, interviewed for 'Basic Cutting' in Laurent Bouzereau, *The Cutting Room Floor* (New York: Carol Pub. Group, 1994), p. 200.

23. It is interesting to note the close overlap between Stephen Ziplow's checklist of the sexual acts needed in porn movies (Linda Williams, *Hardcore: Power, Pleasure and the 'Frenzy of the Visible'*, [London: Pandora Press, 1990], pp. 126–7) and the acts included in the films cited here. *Body of Evidence*, for example, includes depictions of masturbation, straight sex in a variety of positions, oral sex, anal sex, and what Linda Williams defines in industry jargon as 'sadie max' (sado-masochism).

24. Nick's detective partner Gus, the voice of masculine reason in *Basic Instinct*, dismisses Catherine's alibi ('That's her pussy talking – it ain't your brain').

25. Stephen Heath, 'Body, Voice' in *Questions of Cinema* (London: Macmillan Press, 1981), p. 189. The emission of sexual sounds is important to the representation of the *fatale* as duplicitous – though her sexual pleasure is presented as genuine, since it cannot be represented visibly, the spectator/auditor must factor in her vocal dissimulation, alongside the contradictory notion that these sounds are involuntary and unforced.

26. For an extended analysis of this exchange, see Peter William Evans '*Double Indemnity* (Or Bringing Up Baby)' in Ian Cameron (ed.), *The Movie Book of Film Noir* (London, Studio Vista, 1992), pp. 168–9. Evans examines the strong sadomasochistic element within this famous scene in some detail.

27. Mary Ann Doane (ed.), *Femmes Fatales: Feminism, Film Theory, Psychoanalysis* (New York: Routledge, 1991), p. 108.

28. Catherine Trammell in *Basic Instinct* interrogation scene.

29. Lucienne Frappier-Mazur, 'Truth and the Obscene Word in Eighteenth-Century French Pornography', in Lynn Hunt (ed.), *The Invention of Pornography*, (New York: Zone Books, 1993). Mazur notes that the introduction of a female narrator will 'frequently obscure, alleviate, or even eliminate the hostile undertones of the obscene words, and complicate their significance' (p. 209).

30. The construction of a pornographic text has traditionally assumed and privileged a reader/viewer/

auditor presumed to be male. I suspect that this address requires the female auditor to perform a kind of aural masquerade, oscillating between male and female positions. For this point, I am grateful to Laura Mulvey who kindly discussed the possible functions of female sexual speech with me while this section took shape.

31. Ariel Arango, *Dirty Words: Psychoanalytic Insights* (New Jersey: Jason Aronson, 1989), p. 15.
32. Sigmund Freud, *Jokes and their Relationship to the Unconscious* (London: Hogarth Press, 1945). Freud conceived of sexually aggressive smut solely as a conduit for male-to-female aggression rooted in arousal, and firmly cast the 'attacked' person as female – since this is usually the case.
33. Frappier-Mazur, 'Truth and the Obscene Word', p. 213.
34. Mary Anne Doane, *Femmes Fatales*, p. 3.
35. Bridget (*The Last Seduction*), for example, even in her good-girl masquerades to the police, is speaking about sex when she passes herself off as the victim of a threatened rape ('The gist of it was ... he was going to impale me ... with his big "thing"'), and as the mother of a threatened toddler ('There's a strange man outside my house. He tried to show his "diddly" to my three-year-old daughter').
36. Catherine MacKinnon, *Only Words* (London: Harper Collins, 1995), p. 46.
37. Fredric Jameson, *The Geopolitical Aesthetic* (London: BFI, 1992), p. 29.
38. Julianne Pidduck, 'The 1990s Hollywood Fatal Femme: (Dis)Figuring Feminism' in *CineAction* pp. 64–72, September 1995. Not all female critics are this positive about the new *femme fatale*. As Linda R. Williams writes: 'the shock of the icepick isn't the shock of a woman taking up arms, it's that someone has bothered to lay out their fantasy of female sadism made in the image of male masochism so explicitly and expensively while pretending it's something else' (*Sight and Sound*, July 1994).
39. Both the violent death-dealing and the active physical cruelty of the *femme fatale* suggest a strong link with the increasing instances of real-life females 'acting out' violently on the male body – Lorena Bobbitt, Aileen Wournos, Tracie Andrews, et al.

13

'The Dark Continent of Film Noir': Race, Displacement and Metaphor in Tourneur's *Cat People* (1942) and Welles' *The Lady from Shanghai* (1948)

E. Ann Kaplan

White critics' blindness to the importance of blackness in a racial sense to film noir has still not been adequately addressed. Race is film noir's repressed unconscious Signifier. It was convenient that French critics first named these films 'noir'; however, English-speaking critics could, theoretically, have translated the term and talked about 'black' film. But that would have forced us to confront the problem of 'black' as a category we were still 'forgetting' about – at least in relation to film analysis – in the late 70s. 'Black film' would have opened up the concept of 'blacks in film' which white feminist film critics were not then thinking about for complex historical and social reasons (Doane, 1991; Kaplan, 1997). It was easier for Anglo-American critics to accept the French term 'noir' for the genre.

As research since then has amply shown, the *literal* absence or stereotyping of black characters is a result of Hollywood's collusion with American racism that rendered Hollywood basically apartheid: blacks could not act in Hollywood for a long time, and whites in blackface played ugly black stereotypes. As Michael Rogin has shown, Hollywood capitalised 'on the surplus symbolic value of blacks, the power to make African Americans stand for something besides themselves' (Rogin, 1992: 417). As the first blackface film, Porter's *Uncle Tom's Cabin* straddled the border between popular nineteenth-century black face minstrelsy and twentieth-century film (p. 418). When blacks could finally act in Hollywood, they were at first mandated to play only in all black films. Finally, they were allowed to play demeaning roles such as waiters, drivers, mammies, prostitutes, etc., when working with a white cast. This situation by itself does not pertain specifically to films noirs, but it is something which critics might have commented on in studying these films.

So in what ways is noir as a genre or group of films in any special sense related to race? Are representations of race in noir any different from those in other Hollywood films? And if so, in what ways, and why and how? Had we asked these questions at the time, it might also have prompted the task I now undertake in this essay, namely to think through the relationship of 'black' film (i.e., film noir) to race as well as to sex in the political unconscious.

The feminist analysis in our 1978 volume stressed how the visual style of film noir – the dark shadows, ominous lighting, disturbing architecture and awkward visual compositions, etc. – represented white male culture's dis-ease with femininity, with the Otherness of woman: it marked male fear of the not-male. Although we did not yet have Judith Butler's phrase to hand, we were in effect arguing that film noir was preoccupied with 'gender trouble' – the fear of the *order* of heterosexuality being reversed, leaving the female dominant; or, as Richard Dyer showed in relation to *Gilda*, with the fear of heterosexuality slipping into something else.

This was the originality of our volume at the time. As I indicated in the Introduction, male critics in 1978 were debating whether film noir *was* a genre or not; which films belonged in it; what the time-frame for film noir should be; how film noir differed from the thriller or crime genre, the historical relationships among noir and crime films, which noirs were the greatest aesthetically, etc.; and they were researching the background of the directors and scriptwriters, the links with crime stories and novels, the iconography of noir, and the historical reasons for the gloomy view of human nature. But we took a different approach in our book: we argued that the strangely twisted relations between the sexes made a film 'noir'. We focused on the unusual prevalence of the powerful, sexual, often evil woman in this group of films, and on the absence of woman in her 'normal' place, i.e., safely located in the family.

I still think that the problem of gender – or gender trouble – is one of the main unconscious formations for the style and themes of film noir, and the new authors writing in the 90s seem to agree, however differently organised sexualities are in the neo-noirs. But I would now add that another powerful and troubling difference is also at work in the 40s films, namely the problem of racial difference. It is this troubling other 'difference' that I shall explore in two noir films, *Cat People* (1942) and *The Lady from Shanghai* (1948).

My task differs from, if it is linked to, both Manthia Diawara's interesting project in his essay 'Noirs on Noir', and Eric Lott's work on 'The Whiteness of Film Noir', which I briefly summarise in what follows as preparation for my own analyses. In 'Noirs on Noir', Diawara addresses the ambivalence of the French term, 'noir', for this group of films, given that the term for African peoples the French colonised was 'Noirs'. In addition, Diawara notes that 'Women, bad guys, and detectives in *film noir* are "Black" by virtue of occupying indeterminate and monstrous spaces that Whiteness traditionally reserves for Blackness in our culture' (1993: 525). Diawara usefully distinguishes films labelled noir in Borde and Chaumeton's pioneering volume because of their style, from the use of noir style by black film-makers to focus on themselves.[1] While the classic noir style uses tropes of Blackness as metaphors of White characters' falls from grace, black directors use the style to focus on the desperate plight of blacks in US society. Diawara discusses Chester Himes' *A Rage in Harlem* – a novel that 'deploys the noir style to shed light on the desperate condition of people who are forced to live below whites, but who have not fallen from grace or are misogynists, cowardly or duplicitous' (as are white characters in the films noir).

Diawara points out that 'The noirs in Himes's text are Black people trapped in the darkness of White captivity, and the light shed on them is meant to render them visible, not White' (p. 526). Diawara further argues that critics should not compare the detectives and *femmes fatales* in noir films by black directors to their white counterparts in film noir; he suggests that black film-makers 'redeem blackness from the genre by recasting the relation between light and dark on the screen as a metaphor for making Black people and their cultures visible. In a broader sense, Black film noir shines light (as in day*light*) on Black people' (p. 527).

Diawara here shows how black directors have *literalised* the unconscious of film noir – how they have turned the genre on its head to expose what it repressed, namely the realistic plight of blacks. Black directors show how 'black' black life really is, while whites have used the film noir's 'blackness' to represent whites' moral evil, ignoring real blacks altogether. While Diawara does not always make it clear how 'noir' (in the classic senses) the noir style is in films by black film-makers, none the less, his is a highly suggestive and fascinating thesis.

Eric Lott's argument in 'The Whiteness of Film Noir' complements Diawara's in showing how the film noir style – with its shadows and dark/light sharp contrasts – shows characters literally changing from 'black' to 'white' as they, for example, step out from a dark shadow into a bright light. He cites the instance of Walter Neff in *Double Indemnity*, giving an account of Neff at the film's opening. As a man scarred by his deceit, violence and cunning, he is 'so fully immersed in blackened cinematic compositions that his darkness threatens to manifest itself on his very skin' (Lott, 1997). In this the way, whites in film noir are 'blackened' in visual terms – as if the repressed must return. Lott's larger thesis is that 'at a moment when bold new forms of black, Chicano, and Asian activism and visibility confronted resurgent white revanchism and vigilantism, film noir's relentless cinematography of chiaroscuro and moral focus on the rotten souls of white folks ... constantly, though obliquely, invoked the racial dimension of this figural play of light against dark'.

I want to extend such arguments and show that the visual style of film noir refers to western culture's unconscious linking of the 'darkness' of the psyche (especially the female psyche) not only with the literal darkness of racial others, but also with unconscious fear/attraction for the racial others that the 'Imaginary' of dominant white culture represses both literally and symbolically.[2] Most critics agree that in the immediate context of World War II, American film turns increasingly to the dark side of the psyche in the type of film called 'noir'. I have, however, deliberately used the phrase 'dark continent' in my title (referring to the psyche) rather than simply 'dark side' to connote what was readily referred to at the time – carrying over from the heights of colonialism a century earlier – as the 'dark continent' of Africa. Africa was 'dark' (as many critics have now argued) both because its inhabitants happened to have black skins, but more so because the western Imaginary superimposed on this literal darkness connotations of savagery, cannibalism, immorality, backwardness (see Said, 1992; Stam and Spence, 1988; Shohat and Stam, 1994).

But as colonialism began to wane under the challenges made effectively by subaltern groups in the 40s, so white culture's unconscious searched for other 'dark continents' to fill the gap left by Africa. One such continent was the psyche of women, now coming into consciousness as Freud's theories spread in the wake of World War II. But this dark continent of the female psyche never quite lost its links to displaced reference to racial darkness. This was because the differences of both women and 'dark' others from the white male centre were often collapsed, uncon-sciously, in an effort for white patriarchy to keep its image of itself. As scholars now know from post-Structuralist theories not available to us in 1978, dominant (white, male) culture has to manage the boundaries between male and female, white and black. In relation to sexuality, Foucault, for instance, has shown that, in his words, 'sex was not something one simply judged; it was a thing one adminis-tered; it called for management procedures' (Rabinow, 1984: 307). Although Foucault never dealt extensively with race matters, he suggests that race similarly has to be 'managed' when he says: 'There also appeared those systematic campaigns which … tried to transform the sexual conduct of couples into concerted economic and political behavior. In time, these new measures would become anchor points for the different varieties of racism in the 19th and 20th centuries' (p. 309). Through analysis of the two chosen noir films, I shall argue for the simultaneous production of potentially useful knowledge about blacks and women, and a narra-tive address that satisfies the need to control or manage fear of women and blacks.[3] Discourses in the films reveal white culture's fears of what might happen if gender and racial boundaries were not managed and kept in place.

In the following discussion of the noir films – deliberately chosen to represent early and late noir (one made during, and one after, World War II) – I hope to il-luminate two somewhat different ways in which a racial unconscious speaks through noir visual style and narrative themes. In each case, however, the need to manage or control the boundaries between male and female, and between white and black, are intertwined. In each film, also, there is an almost endless play with varied connotations and symbolisms for whiteness and blackness. If Tourneur's 1942 film makes issues to do with the unconscious evident in its surface narrative, which involves a typical 'Hollywood' psychoanalytic investigation of the heroine, *The Lady from Shanghai* is equally concerned with the dark continent of the fe-male psyche as this concern slips into unconscious fears of racial darkness.

Tourneur's *Cat People* is an early film noir which departs slightly from the classic mould in that here the investigation of the heroine is undertaken not by a detective but by his surrogate, a psychoanalyst. In addition, if the heroine Irena is a *femme fatale*, she is represented as one *in spite of herself*. In other words, Tourneur's film explicitly investigates the noir heroine's unconscious – the dark continent of her psyche – rather than this dark continent being implicit, as in a noir film like *The Lady from Shanghai*, which I dicuss below.

Made in 1942, when western culture's racism was still dominant, *Cat People* man-ifests the Foucaultian cultural practice of at once attempting to control social enti-ties creating tension while, in the same move (paradoxically) producing knowledge about them. Thus the film unconsciously lays bare oppressive racial mechanisms which were putting pressure on American culture at this time while ostensibly 'man-aging' the threatened boundaries. World War II was under way and the experience of black GIs in the various armed forces highlighted American racism. The Army or-ganised a form of apartheid for white and black soldiers, and often embarrassed it-self in foreign nations by insisting on separate facilities for white and black soldiers. Wartime, then, forced Americans to become aware of a racism they were in the habit of denying, producing a need for further denial mechanisms, further 'management'. But the repressed returns, as we know: hence the racial unconscious of film noir.

Fig. 1. This publicity shot plays with the split between surface domestic, white middle-class normality, and the dangers of blackness and female sexuality lurking beneath the visible. The shot's structure mimics that of Freud's conscious/unconscious topography.

Cat People, then, unconsciously comments on patriarchal, nationalist and racist oppressions in the course of producing knowledge about them, while unable to take a fully resisting (or conscious) stance on these issues. US xenophobia produces Irena's foreignness as monstrous, and surely in 1942 specific reference is to unconscious fears of the Jew. Indeed, the film unconsciously reflects Nazi iconography in the textures of Irena's clothes, in the exaggerated furs and stiff black body of the Cat Woman who greets Irena early on in the film, in the aesthetics of the black panther itself and of the drawings and statue of the animal. Irena's own slinky body and often shiny clothes suggest Nazi body and clothing aesthetics. This can be seen in figure 1, a publicity still for the film, which shows Irena in a close-fitting, shiny black dress; it also figures the Freudian superego/id divide in the split image. The upper part of the image provides the Ideal romantic heterosexual couple of American social law; but below we find the black panther-like *femme fatale,* bursting with sexuality, passion and evil. The still unconsciously produces the film's underlying meanings. Uncannily, *Cat People* echoes Nazism's surprising expression of a fantasy about pure Aryan whiteness through *blackness,* that is through an extreme focus on black leather, black symbols, etc. It is a perfect example of the return of the repressed. Trying to extricate blackness (a black idea in the first place), the Nazis end up inscribing the blackness they hoped to eradicate.[4] The mechanism is rather like that which I argue was taking place in the films noirs discussed here *vis-à-vis* African Americans.

Another resonance is a similar slippage between Jews and blacks that Rogin discusses in relation to a hero not in a film noir, but in melodrama, namely Al Jolson in *The Jazz Singer* (1929). Rogin's analysis focuses on the male Jew in blackface, and he argues that for this figure, 'the interracial double is not the exotic other but the split-off self, the white in blackface' (Rogin, 1992: 419). Rogin suggests that Jews 'appropriated an imaginary blackness to Americanise the immigrant son' (p. 421), since 'Blacks may have seemed the most distinctively American people, the furthest from the old-world identities of Americanizing immigrants' (p. 439). While this strategy did ultimately exploit and silence African Americans, Rogin argues that 'A common set of racial stereotypes (later to bear fruit in the 1924 immigration restriction bill) ... bound together Jews, Asians, and blacks under the Orientalist umbrella.' A redemptive meaning, however, resided in the combining of 'racially alien, primitive qualities ... that would revivify American life' (p. 440).

Tourneur's film exposes a similar slippage, but now working from the paranoid white imaginary centre rather than from within one of the immigrant groups' consciousness, such as that in *The Jazz Singer*. *Cat People* more or less reverses the positioning in *The Jazz Singer*, using the 1924 immigration bill's common set of stereotypes to collapse Jews, blacks and 'foreign' women together in the complex, ambiguous figure of Irena. Irena's cross between a white woman and a dark black animal figures forth ambiguity about the Other. Unconscious fears about white/African-American boundaries, and specifically, fears of the black *woman* are mixed with a desire evident in the beauty of both Irena and the panther – in both their power and their elegance. The monstrosity of woman/animal displaces fears of African American/white American 'mixing', yet it images forth a repressed desire for such mixing in Dr Judd's erotic fascination for Irena. Yet, linking Irena to the panther (who also stands in for black Americans) re-inscribes the western linking of Africans with animals in an attempt to denigrate, and lower, Africans *vis-à-vis* white culture (see Jordan, 1968: 216–265; Haraway, 1989). But such linking is, as noted, contradictory in yet more ways. It masks an envy of the imagined greater virility and physical power of African males over that of white males. Animalising, then, is both a defensive move (i.e., virility is jeopardised by being linked to non-humans), and it also exposes displaced envy.

Irena Dubrovna is from the start marked as 'foreign'. Indeed, part of her attraction for the hero, Oliver Reed, is this difference. To the rather ordinary Oliver, Irena appears as exotic and exciting, with her attractive accent and svelte, European look. Irena, meanwhile, paradoxically yearns to be normal. Oliver soon finds out that he cannot fulfil the promise of Irena's body: she is afraid to consummate their marriage because of legends passed down to her from her remote country, Serbia. But she wishes to be a normal wife: 'They're happy,' she says, 'they make their husbands happy, they lead normal, happy lives.'

Oliver at first belittles Irena's fears, but in so doing significantly uses myths about America – myths that insist on America being the only really safe nation. 'They're fairy tales', Oliver says. 'They've got nothing to do with you, really. You're here in America. You're so normal. You're even in love with me, Oliver Reed, a good plain Americano.' Oliver implies that Irena's abnormality is a result of her not being 'American', whereas Oliver's normality is part of his Americanness.

When Irena's problems do not go away, Oliver turns for comfort to his co-worker, Alice – the 'All-American girl' who corresponds to Oliver's solid Americanness. Meanwhile, Irena turns to the impressive statue of King John slaying a leopard (see fig. 2). Finally, Oliver says: 'We've got to have help, Irena. ... Not that sort of help [i.e., the King John sort]. There's something wrong and we have to face it in an intelligent way. We don't need a King John with fire and sword, we need someone to find a reason for your belief and cure it. We need ... a psychiatrist.' Important here is the opposition set up between Irena's irrational form of purgation through the violence and exorcism of King John (seen as belonging to the East) and 'intelligence', 'reason' and (implied in the mention of a 'cure') Science, linked to America and the West. It is Alice who suggests that Irena get help from Dr Judd, the psychoanalyst, with fatal consequences. The already obvious nationalism of the film is clinched at the end, when that which is foreign and dark is excluded, and the all-American couple go off together.

Fig. 2. Here Irena's black dress, the looming statue of King John slaying a leopard and the shadows edging the frame build on film noir's usual lighting contrasts to suggest her descent into darkness.

But if by the end the film stabilises gender relations, it subverts normal gender positions in Irena's very resistance to the psychoanalytic transference and her inability to accommodate herself to her husband's needs, desires and image of her. Lest this destabilising throughout the narrative gets out of hand, the film makes sure to stabilise black/white relations. For dominant culture can only tolerate the destabilisation of one binary at a time. *Cat People*, then, reinforces white stereotypes of blacks as dangerous and 'savage' but it does this indirectly, through displacement into literal images of the black panther, and through suggesting links between the dark continent of the psyche and the dark continent of Serbia (which references 'Africa'). Irena's subversiveness – her destabilisation of normal male–female power relations – *requires* the film's stabilising white/black race hierarchies and positions.[5]

Part of the stabilising of race hierarchies generally involves the repression of the figure of the black female, who is rendered invisible, or a marginalised object, both within film narratives and within psychoanalytic film discourse. In *Cat People*, this figure is doubly displaced, first through the body of the white woman, and then through that of the black leopard. Such repressions produce the 'monster' Irena I've referred to – that is a mixture of woman and panther, and a mixture of white and black. Her monstrosity is specifically marked as part of her foreignness.

Dr Judd in the film occupies the arrogant, imperial position, assuming he controls the gaze, the narrative, Irena. Like the colonists, the psychoanalyst is sure that he can do what is best for Irena, that is, bring her into 'civilisation', and also rationalise his lustful, illicit desires as part of the process of 'cure'. Given this, his violent death by the black, wild woman/animal at once represents Empire's deepest fears of revenge by the racial Others whom colonists dominate, *and* the film's ambivalence toward this arrogant scientist, who thoroughly deserves his death. Interestingly, then, in this film the arrogance of the scientist is critiqued and seen to be insufficient. Psychoanalysis is revealed as a negative tool of containment, and in this case it fails in its mission. As Deborah Linderman argues (Kaplan, 1990), it is the cinema that comes in to constrain Irena in its resolution of her unendurable duality in her confinement in the cage as a panther.

One might ask why this 1942 film is willing to jeopardise Science, given the general western hierarchy of knowledges such that Science sits at the top and literature quite near the bottom. The answer to this lies in the much broader question of how Science is represented on film. While this question lies beyond detailed attention here, it is obvious that Hollywood produces divergent images of Science, depending on the film genre involved. Science is both ridiculed and presented as all-powerful, all-knowing. Hollywood's need to address a middle-class audience requires humanist perspectives, and, loosely liberal-democratic views. Science often scorns the general public (Hollywood's audience) so that it can easily become the object of Hollywood's scorn as well. Hollywood and Science, then, are both arrogant in diverse ways but do not respect *each other*.

In *Cat People*, the arrogance of Science means that its representative suffers at the hands of the inexplicable – something that Science abhors, or rejects. Nevertheless, the impossible and the irrational in fact are seen to be so: Irena is a Cat Woman, unable to make love to a human and able to move between panther and human. Irena crosses the boundaries and demarcations of western culture between animal and human. She also anticipates white culture's fantasies of both the female serial killer of neo-noir, and the young black of post-60s America, ready to kill (but not necessarily *serially* or *pathologically*).[6] Irena combines these two figures of the white imaginary, allowing Hollywood to double the terror she produces for the spectator. Irena/black panther[7] would keep on killing whenever she made love or was jealous. In the classic noir, the *femme fatale*'s gunshot is premeditated, collected, seen as necessary for her crazed ends. And the killing is clean and quick. The way Irena/panther is seen to kill in *Cat People* is far from clean or quick: we first see her face in close-up looking strange and in the midst of a were-wolf-like change; next she is locked on to Dr Judd, now as the panther. The film cuts to a shadow play of the intense struggle, and there are shots of Judd trying to kill his attacker with the spear hidden in his cane. Irena/panther has already come close to killing Alice twice before. Alice's torn bathrobe in the swimming pool scene stands in for the flesh Irena wanted to tear. Irena/panther's deadly attack on the sheep is shown to viewers in all its gory details. So that in some way, Irena/panther looks towards the 90s fascination with the 'wound culture' which Mark Seltzer has defined (and as I discussed in the Introduction). She anticipates the fascination with torn bodies, wrenched flesh, bloodied clothes, floors and cars which is *de rigueur* in 90s films.

Just as Chris Straayer and Kate Stables in this volume have shown the way 90s neo-noir heroines make literal the sex that classic noir represses, so 90s 'wound culture' makes explicit what, in *Cat People*, has to be relegated to the irrational level of a woman/animal monster. If 90s 'wound culture' marks transgression of the boundary between inner and outer body, the analagous 40s transgression was that between human/animal. In between these fantasies is the figure of the cyborg which Donna Haraway theorised in the mid-80s, and which still remains the most hopeful image for the future. Haraway argues that the human/animal boundary has been breached by the 80s (Haraway, 1985),[8] and she also transvalues the very term 'monster' to signify beneficial refusal of 'the imperative to recreate the sacred image of the same' (Haraway, 1989: 378).

However, in the 40s, transgressing the human/animal divide could only be viewed with horror. As Haraway notes, 'Monsters have always defined the limits of community in Western imaginations', and have provided the grounding for discourses on 'the natural and supernatural, medical and legal, portents and diseases – crucial to establishing modern identity' (1985: p. 99). The limits that Irena/ monster sets in *Cat People* are especially crucial since the unconscious association in this particular case was to black/white intermixing as well. The Irena/ monster becomes a metaphor for such intermixing. Fear of blacks is displaced into the feared black animal, a killer. Irena's foreignness and difference are not that dissimilar from that of blacks – equally a location of white guilt, fear and desire. The slippage from seductive killer-woman (the *femme fatale*) to black panther to African Americans reveals Hollywood's way of seeing from its dominant (Imaginary) 'white' centre. That is, this Imaginary white centre collapses all that is different from it into one – the Other – since this Imaginary desires only the repetition of that 'sacred image of the same' which Haraway talks about. While in fact there is specificity to each of the entities that differ from this 'white' centre, Hollywood discourse is not able to take such differences into account. Its ideological formation determines that all differences are collapsed. In this way, the Imaginary white centre can contain its mythic uniqueness. Whiteness is not just one category among many: it is the category through which all other differences *are produced as Other*.

It is notable that a scene with an African-American waitress serving Alice and Oliver is followed by a cut to scenes of Irena/panther pursuing Alice on her way home. The juxtaposition of scenes with the waitress in the usual 40s 'invisible' position (significantly, there are more black bodies in films noirs than earlier critics noticed – see Lott, 1997), and scenes with the black animal about to ravage Alice, does not 'prove' white fears arising from guilt at oppressing the Other, but it is suggestive (as is white critics' blindness to black bodies). Irena's illicit border status produces her noncompliance with patriarchy, which in turn must be compensated for by a derogatory white fantasy of blackness as savage and evil. Her desire to be the black animal, and her liminal state, are unbearable to order and the territorial delimitations white culture insists on. Irena must be controlled, constrained and her ambivalent black *and* white status resolved. She cannot be allowed to be black, wild and outside the cage, while *also* white and female within heterosexual marriage.

That *Cat People* is America's 'dream' about its own 'dark' places[9] is borne out by the cinematic techniques themselves, which figure forth the cinema as a dream-text. The focus on the cinema as a dream-text is referenced explicitly in the first psychoanalytic session, in which Irena is hypnotised by Dr Judd. Irena's face appears in a close-up in a small lit circle in the centre of the frame – reminiscent of early cinema's iris technique. And when Irena gets up, the shadows of Irena and Judd are relayed on a large white window blind so that their figures seem like those on a cinema screen. Irena's 'dreams' of the Cat People and her fears of her sexuality then seem equated with cinema's 'dream' of Irena dreaming. The audience is 'hypnotised' by cinema just as Judd has hypnotised Irena. The cinema tells spectators their dreams (their fears, wishes, fantasies) just as Irena tells the psychoanalyst. Irena's 'dream' of being the black animal (the darker, sexual side of herself) parallel's white people's 'dream' of being 'black' – that is, displacing on to blackness the 'darker', sexual, possibly aggressive and evil parts of them (Jordan, 1968; Gilman, 1985).

Cat People represents psychoanalysis as limited, indeed, in Deleuze/Guattari's words, as 'an autonomous territoriality of the ultimate artifice', or 'a little island with its commander, the psychoanalyst'. In this case, the analyst mistakenly reads Irena's problems as familial neurosis, and tries to transform them into 'artificial neurosis' so as to cure her (perhaps). But this film interestingly reads psychoanalysis as irrelevant – in particular, as unable to take account of the 'uncanny'. Psychoanalysis' world view is shown to be narrow and its authority jeopardised by the unethical behaviour of the analyst, which costs him his life. Possibly this stance reveals American culture's long-standing ambivalence towards 'the dark continent' of the psyche – its desire to put the practitioners skilled in this 'continent' – into disrepute.[10]

Cat People addresses powerful issues which were unconsciously troubling its 1942 American spectators. While attempting to control boundaries between white and black, male and female, Jews, foreigners and 'Americans', it manages to produce knowledge that links the realities of violent Nazi racism against blacks as well as Jews with unconscious guilt at America's own dehumanising and violent slavery system. Tourneur successfully mobilises the noir genre – its visual style (Tourneur uses light and shadow especially strikingly in Dr Judd' s office, where shadows of the slats of the blinds appear on the white walls or in the scene in which Irena stalks Alice in the swimming pool); its themes of twisted human nature (viz., especially Dr Judd, Irena) juxtaposed to healthy, rational American sanity (Oliver, Alice); its focus on a beautiful female murderess who cannot have sexual intercourse and therefore cannot occupy her 'normal' place as 'mother', and so on – to address complementary fears of femininity and of racial 'otherness' which American culture was still suppressing in the war, and immediately post-war, years.

But what about the differing ways in which unconscious fears of blackness are expressed in the later film made by the sophisticated director Orson Welles? Interestingly, some of the strategies used by Welles are similar to those of Tourneur: Once again, there is the deliberate (and heightened) play of light and darkness. In *The Lady from Shanghai*, as against *Cat People*, though, Welles does this through light and darkness on the faces and bodies of his two main protagonists, Elsa Bannister and Michael O'Hara. Once again, the director uses animal imagery, linked to the exotic foreign place (in this case mainly Mexico), to reference racial otherness and to link this otherness to savagery, cannibalism, backwardness and evil. As in *Cat People*, Welles' film indirectly references what it has to repress – namely the 'dark plight' of racial others in the USA – through having his hero, Michael O'Hara, be a 'black Irish', known as 'Black-Eyes'. In addition, there is one character, Bessie, who is clearly an ethnic American (Hispanic or black) and whose image is intercut with the heroine, Elsa Bannister, who is whiter-than-white on the outside but 'black' within. Finally, in *Shanghai* there is the linking of this 'black' heroine with China specifically, as the 'foreignness' that parallels Irena's Serbian foreignness. American xenophobia appears in similar fashion to that in *Cat People* in the depiction of the Chinese whom Elsa uses in San Francisco to help her catch Michael. Elsa is fluent in Chinese, and suddenly is made to 'look' Chinese in these later scenes.

Let me say something more about each of these strategies in *The Lady from Shanghai*.

1. The uses of lightness/darkness symbolism

As in *Cat People*, the deliberate, even heavy-handed, ways in which whiteness and blackness are contrasted in the visual style of the film references suppressed knowledge of racial blackness versus the whiteness of the majority of Americans at the time. The film opens in darkness: the titles appear across images of black water accompanied by gloomy musical tones. This is followed by a very black silhouette of Brooklyn Bridge, and then of the Manhattan skyline split between a light band at the top, and a black band at the bottom of the shot.

The entire following sequence in which Michael meets Elsa Bannister in Central Park is filmed as a play between extreme whiteness and extreme blackness: Elsa (Rita Hayworth) is filmed so as to be whiter-than-white: Her face is lit so as to be flawlessly, perfectly white, with her eyebrows sketched in and her mouth shaped by heavy lipstick: her hair is extremely blonde; her dress whiter-than-white, with matching white gloves and bag. This snow-white image is framed within a dark carriage in which she is riding, itself moving through a blacker-than-black night. Framed by the black carriage window, Elsa looks like a painting, photograph or cinema image. Like Tourneur in *Cat People,* Welles seems to deliberately reference the cinema in several scenes that emphasise a frame around the characters.

Meanwhile, this whiter-than-white image is soon linked to a contrasting Otherness, when she tells O'Hara that, a White Russian, she comes from the most evil city of all, Shanghai ('You need more than luck in Shanghai,' Elsa comments, ominously). This link with Chinese Otherness (it's not incidental that the film was made in 1948, when China's civil war between Mao's communist forces and Chiang Kai-shek's US-backed troops must have filled the news) is foregrounded at the end of the film. Elsa's whiteness and apparent virginal Princess quality is immediately put in contrast with an evil foreignness. And when O'Hara discovers a gun in her white pocketbook, suggestions of blackness (not only drugs and sex but now murder, too) are confirmed.

Almost the reverse symbolism is used with O'Hara. Dressed in black, and with black hair as well, O'Hara seems dark. However, his face too in these opening sequences is lit so as to be extremely white, as if to mark his *moral* superiority despite his darkness. We soon learn that Michael is known as 'Black-Eyes', or as 'Black Irish'; when Bannister goes to the seamen's bar and asks for O'Hara, he is asked if he means 'Black-Eyes'. This accords with the by now well-known racial linking of the Irish, historically, with blacks.[11] While this linking originally took ideological form within English culture, its legacies came with the Anglo-Saxon emigrants to the New World. Michael, then, might be seen as this film noir's main 'black' character in the sense of *racial* blackness, while Elsa is the typical *noir* figure upon whom 'blackness' is conferred as symbolism for immorality, greed, danger. In other words, the iconographic 'whiteness' that Welles insists on in Elsa's opening image, and Michael's iconographic 'blackness', are meant to mislead the spectator. The technique leaves viewers confused about the moral status of both protagonists. Welles will continue to play with spectatorial identifications as part of the narrative process.

2. Ethnic others as characters and presences within Shanghai

Michael's 'blackness', actually racialised by white American culture, as noted above, meant that the Irish were discriminated against in America much in the manner of African Americans and Native Americans. Thus, the way Bannister, Grisby (Bannister's business associate) and Elsa play with O'Hara's emotions is exploitative, if not quite as oppressive, as other racism in the film – Michael has a degree of agency and is educated and articulate, after all. In addition to O'Hara, like *Cat People,* this film has an ethnic, female character, Bessie, also a servant, who works for Roger Bannister. Bessie is shown early on in the film encouraging O'Hara to join the crew on Bannister's boat. She says to him, 'She needs you bad; you stay.' Unlike the African-American waitress in Tourneur's film, who is pleasant and cheerful, Bessie is stone-faced and uncanny. In a later scene, she seems even pathological. She is serving Bannister his tea on the boat, and her face is framed in the shot quite close to Bannister's. Bannister is holding forth on how 'money is what we all have in common'. To prove his point about money crossing even racial divides, he turns to Bessie, snidely: 'Take Bessie here,' he says. 'She used to work for Backrack. I pay her well. Her salary means happiness, a home with three bedrooms for two families. Bessie is a grandmother and a widow, and one of the boys is not working. So Bessie goes to Church every Sunday she gets off and prays never to be too old to earn the salary I pay her.' The scene cuts from Bannister and Bessie to the whiter-than-white Elsa in her swimsuit, on top of the boat.

In solidarity wih Bessie against Bannister's exploitation, O'Hara follows Bessie into the kitchen and asks: 'Why do you stand for it? I'm quitting.' The next shot shows Bessie in an awkward wide-angle shot, staring up at the camera and saying with a strange look on her face: 'You heard him. I need the money.' When Michael mentions that the talk of money and murder is crazy, she says: 'That's why I can't leave. Poor child he married. Someone's got to take care of her.' The film cuts to a close-up of Elsa's white face in the frame, as if, again, to contrast blackness and whiteness but with uncertain symbolism. For Bessie is neither 'good' nor 'evil', it seems, but an ambiguous figure. In a shot soon afterwards, we see Bessie settling Elsa on deck and bringing her her dog to cuddle, giving us some evidence for the second of her motives for staying.

This is soon followed by reference to racial otherness now in the sense of foreignness, which is never far away from American otherness. For when O'Hara asks Elsa if she believes in love, she says: 'I was taught to think of love in Chinese: the Chinese say that it is difficult for love to last but one who loves passionately is cured of love in the end.' She continues with the saying: 'Human nature is eternal. ... One who follows his nature keeps his nature in the end.' Compared with the American ideal of true love for ever (that is, against the idea of permanence, safety, and security in love – all-American ideals), Elsa throws up a different, less comforting philosophy of love – that of immersion and 'cure' through satiation. In regard to human nature, whereas the Chinese proverb would satisfy Americans if we are talking of good people, it would not in relation to bad ones; Americans want to believe that one can 'cure' people of their evil. It's as if the Chinese turn American ideals on their head: permanence in love is contrasted with short-lived love; being able to change human nature (the American ideal) is contrasted with following out for ever what one is, even if one is evil.

Elsa is implicitly talking about herself, and giving O'Hara a chance to understand that she is evil, and that she must follow this out to the end. O'Hara, of course, is not ready to 'know' who Elsa is. His understanding only comes at the end of the film when Elsa runs to San Francisco's Chinatown, to seek help in the underground world of Chinese Otherness. The many shots of Chinese people in this sequence are entirely stereotypical: Cantonese is spoken in short, clipped sentences; faces and clothes are dark and figures shadowed; the people seem part of a conspiracy that the viewer is excluded from. People pick up phones and talk in a language we cannot understand. They seem to be plotting something dangerous and evil. The atmosphere in the famed San Francisco Mandarin Theatre, where O'Hara escapes to follow Elsa, is crowded, smokey and noisy with unfamiliar music. Elsa seems absolutely at home in all this Otherness, even speaking Cantonese now as well.[12]

3. Animal imagery linked to racial otherness

While the image of the panther in *Cat People* is central in the film's narrative, in *Shanghai*, the animal references emerge as part of the environment in several key scenes. In both films, the literal and metaphorical levels are fused: the panther is narratively 'real', as are the alligators and huge aquarium fish in *Shanghai*. But one difference is that the human characters in Welles' film play with animal imagery in their speech, self-consciously creating metaphors for humans out of animal references. *Cat People* works instead through displacement and slippages on the level of the signifier. As we saw, the panther is Irena's double, literally, but also metaphorically. What the panther connotes in terms of virility, beauty and power, on the one hand, and of violence, evil and destructiveness on the other, I argued, reflects the ambivalence of the white imaginary *vis-à-vis* both women and blacks.

In *Shanghai*, one driving animal image emerges in a sequence set in an exotic Mexican locale. Bannister has arranged a picnic on the banks of a river near Acapulco. The Bannisters, Michael and their crew leave the yacht and are rowed by anonymous Mexicans up the river. During the course of this, there are shots of skulking birds, of snakes slithering away, and, finally, of an alligator, whose open mouth seems ready to devour the protagonists. Elsa barely turns a hair at these encroaches of the natural world, suggesting her links to the violence and devouring that is routine in nature. When Michael is called by Bannister to talk to their quarrelling threesome (Elsa, Grisby and Bannister), he responds by detailing the worst experience he ever had in some foreign seas when a shark he had caught became snagged by the hook and began to bleed profusely. The other sharks, excited by the blood, turned the scene into a veritable frenzy of sharks eating each other, eating of themselves. He continues: 'I never saw anything worse than that until this picnic tonight', using the sharks metaphorically to refer to the Bannisters.

But the reference cuts, as it were, both ways. It is clearly an image for the white rich people, but it strangely echoes an image that Manthia Diawara, in the essay referred to earlier, quotes from Chester Himes' novel when discussing the desperate plight of black poor people. Whether or not Orson Welles had read Chester Himes, this image recalls vividly Himes' description of blacks in their city below the 'white' city, as 'a city of black people who are convulsed in desperate living, like the voracious churning of millions of hungry cannibal fish. Blind mouths eating their own guts.' The paradox is not so strange if one recalls Diawara's thesis that film noir intends to present whites who are evil as 'black', in the sense of immoral and evil. But of course for Himes the black people are not evil but driven to metaphoric 'cannibalism' by poverty and rejection by white society. The rich whites become cannibalistic through sheer greed.

Even in the final scenes in Chinatown, the film manages to link the Chinese to animal imagery. At one point Elsa runs into a Chinese shop. Since this is a short scene, the viewer barely has time to note the objects in the place, but a prop list from the production studio shows what was at least planned to be there, and that included things like preserved snakes, frogs and dried lizards.[13]

196

4. *Class and Race in* Shanghai

As one might expect, Welles' film has more understanding of class issues than in Tourneur's. Welles has to be very subtle about this, of course. O'Hara has already several times expressed his disgust at what rich people do to themselves and others. But in the following scene, there is another reference when Grisby takes O'Hara on a tour of Acapulco. Welles inserts shots of rich tourists, who are parodied as talking only of money, and making deals in high effeminate voices; but when Grisby says Elsa adores Acapulco and that he likes it here, O'Hara asks what is beautiful, the beaches or the tourists? He follows this with: 'The fair face of the land can't hide the hunger or the guilt,' a telling statement about white Americans' exploitation of Mexican labour and natural beauty.

As if to demonstrate this thought, shots follow of Elsa in a glowing, beautiful sheer white dress, with her white skin and platinum blonde hair, as she floats ethereal-like through the cobbled streets and cave-like stone bars of downtown Acapulco, where we catch sight of Mexican musicians in straw hats playing their instruments and singing. In the ensuing dialogue between Michael and Elsa, which takes place in this dark, low-life environment, we learn that Michael wants to take Elsa away. His voice-over, commenting on Elsa's world, says: 'Rich and rare and strange, but I had no taste for it.' Then, continuing the devouring/cannibal metaphor, he says: 'But even without appetite for it, it was amazing how much a poor fool like me can swallow.'

Shortly after the arrival in San Francisco, the Chinese driver of Bannister's car tells Michael to meet Elsa in the aquarium at 9.00 a.m., that is, he says, 'before many people'. The man's pidgin English evidences his 'otherness' through the Hollywood stereotype – one that will be repeated in the court scenes, in which two Chinese women are seen talking to each other, briefly, and in the scenes in San Francisco's Chinatown, when O'Hara flees there. The sequence of shots of Elsa and O'Hara's conversation in this aquarium parallels the one they had at the start of the film in Central Park on the other coast of America: There, their faces were brightly lit, and white; in this scene, there is a progressive darkening of their faces: shadows begin to fall over the faces as they continue to talk. At one point, Elsa's face is half light and half dark: Michael is trying to gauge her complicity with Grisby's plot, but is still unsure about her. Meanwhile, his own face is now completely black, as if to mark his fall into evil through believing in Elsa. By the end of the scene, both their faces have become large black silhouettes in the front of the frame. Meanwhile, behind them, huge images of the fish continue the image of the sharks Michael talked about – images of devouring, of cannibalism, greed, murder, blood.

Michael has become as 'black' morally as he is racially as the Irish Black-Eyes. His trial for the supposed murder of Grisby is a farce: he is defended by Bannister who wants to see him executed. The trial continues the investigation of Elsa as *femme fatale* which is a concern of the film running parallel to the concern about race. Elsa 'troubles' gender in ways not that dissimilar from Irena in *Cat People*: that is, her 'feminine' is not complete or normal because, like Irena, she does not have children. The film makes sure to mark this absence, as it does in Tourneur's film. During the court scenes, when Elsa is called to testify, the prosecution lawyer queries Elsa about having children. In reply to his question she affirms 'No children.' He repeats 'No children,' a repetition as unnecessary as the question is in the first place, since it has no literal bearing on the case. The film needs to situate Elsa as an 'unnatural' woman (lacking children, not being a mother) before it allows us to truely know that she is evil and that she has in fact murdered Grisby herself.

Elsa's links to the San Francisco Chinatown seem as unnecessary to the plot as the question of children, on the surface level. Both the fact that she does not have children and her connection to the Chinese community are, however, central to the unconscious level of the film. Not only is she unnatural as a *woman*; she is also unnatural in being *close to the Chinese*. The entire sequence in Chinatown takes viewers into a strange world, as noted earlier. We hear a language we cannot understand; we are shown a performance in an alien style and language, with people dressed in strange clothes.[14] Elsa makes phone calls and speaks in Chinese so that we cannot understand what is going on. Elsa is as 'other' as Irena, and as capable of murder as Irena *because* she is linked to Otherness. A regular white American woman (the film, like *Cat People*, suggests), safely located in the family with children, would not be capable of such things.

The final scene of the film, which takes place in a Crazy House in a fairground, is a fitting metaphor for O'Hara's entire experience of being the 'fall guy' for the mad rich people who used him for their crazed greedy desires. O'Hara leaves Elsa lying in black on the floor, looking not unlike the panther in *Cat People*, to die like an animal, alone.

As a quite classic *femme fatale*, Elsa pays for her independence, agency, desire for money and her sexual allure. Her moral blackness refers metonymically to white culture's fears of ethnic 'blackness' that it cannot deal with, as well as to the same culture's fears of female sexuality. O'Hara's 'blackness' as a 'black Irish' is also not confronted directly, but the film at least affirms him: he is the only one able to extricate himself from the evil he finds himself enmeshed in during the course of the film. He walks out into the sunlight, evidently cured of his passion for Elsa. As a man, he has at least triumphed over woman's sexual seduction.

Irena is less classic a figure: in some ways, she is closer to James Maxfield's 'fatal' woman, who endangers the hero without fully intending to (Maxfield, 1995). On the other hand, in the context of the slippages and displacements outlined earlier, Irena expresses equally as dramatically as Elsa what 40s American culture was unable to address and which thus found indirect expression through film noir narratives. Similar racial metaphors, intertwined closely with gender trouble, could no doubt be found in many films noirs. I hope this topic will be taken up in other research.

Notes

1. 'NetNoir' appeared recently on the Internet, dealing with films by black film-makers. This shows the general acceptance of 'noir' as a term for films by and about blacks.
2. Let me make clear at the start that when I use the terms 'white culture' or 'patriarchy' I am referring to dominant, but largely unconscious, American cultural fantasies about the 'Other'. I am not saying that all white people accept prevailing cultural notions about the 'Other', but that cultural forms (which include but are not limited to film) manifest in their discursive organisation such fantasies. Whether the fantasies precede the formation of particular individuals or whether indi-

viduals produce the fantasies which then become pervasive is still not clear to me: we do know that cultures produce over time certain discursive formations which become dominant. Foucault spent his life trying to understand how such formations functioned. The Imaginary of a culture is all but impossible to study. Popular culture offers one space, I would argue. I use the term 'white culture' when talking about the Imaginary *vis-à-vis* race; and the term 'patriarchy' when talking about the Imaginary *vis-à-vis* gender. The categories are not collapsible into one another in reality, but in film discourses they may be mobilised as if they were homologous. As I argue below, popular culture embodies pressures felt in a culture about a culture's oppressive mechanisms. But in the course of addressing tensions in a culture, popular works lay bare repressive mechanisms: they produce knowledge about them, and, as Foucault would argue, this is at the same time beneficial.

3. As Alan Sheridan notes, for Foucault power is not mainly 'repressive'. It *produces* knowledge which is positive. In Foucault's words, 'power produces; it produces reality; it produces domains of objects and rituals of truth' (Foucault, *Discipline and Punish*, p. 194. Quoted in Sheridan, 1977: 165).

4. From what I have been able to find so far, it seems that scholars have not developed this particular argument. Some books concentrate on the rationalised Nazi aim of substantiating, in Jonathan Petropoulos's words, 'the triumph of the Aryan race'. Petropoulos continues: 'Hitler believed that race formed the basis of both nationhood and culture and therefore linked the three concepts in an inseparable manner' (Petropoulos, 1996: 246–247). Eric Rentschler, meanwhile, correctly points out how Hitler's Germany 'was an exercise in emotional engineering' (Rentschler, 1996: xi). He notes the double face of fascism, at once sinister and pleasing, and how Hitler's 'cinema embodies the agreeable façade in its most scintillating incarnation'. Rentschler also reminds us of how the 'spectacles and paraphernalia of National Socialism have assumed a privileged place in American mass culture. SS uniforms and party regalia provide props for both alternative fads and mainstream trends in fashion' (p. 6). While I have not found research that focuses on the return of the repressed, namely the irruption into symbolic forms of the racial 'blackness' Nazis were trying to separate themselves from, readers interested in this topic should explore Rentschler's exhaustive bibliography for books and articles that deal with Nazi aesthetics.

5. See, for example, Judith Mayne's interesting comments in 'Lesbian Looks: Dorothy Arzner and Looking Relations', in *How Do I Look?*, ed. Bad Object Choices.

6. It is interesting that most of the filmic serial killers I can think of (like their historical real-life counterparts) are, whether male or female, white. Speculating on why this is so would take me beyond my topic here. But it perhaps has to do with a cultural construction such that all young blacks are, in the white imaginary, killers, automatically, but not necessarily 'sick'. The white serial killer construction is always of a person whose psychopathology is never in doubt. Whites only kill if they are sick; blacks just kill, it seems, in the white imaginary. (Of course, implied behind this 'blacks just kill' is the social injustice that produces for blacks a desire to get revenge on white cultures.)

   For female serial killers, see *Black Widow, Basic Instinct*, and the spoof of the genre in John Waters' *Serial Mom*. An early version of this figure might be found in *The Eyes of Laura Mars*.

7. It's just possible that the well-known 'Black Panther' movement named itself in direct parody or play with Tourneur's film. Certainly, the term as applied to living African Americans suggests that the organisers saw what *Cat People* was all about, with its slippages between the evil, killer heroine and her alter ego black panther self. In line with Manthia Diawara's arguments regarding film noir as a whole, the Black Panthers deliberately took over the negative valences of Hollywood's meanings, and revisioned the phrase to mean war on white culture to 'correct' the repression of African Americans.

8. While people mainly recall Haraway's definition of cyborg as pertaining to a machine/human interface, Haraway does see a link between the new machine/human interface and the breached boundary between human/animal. 'The cyborg appears in myth', Haraway notes, 'precisely where the boundary between human and animal is transgressed' (Haraway, 1985: 68). The monster in *Cat People* is the 40s version of the more frightening 90s machine/human interface: the horror of the human/animal connection has now been superseded by that of the machine/human. Haraway continues: 'Far from signaling a walling off of people from other living beings, cyborgs signal disturbingly and pleasurably tight coupling. Bestiality has a new status in this cycle of marriage exchange' (p. 68).

9. Eric Lott's paper, 'The Whiteness of Film Noir' (1997), read at The Humanities Institute, Fall 1995,

argued (partly) that the use of darkness, the way shadows fall across the faces of white people, in film noir shows that the genre is about race. This is persuasive and fits in with some of my own concerns in this chapter. However, I have linked stances in *Cat People* to earlier and later legacies in other film genres. In other words, the dark continent pertains also to film noir, but is not exclusively its own.

10. This obsession with putting psychoanalysis into disrepute continues in the 90s. Indeed, there is an increasing group of scholars apparently obsessed with doing in Freud himself—a project which began with maverick scholar Peter Swales, continued with Jeffrey Masson, psychoanalyst, and has entered the academy proper with the discrediting efforts of Shumway and Frederick Crews (the latter, at least, with the passion of a previous convert!). Much more reasoned critique has come from leftist scholars, such as John Brenkman.

11. There is now a substantial body of scholarship which shows that the Irish were racialised and conceptualised as 'black', for various historical reasons. The change seems to have reached its height in nineteenth-century England, where early ethnologists and anthropologists were busy searching for the racial origins of the modern British, usually with a view to situating the Anglo-Saxons considerably 'higher' on some Darwinian-influenced 'tree' of the 'races' than the Celts of Scotland and Ireland. The most thorough exploration of changing images of the Irish in Victorian England is that by L. Perry Curtis, Jnr. Curtis goes to caricatures in popular magazines to chart 'the gradual but unmistakable transformation of Paddy, the stereotypical Irish Celt of the mid-nineteenth century, from a drunken and relatively harmless peasant into a dangerous ape-man or simianised agitator' (Curtis, 1971: vii). He explores connections between 'Victorian images of the Irish, the lore of physiognomy, the Darwinian debate over evolution, and the art of caricature' (p. vii). Curtis shows how the eminent ethnologist DrJohn Beddoe developed his 'Index of Nigrescence' in order to confirm the impressions of many Victorians 'that the Celtic portions of the population in Wales, Scotland and Ireland were considerably darker or more melanous than those descended from Saxon or Scandinavian forebears' (p. 20). Curtis argues that Beddoe's 'index of nigrescence and of Africanoid Celts ... verified attributes as melanous and prognathous features, receding foreheads, and upturned noses', producing 'a composite caricature of a Caucasian Negro with simian features' (pp. 20–1).

Another historical link produces the same linkage of Irish with blacks but from quite another direction. In his book, *Whence the 'Black Irish' of Jamaica?* (1932), Joseph J. Williams traces documents showing the capture and deportation of young Irish men and women to be sent to England's West Indies colonies, especially Barbados, in the seventeenth century. There they worked basically as slaves, sometimes under the title of 'bond-servant'. Clearly, they were identified already with the black slaves, whose lot, according to Williams' documentation, was sometimes better than that of the Irish. What puzzles Williams is the fact that, as of his writing in 1932, many black Jamaicans have Irish names. Photos in the volume show black boys named Collins, O'Hare, McCormack, McDermott, McKeon, Kennedy, and so forth (pp. 48–49). He concludes that 'there was a large proportion of Irish ... in the make-up of the population, and that not only Irish names but Irish blood as well is widely diffused throughout the Island today' (p. 75). Here again, then, is a link between blacks and Irish such that the term 'black-Irish' has a literal racial element to it.

12. According to information in the archives of The Academy of Motion Pictures, Rita Hayworth 'crammed' Chinese for her role in *Shanghai*. The note says in part, 'In preparation for this difficult characterization, Rita took three-hour lessons daily for five weeks from Wong Mee Loo, a teacher brought to Hollywood from San Francisco.'

13. Again, this information is from The Academy of Motion Pictures. The note is a list of 'Movie Props For Chinese Scene' and betrays stereotypes of the Chinese. The Chinese Shop that Elsa goes into was to have items westerners might find disgusting and that again link the Chinese to animals: the list reads in part: '2 dried lizards (large); 4 serpent skins; 2 jars of preserved snakes; 4 dried shark fins; ... 1 human skull.' The skull is thrown in to suggest cannibalism, savagery and so on, in ways we have already seen in relation to other Others.

14. Interestingly, a 90s neo-noir, *Jade* (discussed in other essays in this volume), deliberately references *The Lady from Shanghai* in its sequences also set in San Francisco's Chinatown. That the reference is deliberate is evident in the camera's lurching up to a sign during the car chase between the hero and the serial killer that reads, in capital letters, SHANGHAI. ... But the most obvious visual reference is in the sequence in which the hero chases a prostitute, who flees into the same Chinese

Mandarin theatre (or one just like it!) that O'Hara runs into in *The Lady from Shanghai*. The car chase through Chinatown, during one of the big annual festivals, recalls the chase within the Crazy House at the end of Welles' film. Clearly, Friedkin is having fun linking classic and neo-noir.

14

'Gilda Didn't Do Any of Those Things You've Been Losing Sleep Over!': The Central Women of 40s Films Noirs

Angela Martin

When Rita Hayworth played the title role in *Gilda* she had been a major star since the early 40s, and her picture in *Life* magazine was so much in demand (by the armed forces) that millions of copies were printed and distributed. Her image was painted on 'Able Day', the H-bomb which was dropped on Bikini Atoll, at the same time as *Gilda* was 'making the rounds' of the theatres on the Kwajalein Islands where the bomb was based (*New York Times*, 30 June 1946). The combination of the hugely popular 'love goddess' and a very phallic expression of destruction is, to say the least, interestingly perverse, and significant to the social background of film noir. But Rita Hayworth was also popular with women:

> [she] could be a sex symbol for servicemen without offending the women back home; she possessed an air of romance that made it possible for her to exude those elements of mystery, formerly the stock-in-trade of foreign *femmes fatales*, without reminding the wives and sweethearts of the sort of women their men might find overseas. (Kobal 1977: 139)
> she was just the personification of beauty, glamour and sophistication to me and to thousands of others. Self-assured, wore gorgeous clothes beautifully, danced gloriously and her musicals were an absolute delight. (Mary Marshall, in Stacey 1994: 142; see also pp. 202, 206, 209–10)

Hayworth had starred, two years earlier, in Columbia's second Technicolor film, the fashion musical *Cover Girl* (Charles Vidor, 1944, with Gene Kelly). The screenplay was by Virginia Van Upp,[1] and adapted by her, Marion Parsonnet[2] and Paul Gangelin. (The editor was Viola Lawrence.) Harry Cohn, Columbia's boss, had brought in Van Upp 'specifically because he needed a writer to come up with some star material for Rita Hayworth'. She also 'paid attention to the grooming of the actress into top-line material right down to organising her costumes' (Francke 1994: 63; see also Thomas, B. 1967: 236). When Cohn wanted Hayworth to play Gilda, she 'refused ... unless Miss Van Upp produced the film' (Thomas: 236).

Women stars were not new, of course, but the 30s saw their increasing appearance in female-interest films, and the rise of female scriptwriters,[3] like Van Upp, producing scripts specifically for them.[4] The 'woman's film' of the late 30s and during the 40s dealt with the conflict between female desire and the social demands of femininity and/or motherhood, usually in the form of melodrama.

Gilda was released a year after the end of World War II, which (like World War I and the Vietnam War) threw up enormous problems for the men returning and those they were returning to; there followed an unusually high divorce rate:

> Part of the problem for the returning male troops was the discovery that the pliable, passive wife or lover was yet another casualty of the war, and ... In March 1946 the *New York Times* magazine published an article headed 'The American woman, not for this GI'. (Willett, in Davies and Neue (eds), 1981: 71)

As many writers have indicated, 'the American woman' had become capable and independent, having been 'reclassified almost overnight' as fit for heavy industrial work, after Pearl Harbor; in the munitions industry alone, where women 'provided the basic labor force',[5] over 4 million women were working in 1943 (ibid.: 64). Hollywood addressed itself to this increasingly dominant female audience, in terms of pleasure, but also in terms of the war effort, showing women as workers, as well as patriotic, optimistic and supportive wives, mothers and sweethearts.[6]

However, coinciding with the peak of women's involvement in the labour force, the armed services began, in late 1943, 'discharging psychoneurotic veterans at the rate of 10,000 cases a month' (Waller, 1944: 155, quoted by Fischer, 1993: 77), leading to the hospitalisation of 850,000 soldiers and the addition of 2500 army medical officers to the 25 thus far working in psychiatry (Walker, 1993: 2, citing Starr, 1982: 344). Then, as early as 1944, there was growing governmental optimism about the outcome of the war; women began to be described as 'excess labor', and would soon be pushed back into their strictly domestic roles.

The tension of holding these conflicting interests, illusions and disillusions together surfaced in 1944,[7] and, as Renov suggests, it is not surprising that this year saw 'the re-emergence of the noir "tough" thriller' (1988: 37, cited by Krutnik, 1991: 59). However, by the same token, it is also not surprising that between 1944 and 1946, five films noirs were released which had women's names in the titles, central female characters and female stars in the lead: *Laura* (1944) with Gene Tierney; *Mildred Pierce* (1945) with Joan Crawford; *My Name is Julia Ross* (1945) with Nina Foch; *Gilda* (1946) with Rita Hayworth; and *The Strange Love of Martha Ivers* (1946) with Barbara Stanwyck. These were followed in 1947 by *Ivy* with Joan Fontaine and *Nora Prentiss* with Ann Sheridan. It is further not surprising that two of these films (*Gilda* and *Mildred Pierce*) were the focus of essays in the first edition of *Women in Film Noir*, along with *Double Indemnity* (1944), starring Barbara Stanwyck, and (from a little later) *The Blue Gardenia* (1953), starring Anne Baxter, but the status of all of those listed above *vis-à-vis* the 'canon' of the film noir cycle/genre fluctuates according to the critic/theorist and his understanding of the term (thus far it is only male writers who have compiled lists of films noirs).

For example, Belton includes *Mildred Pierce, My Name is Julia Ross* and *The Strange Love of Martha Ivers* in his (admittedly small) select filmography of relevant titles (1994: 205), but not *Gilda, Laura, Ivy* or *Nora Prentiss*. Tuska, in his chapter on the film noir canon (1984: Chapter 5), includes *Gilda* (but only as one of the films shot by Rudolph Maté), *Laura* and *The Strange Love of Martha Ivers* (which do not qualify as *films gris* because of their 'happy' endings), calling them melodramas (ibid.: 165, 177); *Ivy* is a film noir (p. 181), but 'just narrowly escapes being a melodrama' (p. 182).[8] Telotte lists all except *My Name is Julia Ross* in his 'noir filmography' (1989: 224–35). Silver and Ward (1980) list all except *Ivy*. In their survey, *Hollywood in the Forties*, Higham and Greenberg include *Laura*, *The Strange Love of Martha Ivers* and (mainly for its setting) *Mildred Pierce* as films noirs (1968: 25–7), but call *Gilda* and *Ivy* melodramas (pp. 45, 33), list *Nora Prentiss* under 'Women's Pictures' (p. 150), and exclude *My Name is Julia Ross*. McArthur lists *Gilda* only as one of the films 'related by mood, iconography or theme' to both the gangster film and the thriller (1972: 8) and *Laura* only for its inclusion of the film noir aesthete-villain (p. 44), but none of the others. Schrader, in his early piece on film noir, includes *Laura* (one of 'the first uniquely film noirs') and *Mildred Pierce* ('romantic noir'), but none of the others (1996: 155, 158).

'Film noir'

The genesis of the term 'film noir' is understandable: American 'hard-boiled' novels had been translated into French as the *série noire* (defined in the *Petit Larousse* as: 'suite de mésaventures, de malheurs' – series of misadventures, of mishaps). But the films based on some of them, which had begun to appear in America from 1941, did not appear in France until 1946,[9] when they surfaced rapidly in Paris, one after the other, between July and August.[10] Inevitably, something unusual and new appeared to the French to be happening in American cinema,[11] equally inevitably inviting the coining of an all-embracing phrase. The borrowed word *noir* was suggested by Nino Frank in recognition of the films' similarity of stylistic and narrative concerns with those translated 'hard-boiled' novels.[12] In fact the original term 'hard-boiled' (although perhaps a less 'sexy' one) seems, somehow, more, or at least equally helpful, partly because the doom-laden and threatening world depicted is where the similarity lies, but also since its meaning is more open, given variously as: callous; unfeeling; unsentimental and practical; tough; realistic; cynical. Talking about *Black Mask*, the pulp detective monthly that ran between 1920 and 1951, Herbert Ruhm writes:

> The world depicted in *Black Mask* was irrational and disorderly. Violence was the means to all ends. It was a matter of knives or guns, rather than of reason. At the top of the social hierarchy were the corrupt lawyers and politicians, the gangsters and the bootleggers, while the lonely representative of order, such as the honest cop, was at the bottom.
> *Black Mask* found that the streets of the cities best reflected the moral disorder of the era. Events were depicted in the language of these streets: mean, slangy, prejudiced, sometimes witty and always tough. (1979, p. viii)

American critics of the period had also recognised the films as a phenomenon, and also talked about them as a group (sometimes in language as vivid as that of the original writers).[13] For example:

> Hollywood, according to present indications, will depend on so-called 'red meat' stories of illicit romance and crime for a major share of its immediate non-war dramatic productions. ... This renewed interest in certain types of storied sordidness and ultra-

sophistication … (Fred Stanley, 'Hollywood Crime and Romance', *New York Times*, 19 November 1944)

Of late there has been a trend in Hollywood toward the wholesale production of lusty, hard-boiled, gat-and-gore[14] crime stories, all fashioned on a theme with a combination of plausibly motivated murder and studded with high-powered Freudian implication. (Lloyd Shearer, 'Crime Certainly Pays on the Screen', *New York Times*, 8 November 1945)

But 'film noir' is the term that stuck, becoming, it would seem increasingly, something of a *phrase fatale*, and posing more problems of definition than it has helped. Critical texts often deal with the genre/cycle question; the problem of style or historical moment; or that of misfitting films: films with certain crucial (generic) elements missing, or films which also belong to another genre – particularly (though not always, and this is never signalled as such) when they have central female characters. These films with central female characters constitute perhaps the greatest source of 'misfit' in 'film noir' because they all in some way problematise the conventional film noir discourse in which, as Elizabeth Cowie puts it: 'a particular *masculine* fantasy of sexual difference is played out' (in Copjec (ed.), 1993: 145 – my emphasis). These films are very often called melodramas or examples of the 'woman's film' as if to keep them in their 'proper' and lesser place.[15]

It is extremely difficult to know whether the term 'film noir' can be pushed sufficiently to retain the useful meaning of the original, but includes, theoretically, those films uncomfortably referred to as melodramas or the 'woman's film'; or whether it should be replaced – but, in that case, by what? Hence my use of quotation marks.[16] One cannot talk about 'feminine noir' and mean the equal of 'masculine noir', and both the 'woman's film' and 'melodrama' face a similar problem. The following terms have all been used: Pulp Fiction Films; Pulp Thrillers; Crime Thrillers; Crime Drama (*To-day's Cinema*, 23 July 1948, on *Lady of Deceit*); Murder Melodrama (*Motion Picture Herald*, 19 April 1947, on *Born to Kill*); and Pulp Melodrama (Katz, 1979).[17]

The *femme fatale* and feminist readings

Many accounts of 'film noir' only see a bleak cityscape in which (the) man is threatened by (a) woman – frequently defined as a *femme fatale* (even when this is inappropriate),[18] and the language used to describe her[19] is often even stronger than her supposed ubiquity:

here is a world where it is always night, always foggy or wet, filled with gunshots and sobs, where men wear tuned-down brims on their hats and *women loom in fur coats, guns thrust deep into pockets.* (Higham and Greenberg, 1968: 20)

Most uncertain of all is the commitment of *the central female character*, who may prove true to him [the morally equivocal hero of the thriller] … or false …, but *who will almost certainly sexually enslave him.* … The Circe figure quite often entices the hero by her song, … or by her dance. … The dissembled passion of the *femme fatale* is characteristic of the *film noir.* (McArthur, 1972: 46)[20]

The world of the film noir and its heroes did show the seamy side of a section of American life: the poor detectives operating from shabby offices, insurance embezzlers, *scheming and unfaithful wives, neurotic femmes fatales*, impassive hired killers, frightened little men, and corrupt police officers. These people are the negation of the

American dream and Hollywood-made optimism. *Sam Spade and Philip Marlowe are expressions of the powerlessness of the honest and decent individual* against the nightmare world of crime and corruption and an anonymous social system. (Karimi, 1970: 148; my emphasis throughout these quotes.)

And despite feminism (and after the first appearance of *Women in Film Noir*), we continue to find a perpetuation of the mythic stereotype: 'the simply evil (perhaps psychopathic) *femme fatale* of 1940s *noir* films.' (Maxfield, 1996: 9); 'women in film noir tend to be characterised as *femmes fatales, intent on castrating or otherwise destroying the male hero*' (Belton, 1994: 199); and, 'No situation depicted was without its *femme fatale*' (Taylor, J. R., 1991: 171). And the depiction is carried through to the women who played the '*femme fatale*': for example, McArthur claims that 'The Circe figure ... is usually played by actresses of startlingly sensual unreality' (1972: 46), and Maxfield makes an extraordinary slippage between (male) critic/theorist and male protagonist:

> It is perhaps only my personal tastes that lead me to conclude that Jane Greer is the most attractive female lead of all the *noir* films of the forties; but certainly the character she plays [in *Out of the Past*], Kathie Moffett, is a more plausible deceiver of men than earlier fatal females such as Phyllis Dietrichson or Helen Grayle. While it is difficult to imagine any man with reasonable intelligence and a survival instinct being taken in by the hard, obviously experienced, dyed blondes, Phyllis and Helen, it is much easier to believe that an otherwise intelligent private detective like Jeff Markham would accept the word of a soft, young, natural brunette like Kathie. (1996: 54)

Inevitably, both the definition of the generic term and the definition of the ubiquitous *femme fatale* were essentially determined by film theory when it was still male-dominated, in relation to what had – following the pre-war 'hard-boiled' literature tradition – been considered a masculine genre,[21] and which assumed a male protagonist. No wonder that there was some difficulty in dealing with films with *central female* characters who did not fit the prescribed picture of the *femme fatale*, as is arguably the case of, for example, *Laura, Mildred Pierce, My Name is Julia Ross, Nora Prentiss*, and *Gilda*.

The literal translation (and meaning) of the French term '*femme fatale*' is the 'fatal woman'; dictionary definitions of 'fatal' include: (1) causing or capable of causing death, (2) ruinous, disastrous, (3) decisively important, (4) destined, inevitable. The *femme fatale* carries all these levels of meaning, hence the easy slippage from deadliness to sexuality as weapon. The image in cultural production arose at the end of the nineteenth century, and became, as Mary Ann Doane indicates, 'a clear indication of the extent of the fears and anxieties prompted by shifts in the understanding of sexual difference' towards the end of the century within science – particularly in terms of a newly defined female sexuality and including the work of Freud – which coincided with the period of industrialisation and the development of mechanical means of (visual) reproduction (1991: 1–2). Comolli describes the second half of the nineteenth century as living 'in a sort of frenzy of the visible ... the whole world becomes visible at the same time as it becomes appropriatable' (1980: 122–3). It was equally important to appropriate female sexuality within this project, given the early twentieth-century rise of feminism,[22] and, as Doane writes, 'femininity in modernity has become very

Alison Courtland (Claudette Colbert) caught between two 'wrong men' in Sleep My Love: *a treacherous husband and his accomplice as bogus psychiatrist (played by Don Ameche and George Coulouris respectively).*

much a question of hypervisibility' (1991: 14). It was in this *fin de siècle* period that we see a whole series of eroticised and stereotypic images within painting and literature, defined by Dijkstra as, for example, dead ladies (invalidism), the collapsing woman, the nymph with the broken back, virgin whores, lesbians, clinging vines, poison flowers, metamorphoses of the Vampire and sirens, all resulting from an appalling and devastating male ignorance and/or misogyny:

> What the middle-class male knew about women inevitably came first of all from observing his mother and, if he had any, his sisters. [But] his sisters, [and] her friends … would not at all tend to live up to the ideal transmitted to him by his father, whose mid-century generation had created the image of the household nun. Frightened, fascinated, feeling strange,… he would, more often than not, enter adulthood full of strange scientific knowledge about the perversions to which woman's nature was prone. (1986: 235–6)

Dijkstra includes in his book (p. 252) a contemporary reading by Nordau of Lucchesi's sculpture of a female nude ('The Myrtle's Altar', *c.* 1891), who eyes her viewer in such an aggressively sexual way as to put (him) into a 'morbid state of degeneracy which renders a man a woman's plaything and the victim of his own temperament' (1886: 258). If an enormous number of paintings of this period carry the image of 'feminine evil' (as Dijkstra refers to them in the title of his book), only a relatively small proportion saw this evil as *deadly*. Those that did, show women enticing men down into 'the abyss', or to the depths of the sea, but again displayed the women in totally sexual ways for the viewer (ibid.: 252–271). Circe (cited by McArthur), for example, the Greek sorceress 'of the lovely hair', enticed Odysseus' crew with her beautiful singing, then 'stirred up a mixture of cheese, flour and pale honey with wine [and] some dire drugs' which turned them into pigs and made them 'quite forget their homeland' (Homer, trans. 1993: 399–406). (Odysseus brings them back, thanks to an antidote given him by Hermes, and Circe falls in love with him, surprised that someone could break her spell.) However, as a popular subject for artists at the turn of the century, she became an 'animal woman', 'gleefully hauling the male back into her nature-ordained prison house of degenerate materialism', using, precisely, only her sexuality (Dijkstra, 1986: 324). In other words – and this is the major problem with the characterisation – the fatal woman is *by nature* deadly; she doesn't necessarily have to kill or harm anyone, she just carries the threat by her very presence. Following this trend, 'It is not surprising', writes Doane, 'that the cinema, born under the mark of such a modernity as a technology of representation, should offer a hospitable home for the *femme fatale*' (having already produced the flapper and the vamp) (1991: 2).

Of course, even though the paintings cited by Dijkstra contain narratives, the *power* of the image is in the still and silent representation; this does not mean that they can never be read ironically, but additionally in films, characters move from one setting to another, they move through a number of narrative scenes, encounter other characters, and interact with and speak to them. (*Laura* is, of course, particularly interesting in this respect, being both a moving picture and being, partly, about a painting; see also, Mulvey, 1975: section IIIA; and Dyer, in this volume.) So the narrative structure and concerns of a film may indeed focus on, and present, the deadliness of the *femme fatale*, but may equally well modify, or even counter, its power as a representation: this may take place in the performance of the part, or in the misfit between characterisation by the narrative, and character. Dyer is making the first point in his discussion (in this volume) of Gilda's resistance to her film's attempt to define her sexuality as bad, and Ann Kaplan makes the second point about Nora in *The Blue Gardenia*.

Thus the *femme fatale* is interesting to feminist film theory of 'film noir' in two ways – first, as a powerful image, expressing activity[23] and open to positive reading; second, as an image often re-presented and expressing a masculine view of female sexuality. ('Male' theory, on the other hand, has tended to reinforce the simple presence of the image and its 'inherent' danger to the hero.) This duality is quite clear in Haskell's early feminist description of the woman in the 'dark melodramas of the forties':

> She had sensual lips, or long hair that, passing over her face like Veronica Lake's, cast a shadow of moral ambiguity … her long hair was the equivalent of a gun, where sex was the equivalent of evil (1974: 190–1)

which reads remarkably like some of the quotes above, but, unlike them, went along with:

> She was, in fact, a male fantasy. She was playing a man's game in a man's world of crime and carnal innuendo,… where her power to destroy was a projection of man's feeling

impotence. Only this could never be spelled out; hence the subterfuge and melodrama. (Ibid.: 190–1; see also Dyer, in this volume)

And Mary Doane writes in the introduction to her book, *Femmes Fatales – Feminism, Film Theory, Psychoanalysis*, that it 'is not really *about* the *femme fatale*. … Instead the *femme fatale* acts as a kind of signpost or emblem for many of the issues and concerns addressed [in it]' (1991: 3) because of:

> her function of articulating questions of knowledge and sexuality, of vision and episte-mological reliability. … As soon as the relation between vision and knowledge becomes unstable or deceptive, the potential for a disruption of the given sexual logic appears. Perhaps this disruptiveness can define, for feminist theory, the deadliness of the *femme fatale*. (Ibid.: 14)

There is no question, where the *femme fatale* is truly present, of her deadliness. What is in question here is the seeming inability of (male) film noir theory to recognise female characters as performing other narrative functions – to see them as other than expressions of female sexuality which threaten the hero (or express the total opposite: passivity and benignity). But what is clear from the thematic strands listed in the appendix (which bear very much in mind the 'five main structural features of film noir that together produce a specific location for women', identified by Christine Gledhill in this volume), is that women in films noirs are more often subjected to male definition, control and violence, not because they are a threat but because the male characters are themselves psychotic, or project a neurotic sense of threat on everyone and everything around them. Sometimes the films support that view by presenting the female as threat, but sometimes the male psychosis at work stands by itself quite nakedly. Thus, the films which have central female characters (some of whom may be *femmes fatales* but more are not) throw back implications for that model of film noir that has emerged *critically* without taking into account the existence of both men *and* women as *central* characters.[24]

Central women in pulp thrillers – writers, central female characters and female spectators

This essay, and the lists appended to it (one of thematic strands and one of films), arose from my problem with the ending of *Gilda*:[25] why would Gilda want Johnny to go home with her after everything that's happened? The subsequent realisation that it was produced by a woman and co-written by women was followed by the discovery of the women writers involved in *Laura*, *Mildred Pierce* and *My Name is Julia Ross*.[26] None of the central characters of these films is a *femme fatale* as such. In fact, of the eighty films listed (I am talking here only about films with central female characters), it seems to me that only eight of them really have that role (although this is undoubtedly disputable):[27] Barbara Stanwyck in *Double Indemnity*, *Ivy* and *The File on Thelma Jordan*; Jean Gillie in *Decoy*; Lana Turner in *The Postman Always Rings Twice*; Rita Hayworth in *The Lady from Shanghai*; Bette Davis in *Beyond the Forest*; Peggy Cummins in *Gun Crazy*. Two of these films were scripted by women; one-third of them were based on a story by a woman writer.

However, thirty-three of the films listed with central female characters have women writers credited, either for the script or for the original story.[28]

I do not want to suggest, however, that the presence of women writers in the credits or central female characters on the screen makes a *definitive* or automatic difference to how a film works – especially not in Hollywood during the 40s. Indeed, as will be clear in the discussion of *Laura* and *Gilda* below, there were many contradictions at work. But there does seem to me to be a greater possibility of a 'woman's discourse' at work in these films than is generally suggested within film noir criticism (as Cowie proposed, in Copjec (ed.), 1993).

As indicated earlier, women formed the predominant part of the American cinema audience at home during World War II, hence the growth of a large number of films ('women's pictures') addressed specifically to their interests. All the major studios had stars, whose personal and screen image was crucial in relation to box-office profits. Creating the right image involved, of course, publicity, costume, parts – and scripts: Lenore Coffee wrote for Bette Davis, Jean Harlow and Joan Crawford (indeed, she was called on to change Crawford's image from the flapper roles she had been playing before *Possessed*, 1931; see Coffee in McGilligan (ed.), 1986: 143–4);[29] Catherine Turney wrote for Crawford, Davis and Barbara Stanwyck (Francke, 1994: Chapter 3). Despite these references, we know very little about the women screenwriters of this period,[30] and it is difficult, therefore, to know how much they were able (or indeed, sought) to *create* the 'disruptiveness' within the text that Doane is talking about. Several writers' names only appear once in the appended list, but among the more frequent appearances are: Ketti Frings, Joan Harrison, Virginia Kellogg, Alma Reville (all for Hitchcock) and Marguerite Roberts. But a useful question to ask is whether these writers were being 'used' to write convincingly 'bad' female characters or were being asked to write *in* a woman's point of view.

There is no room here to go over the theoretical debate between the 'textual spectator' and actual spectators, though it is an important one in relation to feminist writing on 'film noir', but I have to admit a tendency towards sympathy with the latter. At the same time, I entirely recognise that without the kind of work conducted by Helen Taylor on *Gone With the Wind* (*Scarlett's Women*, 1989) and Jackie Stacey on female audience responses to Hollywood stars in the 40s and 50s (*Star Gazing*, 1994), one cannot do more than imagine what the responses to 40s pulp fiction films were. However, what I want to do now is look briefly at two films – *Laura* and *Gilda* – in the context of women's centrality behind and in front of the camera, while bearing in mind the following kind of comment (about *Gone With the Wind*) from Pat West, a trainee nurse 'trying to impress both sides of the family by following in the two most admired aunts' footsteps':

> I saw Scarlett O'Hara enter that barn, take one look at the wounded men – and walk out! That was a real turning point in my life. I realised in an instant that you could walk away from illness and from what everyone expected of you. (Taylor, 1989: 38)

There *had to be something* in these films noirs for female spectators – whether it was the treat of seeing women giving as good, if not better, than they got; the idea that men and women can be equally evil or equally innocent; confirmation of the existence of masculine perversity; or, simply, the refreshingly life-size image of male fallibility.[31]

Laura

Laura is described by Higham and Greenberg not as a *femme fatale*, but instead as 'the Eternal Woman [who] remains beyond reach of the mire' in one of Preminger's two 'remarkable contributions to the genre', whose director and writers – here they are only talking about the two male scriptwriters – 'turn the women's magazine conventions of the story inside out' (1968: 25). Betty Reinhardt (about whom very little is known, except that she scripted the *Maisie* films between 1940–42) co-scripted the film with Jay Dratler and Samuel Hoffenstein, from the story by Vera Caspary, herself a screenwriter as well as a novelist and magazine writer, who also provided the story for *The Blue Gardenia*. Caspary was a member of the Communist Party, and decided to write a mystery play, at a moment of disaffection, in order to get away from politics. Yet:

> Mysteries had never been my favorite reading. The murderer, the most interesting character, has always to be on the periphery of action lest he give away the secret that can be revealed only in the final pages. If mystery writers were to expose character in all of its complexity, they could never produce the solution in which the killer turns out to be the butler, the sweet old aunt or … Most of my originals [stories] had been murder stories, but I never thought of them in the same class as a novel. The Novel demands a full development of each character. This was my problem. Every character in the story, except the detective, was to be a suspect – particularly the heroine, with whom the detective was to fall in love. If her innocence was in doubt, how could her thoughts be made clear to the reader? I did not want to cheat. If she and the other characters were to be made more than detective-story stereotypes, I had to find a way to show them alive and contradictory while keeping secret the murderer's identity. (1979: 194–5)

Despite spending many hours developing Lydecker's background and character, and enjoying 'writing in his style', Caspary writes that she equally enjoyed contrasting his version with the 'direct prose' of the detective and 'the girl's version, showing the vagaries of the female mind' (*sic*; ibid.: 195). The play was finished in October 1941; Pearl Harbor was bombed in the December, and a week later, Caspary was laid off by Paramount, where she had been working as a screenwriter. Theatre producers were keen on the play and an initial idea was to tour it with Marlene Dietrich as Laura. But Caspary wanted to sell it to the movies because 'Once a story is sold to the movies, the author can forget it.' However, 'In 1943 retail murder was out of fashion'; Otto Preminger suggested that 20th Century-Fox buy the story and Darryl Zanuck 'gave a vigorous *no*'. Preminger fought and won, but Caspary's contract 'was one of the worst ever written'. Then Caspary fought vigorously with Preminger, after he had shown her the screenplay ('Ordinarily… not allowed,' p. 208), because he had turned her play into 'A commonplace detective story', dulling the characters, 'especially Laura':

> I'd given Laura a heroine's youth and beauty but had added the strength of a woman

If Laura *has a dubiously happy ending, McPherson (Dana Andrews) casts a less neurotic shadow than the other male characters, and certainly less than …*

who had, in spite of the struggle and competition of success in business, retained the feminine delicacy that allowed men to exercise the power of masculinity. (*sic,* p. 209)

When she told Preminger that (book) editors in New York had asked her to write another sexy heroine like Laura, he replied, according to Caspary, that Laura '"has no sex. She has to keep a gigolo". … Couldn't Otto understand that a woman could be generous, find jobs, lend money to a man without thought of paying for his sexual services?' (Shelby is a gigolo, of course, and one kept by Laura's aunt, Ann, but he is engaged to Laura.) However, Caspary claims that the script was then rewritten and that the 'charm, the gaiety, the brilliant humor of the finished film … could only have been the work of Samuel Hoffenstein, distinguished as a wit long before he came to Hollywood'. Betty Reinhardt's name is not mentioned. Elsewhere, in her autobiography, Caspary writes that when she finally saw the film, she was disappointed: the play she had written had been set in a time when 'nice girls' expected husbands to support them and 'working girl' was a term of derision, socially the basis of the heroine's character and crimes; the film was set in this 'contemporary' context (p. 226). Of course, we cannot make too much of Caspary's version, but nor should we ignore it or, if we had access to them, the views of the film held by spectators. But perhaps we can view the film as one offering something positive to female spectators.

As is often the case, Laura only expresses *anything* of the '*femme fatale*' inasmuch as that is projected through the behaviour of the men around her. Her attraction for them becomes 'fatal', not because of anything she does, but because

... Waldo Lydecker (Clifton Webb).

they make the mistake of thinking they can own her and then speak for her/speak her; doing so, vociferously, when she is assumed to have been the murder victim found at her flat. Laura herself becomes a silent and still (painted) image during her long weekend absence, which gives the other characters limitless space to re-create her in their own terms. The other female characters are perfectly 'straight-forward' – one good (the maid), one honest (Ann). There is a central male protagonist, McPherson, who is the hero, and who, being a detective, fulfils the dominant film noir function of the investigator. He also (conventionally) becomes trapped in his own romantic projection of her (which he switches into without warning, after having earlier referred to her painted image, 'hard-boiled'-style, as 'Not bad'). This means that his investigation shifts between murder enquiry and voyeuristic curiosity. However, once Laura returns, the shambolic masculinity that surrounds her is blown apart.

So, in this film there are some conventions of film noir: the investigator, sexual curiosity, distorted relationships, the villainous aesthete, one rainy night, a beautiful woman, sexually motivated murder. However, most of the lighting is bright, and there are no noir shadows, except inasmuch as – as Higham and Greenberg observe – 'the characters cast their own shadows' (1968: 25). But it is the *male* characters whose shadows are thrown; it is the male characters who produce 'the fatal': Laura just brings out what is already there (which is, of course, the real female crime in film noir). Laura and McPherson pursue a happy ending, and two interesting points of *mise en scène* 'normalise' his relationship to her: he often plays with a miniature point-scoring game, but only when he is around the other men, a fact which is marked when, having spent some time sitting alone in Laura's apartment, he is interrupted by Lydecker and immediately gets the game out of his jacket pocket; he also usually wears his hat, even indoors, but on this occasion, he has taken off both his hat and jacket – taking off as well, perhaps, his 'hard-boiled' exterior and making himself – or feeling – 'at home'. Laura, on the other hand, when she returns from her weekend away, keeps her outdoor clothes on, despite their being wet, perhaps as protection against his invasion of her space – and his attempted invasion of her self. If the film, therefore, has a dubiously 'happy' ending, McPherson casts less of a neurotic or selfish shadow than the other male characters.

Gilda

Gilda is a much more complex film and is open to far more readings – as evidenced by those of Dyer (1980), Doane (1983) and Dittmar (1988).[32] Virginia Van Upp produced the film and was centrally involved in the writing of its script. Harry Cohn had enormous respect for her, and had made her Executive Producer at Columbia after *Cover Girl*. Francke reports Van Upp's daughter, Gay Hayden, as saying that Van Upp 'was of the opinion that her women should always find a happy ending in romance' (1994: 65), but suggests that her earlier films, *Together Again* (1944) and *She Wouldn't Say Yes* (1945), 'spelled out a more troubled view of romance and marriage on the way to the happy conclusion' (ibid.: 64). Van Upp is considered to have 'fashioned' *Gilda* to Hayworth's talents (Thomas, B., 1967: 220),[33] and famously Hayworth later blamed her for making every man fall in love with Gilda, only to wake up and find just Rita.

> Virginia knew Rita well and was able to write lines that Hayworth could charge with meaning ... Rita knew by instinct how far she could go with a line or a gesture and never required an occasional toning down as, for instance, Marilyn Monroe did. (Kobal, 1977: 203)

Van Upp had unprecedented control for a woman over the films she was involved with; is it too far-fetched, and textually unsound, then, to suggest that she had in mind, with *Gilda*, a film with a happy ending which recognised and dealt with the problems engendered by the end of the war?[34] (I don't mean to suggest that we should take intention into account when reading a film, but it can add weight to a particular reading.) Glenn Ford himself had just returned from armed service, and did not find it easy to get work. (Bette Davis argued for his participation, with her, in *A Stolen Life*, scripted by Catherine Turney.) Shortly after filming began on *Gilda*, Hayworth announced her divorce from Orson Welles and rumours began about an involvement between her and Ford. The film's script developed on a daily basis:

> We didn't know how the picture was going to turn out. Sometimes we would be on the set in the morning and Virginia would come in with the script and hand it to us. Rita and I were very fond of one another, we became very close friends and I guess it all came out on the screen. Honestly speaking, I'm sure we all sensed something going on there, there was an excitement on the set. (Ford, interviewed by Kobal, 1977: 202)

According to Ford, they discussed 'all possible sexual permutations ... including a homosexual attachment between the characters of Johnny and Mundsen' (ibid.).

Gilda is realised and spoken as *femme fatale* in the film, and written about as such, but she, like Laura, is not one. This is not just, as Richard Dyer rightly suggests in this volume, because Gilda/Hayworth is charismatic and resists that placing of her by the film, or that what most people remember from the film is the strength of her 'Put the Blame on Mame' routine in *that dress*[35] (though the much reproduced image of Rita Hayworth wearing it in the film may be one of the reasons for this by now).[36] A number of writers talk about Hayworth expressing *healthy* sexuality, and dancing, not as if she was performing but as if she actually loved dancing (Dyer in this volume; Rosen, 1973: 226; Kobal, 1977: 160) – wherever she did it. In this respect it seems odd to read the first time we see her (as Doane does, 1983: 7–10), when her health, beauty and all that hair *take over* the empty frame into which she tosses her head back up, as being negated, in advance, by the tilt up – through the floorboards and across the extreme close-up of the dice Johnny has just thrown – to his face in a medium shot. This latter shot, the first one of the film, can just as easily be read as indicating the depths to which Johnny has fallen by the time the film starts, and throwing dice is the only way he has of crawling his way back up again. And these two, as I would argue, different, visual introductions to Gilda and Johnny are indicative of their characters' behaviour throughout the film. Johnny's is further confirmed by the frequent references by Uncle Pio to his being a 'peasant', which in this context is negative; Gilda's vitality is apparent, even when she is seeming to be at her most 'bad' – hence the 're-sistance' Dyer refers to.

On the other hand, Johnny and Gilda are treated in a similar way, as all three writers point out, as objects of desire, for each other, and in relation to Ballin. They are also, in some senses, infantilised: they are both, on occasions, reduced or framed together by Ballin's dominant and ominous presence; when Gilda observes to Ballin that Johnny is 'an attractive man', he replies: 'He's a boy.' She retorts that boys have a habit of growing up; they are referred to as 'kids' by the detective and, emphatically, as 'young' by Uncle Pio, a word which is repeated in

Choosing the wrong man: (top) Ida Lupino's lonely war widow and the itinerant handyman (Robert Ryan) in Beware My Lovely; *and (above) Alison Courtland's near fatal marriage in* Sleep My Love *(Claudette Colbert and Don Ameche).*

the conversation around Captain Delgado's invitation to Gilda to dance; Gilda's maid uses the term 'little one' to her; and Ballin says 'You're a child, Gilda.'

Furthermore, as Uncle Pio equally emphasises, they are both American; they go home – young, married and 'redeemed' – to America. Doane writes that the Bikini bomb soldiers 'completely ignored the final scene of the film' (1983: 15). But what about those in the cinema in America who had not long since 'come home', watching the film with wives, fiancées, girlfriends sitting next to them – all of them (presumably and to a greater or lesser extent) having to deal with the difficulties of adjustment? Difficulties which can arguably be seen as being symbolised in Doane's useful notion of Ballin as 'situated structurally by the text as the third term with respect to the imaginary dyad constituted by Johnny and Gilda' (ibid.: 16 and ff.), which is not contradicted by Dittmar's equally convincing view of him as vampyric (1988: 9–10). But difficulties equally signalled in the sexual innuendo of the exchange about Johnny being out of practice – 'dancing, I mean'.

If Johnny is emulating Ballin and enthralled by him (because there was no question of a *healthy* attraction between them in a 40s Hollywood film, as Dyer points out, in this volume), it is because he has been inhabiting the psychological and criminal nether world that Ballin represents and is a part of. The film plays somewhat on whether it is Gilda who has brought him to this point or whether he is responsible for her being there. But Gilda only has to decide to go home; Johnny cannot be free to go with her and 'properly' be her husband, until he is free of the demonic influence of Ballin (read the demons of war?). At least three times in the film, Johnny turns towards Ballin (or Ballin's criminal narrative) when he could

Olivia de Havilland plays twins in The Dark Mirror, *both investigated by a psychiatrist (Lew Ayres) to see which has committed murder.*

follow Gilda; only when Ballin has been killed at the end does he turn towards her instead. Of course, Gilda has not been sitting prettily playing wife, but what exactly has she been guilty of – apart from the 'stupidity' of marrying 'two insane men in one lifetime' and trying to make the best of it by *enjoying* herself.

I would not wish to claim that this necessarily makes the ending any more credible because there is so much sadomasochism at work in the text against the possibility of the projected ending being happy. But it does seem to me feasible to put Hayworth, Van Upp and female spectators together in a reading of *Gilda* (albeit briefly drawn here) that recognises the presence of a multiplicity of points of view and asserts that of the feminine over the others. And, of course, by implication, I would argue that the same might be said of many of the other films from the cycle with central female characters and, where applicable, women writers.

Appendix: Films with a central involvement of women

This list runs from 1937 to 1959, and is made up from Silver and Ward, whose filmography runs from 1927 to 1976 (1980); Hirsch, 'Selected Filmography' [1941–1976] (1981: 213–20); Tuska, 'Chronology and Filmography of *Films Noirs*' [1940–1959] (1984: 263–271); Krutnik, '"Hard-boiled" Hollywood: 1940–50' (1991: 182–7); and supplemented by the filmographies of women scriptwriters in Francke (1994: 145–64).

I: *Character and theme strands*

Female investigators

Ella Raines in *Phantom Lady* plays a secretary whose boss is arrested for his wife's murder and enlists a detective to help her investigate his assertion that he was with an anonymous woman at a musical show. Nikki (Deanna Durbin) in *Lady on a Train* decides to investigate the murder of a shipping magnate she has witnessed from a train, with the help of a mystery writer. Merle Oberon plays a secretary who investigates the kidnapping of her boss, an elderly statesman, in post-war Berlin, with the help of an American scientist. After seeing her father murdered, Laura (Joyce MacKenzie) in *Destination Murder* dates the killer to discover more and gets caught up in intrigue which a detective then sorts out. Seeking asylum in America from Cuba, a Hungarian refugee (Hedy Lamarr) is persuaded by an American government special agent to become one too, in a plan to break an illegal immigration racket (*A Lady Without Passport*). In *Woman on the Run*, Eleanor Johnson (Ann Sheridan) agrees to help police find her husband, who has witnessed a murder and gone into hiding; she is helped by a reporter – who turns out to be the murderer. Ann Hamilton (Katharine Hepburn), in *Undercurrent*, discovers that the man she has married is disturbed by a deep hatred for his absent and, he claims, bad brother, but other people give her an opposing picture and she decides to investigate, alone, ending up with the right brother after her husband is killed by a horse. In *Deadline at Dawn*, June Goth (Susan Hayward) agrees to help a young sailor who has stolen money from a girl while drunk, later to find her murdered. And Ingrid Bergman (in *Spellbound*), who is given the role of a professional – a psychiatrist – helps Gregory Peck's amnesiac when he believes he has committed a crime.[37] Of course, in most of these films, although the woman is involved in investigation, she enlists or has the help of a man.

Witnesses to murder
Nikki, in *Lady on a Train*; Laura in *Destination Murder*. In *Born to Kill*, Helen (Claire Trevor) finds two bodies at her boarding house as she is about to return to San Francisco, but does not report the fact. The murderer turns out to be on the same train but she does not find this out until he has caused havoc in her family and her head. Cheryl Draper (Barbara Stanwyck) witnesses the murder by a noted writer (who turns out to have Nazi sympathies) of his mistress, in *Witness to Murder*, before his imminent wedding to a wealthy woman. She reports him to the police but he hides the body and they tell her she was mistaken. He then sets her up as a disturbed woman who is threatening him, and tries to kill her.

Female voice-over
Abigail (Deanna Durbin) in *Christmas Holiday*; Margot (Jean Gillie) in *Decoy*; Greer Garson's character in *Desire Me*; Louise Graham (Joan Crawford) to doctors in *Possessed*; Mildred Pierce, to the detective at the police station; Celia in *Secret Beyond the Door*.[38]

Confiding/confessing to a man[39]
Abigail to a detective, in *Christmas Holiday*, after attending midnight mass with him, when he is forced to stop over in New Orleans because of a rainstorm; Margot to a policeman in *Decoy*, as she is dying; Greer Garson's lonely wife to a doctor in *Desire Me*; Louise Graham to doctors (using 'narcosynthesis') in *Possessed*; Nora (Anne Baxter) to reporter in *The Blue Gardenia*; Charlie (Teresa Wright) to the detective in *Shadow Beyond a Doubt*.

Women investigated by men in authority – the police, lawyers, doctors or psychiatrists
Wilma Tuttle (Loretta Young) is a psychology professor in *The Accused*, who accidentally kills a student when he tries to seduce her and then attempts to make his death look like a suicide. She is investigated by a lawyer and a detective, both attracted to her (she ends up with the lawyer). Jennifer Jones' amnesiac in *Love Letters*; Mildred Pierce (see below, and Pam Cook's piece on the film in this volume); the twins (Olivia de Havilland) in *The Dark Mirror*, by a psychologist; Louise Graham by doctors, in *Possessed*; Kathy (Lucille Bremer) by a reporter in *Behind Locked Doors*. Sheila Bennett (Evelyn Keyes) is investigated by both the T-Men and a doctor in *The Killer that Stalked New York*, in which the criminal activity she is involved in with her husband is less important than the smallpox (the killer) she is carrying around New York.

Choosing the wrong man (as husband, as boyfriend – or even as handyman – knowingly or unknowingly)
Abigail in *Christmas Holiday*, Laura, Hilda (Faye Emerson) in *Danger Signal*, Mildred Pierce, Julia Ross, Lorna (Michele Morgan) in *The Chase*, Miranda (Gene

Tierney) in *Dragonwyck*, Gilda ('twice in one lifetime'), Roberta Elba (Belita) in *Suspense*, Ann Hamilton in *Undercurrent*, Nora in *Nora Prentiss*, Celia almost has in *Secret Beyond the Door*, Jane (Joan Fontaine) in *Kiss the Blood Off My Hands*, Lily (Ida Lupino) in *Road House*, Leona (Barbara Stanwyck) in *Sorry, Wrong Number*, Alison (Claudette Colbert) in *Sleep, My Love*, Keechie (Cathy O'Donnell) in *They Live by Night*, Merle Kramer (Dorothy Lamour) in *Manhandled*, Marie Allen (Eleanor Parker) in *Caged*, Ellen Jones (Loretta Young) in *Cause for Alarm*, Sheila Bennett in *The Killer that Stalked New York*, Mrs Gordon (Ida Lupino) in *Beware, My Lovely*, Mae (Barbara Stanwyck) in *Clash by Night*, Myra Hudson (Joan Crawford) in *Sudden Fear*, Nora in *The Blue Gardenia*.

Female killers (a), victims deciding to kill (b), accidental murder (c) and suicide (d)

(a) Phyllis Dietrichson in *Double Indemnity*, the bad twin in *The Dark Mirror*, Margot in *Decoy*, Ivy (Joan Fontaine) in *Ivy*, Louise Graham in *Possessed*, Jane Palmer (Lizabeth Scott) in *Too Late for Tears*, Annie Laurie (Peggy Cummins) in *Gun Crazy*; Martha (Barbara Stanwyck) murders her aunt in *The Strange Love of Martha Ivers*.

(b) Hilda Fenchurch (Faye Emerson) in *Danger Signal* decides to poison the charming opportunist and petty criminal who wants to marry her sister for money. In *Sudden Fear*, Myra Hudson learns that her husband (who has married her for money) plans to kill her, from the dictaphone she has accidentally left running when he is talking to his ex-girlfriend on the phone. Terrified and awake all night, she decides to kill him with the ex-girlfriend's gun, but can't when the time comes.

(c) Jane kills a blackmailer in self-defence in *Kiss the Blood Off My Hands*; Wilma Tuttle in *The Accused*.

(d) Ellen Berent (Gene Tierney) in *Leave Her to Heaven*, Martha in *The Strange Love of Martha Ivers*.

Good women turned temporarily bad

Hilda in *Danger Signal*. Abigail Mannette's only badness in *Christmas Holiday* is seen as such by her husband – he hates her for what she has become – and kills her before he is fatally shot by a policemen. When Ethel Whitehead's (Joan Crawford) son dies in *The Damned Don't Cry*, she leaves her husband and goes to New York, where she moves up the social scale through modelling but becomes involved in gang business and murder. Finally she escapes and returns to her parents. In *No Man of Her Own*, Barbara Stanwyck's young pregnant woman pretends to a man's family to be the wife of their son who has been killed in a train crash with his actual wife. Mae, in *Clash by Night*, returns to her home town from New York where she has been disillusioned by big city life. She marries stable Jerry and has his child, but is still attracted by excitement and runs away with his projectionist friend. Eventually she tires of his cynicism and returns to her husband and child. Lilli Marlowe (Ida Lupino), in *Private Hell 36*, works as a nightclub singer and wants money, but when she is questioned in relation to a murder and one of the detectives falls in love with her to the extent of keeping stolen money, she relents; but it is too late and he is shot by a fellow policeman.

Bad blood relatives

One of the first films here was Hitchcock's *Shadow of a Doubt* (1943), in which Charlie's favourite uncle turns out to be, literally, a lady-killer, who tries to kill her when she finds out, though the rest of her (unusually normal) family is unaware. Matilda's (Joan Caulfield) uncle in *The Unsuspected* is a noted radio personality who murders his secretary and makes it look like suicide, and later tries to poison her. Merle Oberon plays a young woman, orphaned during the war in *Dark Waters* whose relatives try to turn her mad so they can get to her inheritance; a similar situation entraps Ingrid Bergman's character in *Gaslight*. In *Dragonwyck*, Gene Tierney's character marries a wealthy cousin who turns out to be psychotic. A different kind of 'bad family relations' arises in *The Window*, when the young son of a working-class family witnesses the murder by a neighbouring couple of a drunken seamen, but cannot get his parents to believe him, since he often tells lies. The murderers find out that he has seen them commit the crime when his mother (played by the leading star, Barbara Hale) forces him to apologise to them for subjecting them to police investigation. Arguably one could include Veda here, in *Mildred Pierce*.

Victims of psychotic males

Some of those characters in the above category. Gilda. Merle Oberon plays a dancer who is nearly killed in *The Lodger*, as is Julia Ross in the film of her name. The owner of a road house and his manager both fall in love with Lily, when she gets a job there as singer and pianist (*Road House*). But when the owner is away she falls in love with the manager and they both become victims of his psychotic behaviour. Ellen Jones' husband in *Cause for Alarm* believes she is having an affair with the doctor treating him for a heart disease, and denounces her in a letter which she posts. In *Beware, My Lovely*, teacher and war widow Mrs Gordon hires an itinerant handyman who turns out to have murdered his former (also female) employer, and attempts to strangle her too.

Female mental instability

Ellen Berent in *Leave Her to Heaven* is excessively possessive of her husband (who resembles her beloved dead father), causing death around her and then making her own suicide look like murder by him and the adopted sister she believes is plotting against her. In *Love Letters*, Jennifer Jones plays an amnesiac whose husband has been murdered, and is helped by the love of a soldier. In *The Spiral Staircase*, Dorothy McGuire plays a maid who has not spoken since a childhood trauma; Nancy Blair (Laraine Day) is denounced as a kleptomaniac as she's about to be married in *The Locket*, and ends the film institutionalised. Louise Graham has a breakdown in *Possessed*, and kills the man she has always loved after he comes back into her life and courts the daughter of her boss, whom she married on the rebound.

* * *

Obviously these categorisations raise many questions and give few answers – about, for example, the visual realisation of these central characters, the status given to their point of view within the narrative, the function of happy endings (actual or apparent) which often lead the films to be called melodramas or women's pictures. It is also clear that in most of these films women have ended up with bad partners and/or are victims of male violence, perversity or authority. But that in itself throws a different perspective on badness, which is, clearly, usually male in these films, not female.

II: The films

Films involving women writers (but not central female characters)

1941
Suspicion (Alfred Hitchcock, RKO), sc: Samson Raphaelson, Joan Harrison, Alma Reville
1942
Saboteur (Alfred Hitchcock, Universal), sc: Peter Viertel, Joan Harrison, Dorothy Parker
1945
Strange Illusion (Edgar G. Ulmer, Producers Releasing Corporation), sc: Adele Comandini, from an original story by Fritz Rotter
The Unseen (Lewis Allen, Paramount), based on the novel by Ethel Lina White
1946
The Big Sleep (Howard Hawks, Warner Bros.), sc: William Faulkner, Leigh Brackett and Jules Furthman, from the novel by Raymond Chandler
The Brasher Doubloon (John Brahm, 20th Century-Fox), sc: Dorothy Hannah, adapted by Dorothy Bennett and Leonard Praskins from the novel *The High Window* by Raymond Chandler
1947
Desperate (Anthony Mann, RKO), sc: Harry Essex, with additional dialogue by Martin Rackin, from an unpublished story by Dorothy Atlas and Anthony Mann
The Pretender (W. Lee Wilder, W. W. Productions), sc: Don Martin, with additional dialogue by Doris Miller
Railroaded (Anthony Mann, PRC), sc: John C. Higgins, from a Gertrude Walker story
Ride the Pink Horse (Robert Montgomery, Universal), prod: Joan Harrison, sc: Ben Hecht and Charles Lederer, from the novel by Dorothy B. Hughes
They Won't Believe Me (Irving Pichel, RKO), prod: Joan Harrison
1948
A Double Life (George Cukor, Universal-International), sc: Ruth Gordon and Garson Kanin
The Paradine Case (Alfred Hitchcock, RKO/Selznick), sc: David O Selznick, adapted by Alma Reville and James Birdie from the novel by Robert Hichens
T-Men (Anthony Mann, Reliance Pictures), sc: John C. Higgins, from an unpublished story by Virginia Kellogg based on the files of the US Treasury Department
1949
The Bribe (Robert Z. Leonard, MGM), sc: Marguerite Roberts, from a Frederick Nebel short story
Chicago Deadline (Lewis Allen, Paramount), sc: Warren Duff, from the novel *One Woman* by Tiffany Thayer
Follow Me Quietly (Richard Fleischer, RKO) sc: Lillie Hayward, from an unpublished story by Francis Rosenwald and Anthony Mann
Raw Deal (Anthony Mann, Eagle Gamma), sc: Leopold Atlas and John C. Higgins, from a story by Arnold B. Strong and Audrey Ashley
The Reckless Moment (Max Ophuls, Columbia), sc: Henry Garson and Robert W. Soderberg, adapted by Mel Dinelli and Robert E. Kent, from the short story *The Blank Wall* by Elisabeth Sanxay Holding
White Heat (Raoul Walsh, Warner Bros.), sc: Ivan Goff and Ben Roberts, from a Virginia Kellogg story
1950
Dark City (William Dieterle, Hall Wallis Productions), sc: John Meredyth Lucas and Larry Marcus, with contributions from Leonardo Bercovici, and adapted by Ketti Frings from an unpublished story by Larry Marcus
In a Lonely Place (Nicholas Ray, Columbia), sc: Andrew Solt, adapted by Edmund F. North, from the novel by Dorothy B. Hughes

1951

M (Joseph Losey, Superior Films), sc: Norman Reilly Raine and Leo Katcher, with additional dialogue by Waldo Salt, based on the 1931 screenplay by Thea von Harbou, with Paul Falkenberg, Adolf Jansen and Kark Vash from an article by Egon Jacobson

Strangers on a Train (Hitchcock, Warner Bros.), sc: Raymond Chandler and Czenzi Ormonde, adapted by Whitfield Cook from the novel by Patricia Highsmith

1952

The Sniper (Edward Dmytryk, Stanley Kramer Company), sc: Harry Brown, from an unpublished story by Edna and Edward Anhalt

Talk About a Stranger (David Bradley, MGM), sc: Margaret Fiits, from the short story *The Enemy* by Charlotte Armstrong

1953

The Hitch-hiker (Ida Lupino, The Filmakers), sc: Collier Young and Ida Lupino, adapted by Robert Joseph from an unpublished story by Daniel Mainwaring

Films involving women writers or producers, and central female characters

1943

Shadow of a Doubt (Hitchcock, Universal), sc: Thornton Wilder, Sally Benson and Alma Reville, from a story by Gordon McDonell, with Teresa Wright

1944

Dark Waters (André de Toth, Benedict Bogeaus Productions 1944), sc: Joan Harrison, with Merle Oberon

Lady in the Dark (Mitchell Leisen, Paramount), sc: Frances Goodrich, Albert Hackett, based on the Broadway musical by Moss Hart with music by Kurt Weill and lyrics by Ira Gershwin, editor: Alma Macrorie, with Ginger Rogers

Laura (Otto Preminger, 20th Century-Fox), sc: Jay Dratler, Samuel Hoffenstein, Betty Reinhardt,[40] based on the novel and play by Vera Caspary, with Gene Tierney

The Lodger (John Brahm, 20th Century-Fox), sc: based on the novel by Marie Belloc Lowndes, with Merle Oberon

Phantom Lady (Robert Siodmak, Universal), prod: Joan Harrison, with Ella Raines

1945

Danger Signal (Robert Florey, Warner Bros.), sc: Adele Comandini and Graham Barker, from the novel by Phyllis Bottome, with Faye Emerson

Love Letters (William Dieterle, Paramount), sc: Ayn Rand,[41] based on a story by Chris Massis, with Jennifer Jones

Mildred Pierce (Michael Curtiz, Warner Bros.), sc: Ranald MacDougall and Catherine Turney, from the novel by James M. Cain, with Joan Crawford

My Name is Julia Ross (Joseph H. Lewis, Columbia), sc: Muriel Roy Bolton,[47] from the book *The Woman in Red* by Anthony Gilbert, with Nina Foch

1946

Dragonwyck (Joseph L. Mankiewicz, 20th Century-Fox), based on the novel by Anya Seton, with Gene Tierney

Gilda (Charles Vidor, Columbia), prod and uncredited script development: Virginia Van Upp; sc: Marion Parsonnet, adapted by Jo Eisinger from the story by E. A. Ellington, with Rita Hayworth (see Notes 2 and 33)

The Spiral Staircase (Robert Siodmak, RKO), sc: Mel Dinnelli, from *Some Must Watch* by Ethel Linda White, with Dorothy McGuire

Undercurrent (Vincente Minnelli, MGM), sc: Edward Chodorov, with contributions from Marguerite Roberts and (uncredited) George Oppenheimer, from the novel by Thelma Strabel, with Katharine Hepburn

1947

Born to Kill (Robert Wise, RKO), sc: Eve Greene and Richard Macaulay, based on the novel *Deadlier than the Male* by James Gunn, with Claire Trevor

Desire Me (George Cukor, Mervyn Leroy, Jack Conway, MGM), sc: Marguerite Roberts, Zoe Akins, with Greer Garson

Ivy (Sam Wood, Universal), from *The Story of Ivy* by Marie Belloc Lowndes, with Joan Fontaine

Possessed (Curtis Bernhardt, Warner Bros.), sc: Sylvia Richards and Ranald MacDougall, from the *Cosmopolitan* magazine novelette *One Man's Secret* by Rita Weiman, with Joan Crawford

Secret Beyond the Door (Fritz Lang, Univeral/Diana), sc: Sylvia Richards, with Joan Bennett

The Unsuspected (Michael Curtiz, Michael Curtiz Productions), sc: Ranald MacDougall, adapted by Bess Meredyth from the novel by Charlotte Armstrong, with Joan Caulfield

1948

Road House (Jean Negulesco, 20th Century-Fox), sc: Edward Chodorov, from an unpublished story by Margaret Gruen and Oscar Saul, with Ida Lupino

Sorry, Wrong Number (Anatole Litvak, Paramount), sc: Lucille Fletcher from her radio play,[43] with Barbara Stanwyck

1949

The Accused (William Dieterle, Paramount), sc: Ketti Frings,[44] from the June Truesdell novel *Be Still, My Love*, with Loretta Young

Beyond the Forest (King Vidor, Warner Bros.), sc: Lenore Coffee, from the novel by Stuart Engstrand, with Bette Davis

No Man of Her Own (Mitchell Leisen, Paramount Pictures), sc: Sally Benson, with Barbara Stanwyck

Under Capricorn (Alfred Hitchcock, Warner Bros.), sc: James Bridie, from the novel by Helen Simpson, with Ingrid Bergman

1950

Caged (John Cromwell, Warner Bros.), sc: Virginia Kellogg and Bernard C. Schoenfeld, with Eleanor Parker

The Damned Don't Cry (Vincent Sherman, Warner Bros.), sc: Harold Medford and Jerome Weidman, from a story by Gertrude Walker, with Joan Crawford

The File on Thelma Jordan (Robert Siodmak, Paramount), sc: Ketti Frings, from an unpublished story by Marty Holland, with Barbara Stanwyck

Woman on the Run (Norman Foster, Universal), sc: Alan Campbell and Norman Foster, from an *American* magazine story by Sylvia Tate, with Ann Sheridan

1952

Sudden Fear (David Miller, Joseph Kaufman Productions), sc: Lenore Coffee and Robert Smith, from the novel by Edna Sherry, with Joan Crawford

1953

The Blue Gardenia (Fritz Lang, Alex Gottlieb Productions), sc: Charles Hoffman, from the short story *Gardenia* by Vera Caspary, with Anne Baxter

1954

Private Hell 36 (Don Siegel, Filmakers), sc: Collier Young and Ida Lupino, with Ida Lupino

Films involving central female characters (but not women writers)

1937

You Only Live Once (Fritz Lang, UA), with Sylvia Sidney

1940

The Letter (William Wyler, Warner Bros./First National), with Bette Davis

1944

Christmas Holiday (Robert Siodmak, Universal), with Deanna Durbin

Double Indemnity (Billy Wilder, Paramount), with Barbara Stanwyck

Gaslight (George Cukor, MGM), with Ingrid Bergman

1945

Lady on a Train (Charles David, Universal), with Deanna Durbin

Leave Her to Heaven (John M. Stahl, 20th Century-Fox), with Gene Tierney

Spellbound (Alfred Hitchcock, UA), with Ingrid Bergman

1946

The Chase (Arthur Ripley, Nero Producers), with Michele Morgan

The Dark Mirror (Robert Siodmak, Universal-International), with Olivia de Havilland

Deadline at Dawn (Harold Clurman, RKO), with Susan Hayward

Decoy (Jack Bernhard, Bernhad-Brandt), with Jean Gillie

Fallen Angel (Otto Preminger, 20th Century-Fox), with Alice Faye
The Locket (John Brahm, RKO), with Laraine Day
The Postman Always Rings Twice (Tay Garnett, MGM), with Lana Turner
The Strange Love of Martha Ivers (Lewis Milestone, Paramount), with Barbara Stanwyck
Suspense (Frank Tuttle, King Brothers), with Belita
1947
The Guilty (John Reinhardt, Monogram), with Bonita Granville
Nora Prentiss (Vincent Sherman, Warner Bros.), with Ann Sheridan
Pursued (Raoul Walsh, Warner/United States), with Teresa Wright
The Woman on the Beach (Jean Renoir, RKO), with Joan Bennett
1948
Behind Locked Doors (Budd Boetticher Jr, ARC Productions), with Lucille Bremer
Berlin Express (Jacques Tourneur, RKO), with Merle Oberon
Kiss the Blood Off My Hands (Norman Foster, Universal-International), with Joan Fontaine
The Lady from Shanghai (Orson Welles, Columbia), with Rita Hayworth
Sleep, My Love (Douglas Sirk, Triangle Productions/UA), with Claudette Colbert
They Live by Night (Nicholas Ray, RKO), with Cathy O'Donnell
1949
Flamingo Road (Michael Curtiz, Warner Bros.), with Joan Crawford
Manhandled (Lewis R. Foster, Pine-Thomas), with Dorothy Lamour
Too Late for Tears (Biron Haskin, UA), with Lizabeth Scott
Whirlpool (Otto Preminger, 20th Century-Fox), with Gene Tierney
The Window (Ted Tetzlaff, RKO), with Barbara Hale
1950
Destination Murder (Edward L. Cahn, Prominent Pictures), with Joyce MacKenzie
Gun Crazy (Joseph H. Lewis, King Brothers-UA), with Peggy Cummins
A Lady Without a Passport (Joseph H. Lewis, Samuel Marx Productions), with Hedy Lamarr
Cause for Alarm (Tay Garnett, MGM), with Loretta Young
1951
The Killer that Stalked New York (Earl McEvoy, Columbia), with Evelyn Keyes
The Thirteenth Letter (Otto Preminger, 20th Century-Fox), with Linda Darnell
1952
Beware, My Lovely (Harry Horner, The Filmakers), with Ida Lupino
Clash by Night (Fritz Lang, Wald-Krasna Productions), with Barbara Stanwyck
On Dangerous Ground (Nicholas Ray, RKO), with Ida Lupino
1953
Niagara (Henry Hathaway, 20th Century-Fox), with Marilyn Monroe
Vicki[45] (Harry Horner, 20th Century-Fox), with Jeanne Crain
1954
Witness to Murder (Roy Rowland, Chester Erskine Productions), with Barbara Stanwyck
1957
Crime of Passion (Gerd Oswald, Bob Goldstein Productions), with Barbara Stanwyck
1959
The Crimson Kimono (Samuel Fuller, Columbia), with Victoria Shaw

Notes

I should like to thank Ann Kaplan, Rosemary Betterton, Steve Neale and Richard Maltby for their comments; the Cultural Research Institute of Sheffield Hallam University; and Fiona Martin for additional research.
1. On Van Upp see Francke (1994: 60–65) and Thomas, B. (1967: particularly pp. 235–9 and 278–9).
2. Perhaps it is helpful, in the context of this piece, to point out that Marion Parsonnet was a man.
3. See Francke (1994 – especially, in this context, p. 30).

4. Lenore Coffee and Catherine Turney both wrote for Bette Davis and Joan Crawford, for example (Francke, 1994: 46–8; Coffee 1973: 106, and 1986: 143–4 and 147–8).
5. 15 million working women in total (Rosen 1973: 201).
6. See, for example, Baker (1980: 126–7); Basinger (1993). In 1944, *Meet Me in St Louis* grossed $5.2 million and *Since You Went Away* $4.9 million; in 1945, *Leave Her to Heaven* grossed $5.5 million, *Spellbound* $4.9 million and *National Velvet* $4.1 million; in 1946 (Hollywood's most successfully commercial year), *The Best Years of Our Lives* grossed the highest – $10.4 million – closely followed by *Duel in the Sun* – $10 million; the same year, *Notorious* grossed $4.8 million and *The Postman Always Rings Twice* $4 million (Finler 1988: 474–5).
7. See Marjorie Rosen on this period (1973: Pt. 4), and, for example, her discussion of the Hepburn–Tracy films of the 40s, and those starring Rosalind Russell (ibid.: 208–14).
8. See also Tuska's filmography, in which he labels films as films noirs, films gris and melodramas.
9. American films had been banned in France during the German Occupation.
10. *The Maltese Falcon, Laura, Murder My Sweet* (aka *Farewell My Lovely*), *Double Indemnity, Woman in the Window*, followed soon after by *This Gun for Hire, The Killers, The Lady in the Lake, Gilda* and *The Big Sleep*.
11. But see Marc Vernet on 'The circumstances of *film noir*'s French invention' in Joan Copjec (ed.), *Shades of Noir* (1993: 4–6); and Ginette Vincendeau on the influence of French films of the 30s on American film noirs in Ian Cameron (ed.), *The Movie Book of Film Noir* (1992: 51).
12. *Ecran français*, no. 61, 28 August 1946.
13. In fact, of course, there was quite a close relationship between newspaper writers and pulp writers, whose sources were sometimes newspaper reports. Also, when speech was introduced to movies at the end of the 20s and there was a shortage of dialogue writers in Hollywood, some of the demand was met by newspaper writers.
14. 'Gat' is American slang for a revolver or pistol, and was shortened from the name, Gatling gun.
15. But see, in this context, Steve Neale's discussion of 'Melodrama and the woman's film' (Routledge, forthcoming: Chapter 4); the collection on melodrama edited by Christine Gledhill (1987); and Basinger (1993).
16 Of course, the use of the word '*noir*' itself is not without implication, as Manthia Diawara rightly points out (1993: 261–3).
17 *Sorry, Wrong Number* was described as a melodrama by *Today's Cinema* (28 September 1948), but the review ended by saying that it 'is not a film for the squeamish, but for those patrons who like strong fare … here is a well-produced and well-played thriller'.
18 For example:

> While certainly many of the leading female characters in the films I have chosen to discuss do qualify as *femmes fatales*, others are more ambiguous or conflicted in their intentions. Evelyn Mulwray in *Chinatown* is almost entirely a victim of her monstrous father Noah Cross, but her ultimate victimization has a devastating effect on the male protagonist of the film Jake Gittes. Judy/Madeleine in Hitchcock's *Vertigo* is used as a tool by Elster in an intricate plot to murder his wife; the destructive effect she has on the hero of the film, Scottie Ferguson, is not something she wills. … Without intending to be *femmes fatales*, Evelyn and Judy nevertheless qualify as 'fatal women' in my terminology because of the extremely destructive effects they have on the male protagonists. (Maxfield, 1996: 9)

There seems to be an extraordinary displacement going on here from the intentionality of the *femme fatale*, to the *un*intentional effect of some 'fatal women, who may all the same – or may not – be destructive.
19. Cf., in relation to this point, for example, Deborah Cameron, *Feminism and Linguistic Theory*, (New York: St Martin's Press, 1985), pp. 76–8.
20 McArthur did acknowledge (inside the quote I have included here) 'this somewhat misogynist element of the *film noir*' (1972: 46), even if he did not foresee it as one of the 'questions [that] remain' about the thriller strand (p. 9; see also p. 67).
21. Dorothy B. Hughes is the only woman writer included in Frank Krutnik's list of film noir sources among 'hard-boiled' novels (1991: 182–7), and none is included in his chapter on that cycle, '"Hard-boiled" crime fiction and *film noir*' (ibid.: 33–44); nor in Foster Hirsch's 'The Literary

Tradition' (1981: 23–51). Yet Cowie reports that Raymond Chandler thought Elisabeth Sanxay Holding to be 'the top suspense writer of all' (1993: 136 and 164, fn. 50), quoting the Ace Giant Double Novel Edition of her *The Blank Wall* (original source of *The Reckless Moment*).

22. Rosemary Betterton's discussion of the representation of suffragettes in terms of sexuality and hysteria is particularly relevant in this context, and includes an interesting consideration of a *Daily Mirror* photograph of Mrs Pankhurst in the context of the *femme fatale* image (1996: 63–9).

23. See Janey Place in this volume. In fact, in painting too, writes Dijkstra, the *femme fatale* came 'as a relief, a sign that woman still existed as a thinking entity – even if all she could think about … was the destruction of man' (1986: 251), and in the first few years of the twentieth century 'it became fashionable among society ladies to have themselves painted as *femmes fatales*' (ibid.: 252). And it is not surprising that scrolling up from the woman's typewriter on the front of Lizzie Francke's book, *Script Girls*, is Gilda in *that* dress, interestingly having just begun her 'strip' routine.

24. In using the term 'central female characters', I recognise that not all of them can necessarily be counted as *protagonists*, as Elizabeth Cowie pointed out (1993: 132–6); see, in this context, Gledhill, '*Klute* 1', in this collection; Cowie's discussion of *Raw Deal* and *Secret Beyond the Door* (1993: 137–59); and Krutnik (who refers to some films as being 'woman-centred thrillers', 1991: 193–7).

25. Previous essays on the film by Dyer (in this volume), Doane (1983) and Dittmar (1988) have dealt with other aspects of the film.

26. Elizabeth Cowie was the first to point out the involvement of women writers in '*films noirs*' (1993: 136).

27. Is Jane Palmer, in *Too Late for Tears*, a *femme fatale* or, more simply, corrupt, for example?

28. Interestingly, Lloyd Shearer relates that Thelda Victor, producer Joe Sistrom's secretary, was 'in the ladies' lounge' for an hour, reading, and when he demanded to know what the fascinating story was that had kept her away from her desk for so long, she produced *Double Indemnity* (written by James Cain in 1935 and 'banned for the movies [by the Hays office] on the ground that it was a "blueprint for murder"'). She told Sistrom it was a 'natural' for Billy Wilder. Shearer continues: 'In Hollywood most opinions of women are considered as interesting as laundry lists and about as important, but Miss Victor's are usually valid.' Sistrom read it, liked it and bought it (*New York Times*, 11 August 1945). This is a slightly different version of the story from the two Richard Schickel reports, but, as he points out, the origin of the film project is debatable (1992: 24–7), so it may be as valid as they are, and is the only one to mention the secretary by name.

29. Coffee, in her interview with McGilligan, said, about writing differently for Davis and Crawford, that: 'The difference was entirely in the dialogue. Bette spits words, Joan doesn't. I gave Bette short sentences, short speeches' (1986: 148). See also Coffee's autobiography (1973: 104–6).

30. In fact, when *Women in Film Noir* was originally published in 1978, a theoretical consideration of screenwriters was not yet 'on the agenda' of film theory. Since then, there has been a rise of interest in scriptwriting on film studies courses, the elevation of the scriptwriter to new recognition (with film scripts attached as 'gifts' to a variety of magazines) and, more recently, the publication of *Script Girls: Women Screenwriters in Hollywood* (Francke, 1994). However, see also, in the context of the current piece, interviews with Lenore Coffee and Frances Goodrich in McGilligan (ed.) (1986), and the autobiographies of Caspary (1979) and Coffee (1973).

31. See also, in this context, D. Thomas (1992: 59–70); and Richard Maltby's comments on spectatorship and *Casablanca* (1996).

32. See also Kobal (1977: 198–211).

33. Martin states that *Gilda* was written by Ben Hecht (1985: 166) but lists the writers, in Hecht's filmography, as 'Marion Parsonnet and unc[redited] BH' (ibid.: 198); an additional note in Francke (1994) reads: 'Nothing that is said about Virginia Van Upp's contribution to the making of *Gilda* should be interpreted as devaluing the role of Marion Parsonnet as a writer of the script.' E. A. Ellington's real name was Elpha Seelin (sometimes written as Seelen).

Later, when Orson Welles' *The Lady from Shanghai* was in trouble, Cohn suggested that Van Upp might be able to help, and she and Welles 'spent the rest of the night devising methods of clarifying the muddled story. (Thomas, 1967: 222).

Interestingly, but not surprisingly, like a number of prominent women working behind the scenes, Van Upp found herself being publicised as if she were also an image (Francke, 1993: 59–60): Columbia put out a publicity sheet headed 'Here's a Hollywood girl you don't see – but she's a big picture personality for all that!', ending with 'Petite red-headed producer Van Upp has green eyes, likes anything green and takes an active part in Hollywood affairs' (no date).

34. The film was a popular one (if not a major grosser) in a year when cinema audience figures in the United States reached their highest yet with 4,060 million admissions (Davies, 1981: 120).

35. Both 'Mame' and 'Amado Mio' were written by Doris Fisher and Allan Roberts. They were written late on in the production and shooting them took place when everything else had finished (see Kobal, 1977: 206–9). Jean Louis (1907–1997) designed Hayworth's costumes for *Gilda* (filmed shortly after she had had a baby), as well as for Doris Day, Judy Holliday, Judy Garland, Marlene Dietrich (when she moved on to cabaret performances) and Marilyn Monroe (including the 'Happy Birthday, Mr President' dress). In her obituary, Veronica Horwell wrote that he 'allowed women elegance and self-possession', but of the Mame dress, he said that Hayworth 'made it sexy because of the casualness with which she wore it. There was something voluptuous about her ease' (*Guardian*, 28 April 1977).

36. Stacey writes, for example, that 'Women's memories of 1940s and 1950s Hollywood often take the form of a particular "frozen moment", taken out of its temporal context and captured as "pure image"' (1994: 67).

37. There do not appear to be many examples of films whose central female characters help men out of neurosis, but *Dangerous Ground* is one; *Secret Beyond the Door* is another (Cowie in Copjec (ed.), 1993: 158).

38. See Cowie's discussion of the first-person narration in *Raw Deal* and *Secret Beyond the Door* (ibid.: 137–59).

39. In *Danger Signal*, Hilda confides in a woman friend, who is, nevertheless, a psychiatrist, and who stops her poisoning Ronnie, but with the help of a male psychiatrist.

40. The order in which screenwriters' names were credited (in fact, their inclusion at all) was somewhat haphazard before the Screen Writers Guild and the producers' negotiating committee agreed, in 1945, the right for the Guild to decide on their credits (Stempel, 1988: 140–1); so the ranking before then cannot, presumably, be assumed to be a correct reflection of the situation, and this is not helped by the relative lack of information on women scriptwriters – despite Lizzie Francke's important contribution in this respect (1994). (Frances Marion was voted the first Vice-President of the SWG when it set up in 1933, and Mary McCall Jnr was elected President in 1942 (–1952) [Francke, 41–3], so was presiding at the time of the above agreement.)

41. Ayn Rand was born in Russia and went to the States in 1926. She wrote her first novel, *We the Living*, in the early 30s while working in the RKO wardrobe department; it was turned into a four-hour film by the Italian company Scalera Films in 1942, but banned by Mussolini's government for being not only anti-Communist, but also 'anti-State and implicitly anti-Fascist' (Elliott Stein, in *Film Comment*, vol. 23, no. 4, July–Aug 1987: 8). Melanie McGrath writes that Rand became 'the leading philospher of the American libertarian movement'. Her novel, *The Fountainhead* – 'a fully-integrated piece of propaganda' – was published in 1943, and another, *Atlas Shrugged*, in 1947. Her admirers include Billie Jean King, Judge Clarence Thomas, the Canadian heavy metal group Rush, and the British politician Teresa Gorman; there are some '5,000 Rand-related websites' on the Internet (*The Guardian* 'Weekend', 2 August 1997: 14–23).

42. Muriel Roy Bolton (1909–1983) wrote for the radio (*Suspense* and *Date with Judy*) and television as well as more than a dozen film scripts. She also wrote four short novels and twenty-seven magazine stories, and a number of stage plays (*Variety*, 16 March 1983).

43. See Matthew Solomon, 'Adapting "Radio's Perfect Script": "Sorry, Wrong Number" and *Sorry, Wrong Number*', in *Quarterly Review of Film & Video*, vol. 16, no. 1, 1995: 23–40.

44. Silver and Ward (1979) also list 'Uncredited contributing writers: Leonard Spigelgass, Barré Lyndon, Jonathan Latimer, Allen Rivkin, Charles Schnee'.

45. From *I Wake Up Screaming*, the novel by Steve Fisher which was made into a film with the same title in 1942.

Bibliography (1978)

Alloway, Lawrence, 'The Iconography of the Movies', in Ian Cameron (ed.), *Movie Reader* (London: November Books, 1972).

Bachofen, J.J., *Myth, Religion and Mother Right* (1861; New Jersey: Princeton University Press/Bollingen Foundation, 1973).

Barthes, Roland, *S/Z* (London: Jonathan Cape, 1975).

Burch, Noel, 'De *Mabuse* à *M*: Le travail de Fritz Lang', *Revue d'esthétiqu'*, 1973.

Cahiers du cinéma, editors of, 'John Ford's *Young Mr. Lincoln*', *Cahiers du cinéma*, vol. 13 no. 3, 1970; *Screen*, vol. 13 no. 3, 1972.

Ciment, Michel, 'Entretien avec Alan J. Pakula', *Positif*, no. 36, March 1972.

Comolli, Jean-Louis and Jean Narboni, 'Cinema/Ideology/Criticism', *Screen*, vol. 12 no. 1, Spring 1971.

Cook, Pam, '"Exploitation Films" and Feminism', *Screen*, vol. 17 no. 2, Summer 1976.

Coward, Rosalind, 'Lacan and Signification: An Introduction', *Edinburgh '76 Magazine*.

Cowie, Elizabeth, 'Women, Representation and the Image', *Screen Education*, Summer 1977.

Davis, John, 'The Tragedy of Mildred Pierce', *Velvet Light Trap*, no. 6.

Dayan, Daniel, 'The Tutor-Code of Classical Cinema', *Film Quarterly*, Fall 1974.

Dyer, Richard, 'Stereotyping', in Richard Dyer (ed.), *Gays and Film* (London: BFI 1977).

—— 'Homosexuality and Film Noir', *Jump Cut*, no. 16.

—— 'Four Films of Lana Turner', *Movie*, no. 25, Winter 1977/78.

—— *Stars* (London: BFI, 1979; new ed., 1998).

Eco, Umberto, 'Towards a Semiotic Enquiry into the Television Message', *Working Papers in Cultural Studies*, no. 3, Autumn 1972.

Engels, Frederick, *The Origin of the Family, Private Property, and the State* (1884; New York: Pathfinder Press, 1973).

Farber, Stephen, 'Violence and the Bitch Goddess', *Film Comment*, Nov./Dec. 1974.

Freud, Sigmund, *Collected Papers* (London: Hogarth Press, 1951).

Giddis, Diane, 'The Divided Woman: Bree Daniel in *Klute*', *Women and Film*, vol. 1 nos 3/4, 1973.

Hall, Stuart, 'Culture, the Media and the "Ideological Effect"', in James Curran et al. (eds), *Mass Communication and Society* (London: Edward Arnold, 1977).

Haskell, Molly, *From Reverence to Rape* (New York: Holt, Rinehart and Winston, 1974).

Heath, Stephen, 'Narrative Space', *Screen*, vol. 17 no. 3, Autumn 1976.

—— 'Notes on Suture', *Screen*, vol. 18 no. 4, Winter 1977/78.

Jensen, Paul, *The Cinema of Fritz Lang* (New York: A.S. Barnes, 1969).

Johnston, Claire, 'Women's Cinema as Counter-Cinema', in Claire Johnston (ed.), *Notes on Women's Cinema* (London: SEFT, 1973).

—— 'Feminist Politics and Film History', *Screen*, vol. 16 no. 2, Summer 1975.

—— (ed.), *The Work of Dorothy Arzner: Towards a Feminist Cinema* (London: BFI, 1975).

Kobal, John, 'The Time, the Place and the Girl: Rita Hayworth', *Focus on Film*, no. 10.

Kristeva, Julia, 'Signifying Practice and Mode of Production', *Edinburgh '76 Magazine*.

Lacan, Jacques, *Écrits* (Paris; Editions du Seuil, 1966); *Écrits: A Selection* (London: Tavistock Publications, 1977).

Lesage, Julia, 'Whose Heroines', *Jump Cut*, no. 1, May–June 1974.

MacCabe, Colin, 'Realism and the Cinema: Notes on some Brechtian Theses', *Screen*, vol. 15 no. 2, Summer 1974.

McGarry, Eileen, "Documentary, Realism and Women's Cinema', *Women and Film*, vol. 2 no. 7, Summer 1975.

Metz, Christian, 'Current Problems of Film Theory', *Screen*, vol. 14 nos 1/2, Spring/Summer 1973.

—— 'History/Discourse: Note on Two Voyeurisms, *Edinburgh '76 Magazine*.

Mulvey, Laura, 'Notes on Sirk and Melodrama', *Movie*, no. 25.

—— 'Visual Pleasure and Narrative Cinema', *Screen*, vol. 16 no. 3, Autumn 1975.

—— and Peter Wollen, '*Riddles of the Sphinx*: A Film by Laura Mulvey and Peter Wollen', *Screen*, vol. 18 no. 2, Summer 1977.

Nash, Mark, 'Notes on the Dreyer-text', in Mark Nash (ed.), *Dreyer* (London: BFI, 1977).

Neale, Steve, 'New Hollywood Cinema', *Screen*, vol. 17 no. 2, Summer 1976.

Nelson, Joyce, '*Mildred Pierce* Reconsidered', *Film Reader*, no. 2.

Nichols, Bill, 'Style, Grammar and the Movies', *Film Quarterly*, vol. 27 no. 3, Spring 1975.

Nowell-Smith, Geoffrey, 'Minnelli and Melodrama', *Screen*, vol. 18 no. 2, Summer 1977.

Panofsky, Erwin, 'Style and Medium in the Moving Pictures', in Daniel Talbot (ed.), *Film: An Anthology* (Berkeley: University of California Press, 1969).

Petley, Julian, *The Films of Fritz Lang: The Cinema as Destiny* (unpublished thesis, University of Exeter, 1973).

Place, J.A. and L.S. Peterson, 'Some Visual Motifs of Film Noir', *Film Comment*, Jan. 1974.

Pollock, Griselda, 'What's Wrong with Images of Women?', *Screen Education*, no. 24, Autumn 1977.

Rosen, Marjorie, *Popcorn Venus* (New York: Avon Books, 1974).

Ruskin, John, 'Of Queens Gardens', in *Sesame and Lilies* (London: George Allen & Unwin, 1960).

Schrader, Paul, 'Notes on Film Noir', *Film Comment*, Spring 1972.

Shklovsky, Victor, 'Art as Technique', in Lee T. Lemon and Marion J. Reis (eds), *Russian Formalist Criticism* (Lincoln: University of Nebraska Press, 1965).

Todorov, Tzvetan, *The Poetics of Prose* (Oxford: Blackwell, 1977).

Warshaw, Robert, 'The Gangster as Tragic Hero', in *The Immediate Experience* (New York: Atheneum, 1970).

Willemen, Paul, 'On Realism in the Cinema', *Screen*, vol. 13 no. 1, Spring 1972.

Wollen, Peter, '*Vent d'est*: Counter-Cinema', *Afterimage*, no. 4, Autumn 1972.

Bibliography (1998)

Arango, Ariel, *Dirty Words: Psychoanalytic Insights* (New Jersey: Jason Aronson, 1989).

Baker, M. Joyce, *Images of Women in Film: The War Years, 1941–1945* (Ann Arbor, MI: UMI Research Press, 1980).

Basinger, Jeanine, *A Woman's View – How Hollywood Spoke to Women 1930–1960* (London: Chatto & Windus, 1993).

Belton, John, *American Cinema/American Culture* (New York: McGraw-Hill, 1994).

Bergstrom, Janet and Mary Ann Doane (eds), 'The Spectatrix', *Camera Obscura*, nos 20–21, May–September 1989.

Betterton, Rosemary, *An Intimate Distance: Women, Artists and the Body* (London: Routledge 1996).

Buchsbaum, Jonathan, 'Tame Wolves and Phoney Claims: Paranoia and Film Noir', in Ian Cameron (ed.), *The Book of Film Noir*, pp. 88–97.

Cameron, Ian (ed.), *The Movie Book of Film Noir* (London: Studio Vista, 1992); published in USA as *The Book of Film Noir* (New York: Continuum, 1995).

Casparay, Vera, *The Secrets of Grown-Ups* (New York: McGraw-Hill, 1979).

Coffee, Lenore, *Storyline: Recollections of a Hollywood Screenwriter* (London: Cassell, 1973).

Cohan, Steven and Ina Rae Hark (eds), *Screening the Male – Exploring Masculinities in Hollywood Cinema* (London: Routledge, 1993).

Collins, Jim, Hillary Radner and Ava Preacher Collins (eds), *Film Theory Goes to the Movies* (New York: Routledge, 1993).

Comolli, J.-L., 'Machines of the Visible', in Teresa de Lauretis and Stephen Heath (eds), *The Cinematic Apparatus* (Basingstoke: Macmillan, 1980), pp.121–42.

Copjec, Joan (ed.), *Shades of Noir* (London: Verso, 1993).

—— 'The Phenomenal Nonphenomenal: Private Space in Film Noir', in Joan Copjec (ed.), *Shades of Noir*, pp. 167–198.

Corber, Robert J., *Homosexuality in Cold War America: Resistance and the Crisis of Masculinity* (Durham, NC: Duke University Press, 1997).

Corrigan, Timothy, *A Cinema Without Walls: Movies and Culture After Vietnam* (London: Routledge, 1992).

Cowie, Elizabeth, 'Film Noir and Women', in Joan Copjec (ed.), *Shades of Noir*, pp. 121–166.

Creed, Barbara, *The Monstrous Feminine: Film, Feminism, Psychoanalysis* (London: Routledge, 1993).

Curtis, L. Perry, Jr., *Apes and Angels: The Irishman in Victorian Caricature* (Washington, DC: Smithsonian Institution Press, 1971).

Dale, Patrick, *Femme Fatale: Images of Evil and Fascinating Women* (London: Ash & Grant, 1979).

Davies, Mary, 'Women in Modern Film Noir' (unpublished master's thesis, Institute of Education, University of London, 1987).

Davies, Philip and Brian Neve (eds), *Cinema, Politics and Society in America* (Manchester: Manchester University Press, 1981).

De Lauretis, Teresa, 'Guerrilla in the Midst: Women's Cinema in the 80s', *Screen*, vol. 31 no. 1, Spring 1990.

—— *Alice Doesn't: Feminism, Semiotics, Cinema* (Bloomington: Indiana University Press, 1984).

Diawara, Manthia, 'Noir by Noirs: Towards a New Realism in Black Cinema', in Joan Copjec (ed.), *Shades of Noir*, pp. 261–76.

—— 'Noirs on Noirs', *African American Review*, vol. 27 no. 4, 1993, pp. 525–536.

Dijkstra, Bram, *Idols of Perversity: Fantasies of Feminine Evil in Fin-de-siècle Culture* (Oxford: Oxford University Press, 1986).

Dittmar, L., 'From Fascism to the Cold War: Gilda's "Fantastic" Politics', *Wide Angle*, no. 3, 1988, pp. 4–18.

Doane, Mary Ann, '*Gilda*: Epistemology as Striptease', *Camera Obscura*, no. 11, Fall 1983, pp. 6–27.

—— *The Desire to Desire: The Woman's Film of the 1940s* (Bloomington: Indiana University Press, 1987).

—— (ed.), *Femmes Fatales: Feminism, Film Theory, Psychoanalysis* (New York: Routledge, 1991).

—— 'Dark Continents: Epistemologies of Racial and Sexual Difference in Psychoanalysis and the Cinema', in Mary Ann Doane (ed.), *Femmes Fatales: Feminism, Film Theory, Psychoanalysis*, pp. 209–248.

—— 'Film and the Masquerade: Theorizing the Female Spectator', in Mary Ann Doane (ed.), *Femmes Fatales: Feminism, Film Theory, Psychoanalysis*, pp. 17–32.

Durbin, Karen, 'PsychoFemmes', *Mirabella*, June 1992.

Dyer, Richard, 'Homosexuality and Film Noir', in *The Matter of Images* (London: Routledge, 1993), pp. 52–72.

Erickson, Todd, 'Kill Me Again: Movement Becomes Genre', in Alain Silver and James Ursini (eds), *Film Noir Reader*, pp. 307–329.

Finler, J.W., *The Hollywood Story* (London: Octopus Books, 1992).

Fischer, Lucy, 'Mama's Boy – filial hysteria in *White Heat*', in Steven Cohan and Ina Rae Hark (eds), *Screening the Male – Exploring Masculinities in Hollywood Cinema*, pp. 70–84.

—— (ed.), *Imitation of Life: Douglas Sirk, Director* (New Brunswick, NJ: Rutgers University Press, 1991).

Fitzgerald, Gerald, '*Basic Instinct*: Feminist and Postmodernist Strategies', *Metro*, no. 93, September 1993.

Francke, Lizzie, *Script Girls: Women Screenwriters in Hollywood* (London: BFI, 1994).

Freud, Sigmund, 'A Case of Paranoia Running Counter to the Psychoanalytical Theory of the Disease' (1915), in Philip Rieff (ed.), *Sexuality and the Psychology of Love* (New York: Collier, 1963), pp. 97–106.

—— 'On the Mechanism of Paranoia' (1911), in Philip Rieff (ed.), *Sexuality and the Psychology of Love*.

—— 'The 'Uncanny'' (1919), in Albert Dickson (ed.), *Art and Literature* (Harmondsworth: Penguin, 1985), pp. 335–76.

—— *The Interpretation of Dreams* (1900; New York: Avon Books, 1965).

—— *Totem and Taboo* (1913; New York: Vintage, 1946).

Gilman, Sander, *Difference and Psychopathology: Stereotypes of Sexuality, Race and Madness* (Ithaca, NY: Cornell University Press, 1985).

Gledhill, Christine (ed.), *Home is Where the Heart Is: Studies in Melodrama and the Woman's Film* (London: BFI, 1987).

Grist, Leighton, 'Moving Targets and Black Widows: Film Noir in Modern Hollywood', in Ian Cameron (ed.), *The Book of Film Noir*, pp. 267–85.

Haraway, Donna, 'A Manifesto for Cyborgs: Science, Technology and Socialist Feminism in the 1980s', *Socialist Review*, vol. 15 no. 2, 1985, pp. 65–108.

—— *Primate Visions: Gender, Race and Nature in the World of Modern Science* (New York: Routledge, 1989).

Hart, Lynda, *Fatal Women: Lesbian Sexuality and the Mark of Aggression* (Princeton, NJ: Princeton University Press, 1994).

Hatt, Michael, 'The Male Body in Another Frame: Thomas Eakins' *The Swimming Hole* as a Homo-erotic Image', in Andrew Benjamin (ed.), *The Body: Journal of Philosophy and the Visual Arts* (London: Academy Group, 1993), pp. 8–21.

Heath, Stephen, *Questions of Cinema* (Bloomington: Indiana University Press, 1981).

Higham, Charles and Joel Greenberg, *Hollywood in the Forties* (New York: Barnes, 1968).

Hirsch, Foster, *The Dark Side of the Screen: Film Noir* (London: Barnes, 1981).

Holland, Norman N. and Leona F. Sherman, 'Gothic Possibilities', *New Literary History*, vol. 8 no. 2, Winter 1977.

Holmlund, Christine, 'A Decade of Deadly Dolls: Hollywood and the Woman Killer', in Helen Birch (ed.), *Moving Targets* (Berkeley: University of California Press, 1993), pp. 127–51.

Jackson, Shirley, *The Haunting of Hill House* (1959; New York: Penguin, 1987).

Jenkins, Henry, 'Post-Classical Cinema', in Joanne Hollow and Mark Jancovich (eds), *Approaches to Popular Film* (Manchester: Manchester University Press, 1994).

Jensen, Paul, *The Cinema of Fritz Lang* (New York: A.S. Barnes, 1969).

Jones, Amelia, 'She Was Bad News: Male Paranoia and the Contemporary New Woman', in *Camera Obscura*, nos 25–26, January/May 1991, pp. 297–320.

Jordan, Winthrop D., *White Over Black: American Attitudes Toward the Negro 1550–1812* (Baltimore: Penguin, 1969).

Kaplan, E. Ann, 'The Couch-Affair: Gender, Race and the Hollywood Transference', *American Imago*, Winter 1993, pp. 481–514.

—— *Looking for the Other: Feminism, Film and the Imperial Gaze* (New York: Routledge, 1997).

Karimi, A.M., *Toward a Definition of the American Film Noir (1941–1949)* (New York: Arno Press, 1976).

Kinsey, Alfred and The Institute for Sex Research, *Sexual Behaviour in the Human Female* (1953; Philadelphia, PA: Saunders, 1993).

Kobal, John, *Rita Hayworth* (London: W H Allen, 1977).

Kotsopoulos, Aspasia and Josephine Mills, '*The Crying Game*: Gender, Genre and "Postfeminism"', *Jump Cut*, no. 39, June 1994, pp. 15–24.

Krutnik, Frank, *In a Lonely Street: Film Noir, Genre, Masculinity* (London: Routledge, 1991).

Linderman, Deborah, 'Cinematic Abreaction in Tourneur's *Cat People*', in E. Ann Kaplan (ed.), *Psychoanalysis and Cinema* (New York: Routledge, 1990).

Lott, Eric, 'The Whiteness of Noir' in Michael Hill (ed.), *Whiteness: A Critical Reader* (New York: NYU Press, 1997), pp. 81–101.

MacKinnon, Catherine, *Only Words* (London: Harper Collins, 1995).

Maltby, Richard, "'A brief romantic interlude": Dick and Jane go to 3 seconds of the classical Hollywood cinema', in David Bordwell and Noel Carroll (eds), *Post-Theory – Reconstructing Film Studies* (Madison: University of Wisconsin Press, 1996).

Marling, William, *The American Roman Noir: Hammett, Cain and Chandler* (London: University of Georgia Press, 1995).

Martin, Jeffrey Brown, *Ben Hecht: Hollywood Screenwriter* (Ann Arbor, MI: UMI Research Press, 1985).

Maxfield, James F., *The Fatal Woman: Sources of Male Anxiety in American Film Noir, 1941–1991* (London: Associated University Presses; Madison, WI: Fairleigh Dickinson University Press, 1996).

McArthur, Colin, *Underworld USA* (London: Secker & Warburg/BFI, 1972).

McGilligan, Patrick (ed.), *Backstory – Interviews with Screenwriters of Hollywood's Golden Age* (Berkeley: University of California Press, 1986).

Modleski, Tania, "'Never To Be Thirty-Six Years Old": Rebecca as Female Oedipal Drama', *Wide Angle*, vol. 5 no. 1, 1982, pp. 34–41.

—— *The Women Who Knew Too Much: Hitchcock and Feminist Theory* (New York: Methuen, 1988), pp. 43–56.

Mulvey, Laura, 'Visual Pleasure and Narrative Cinema', *Screen*, vol. 16 no. 3, Autumn 1975.

—— 'Afterthoughts on "Visual Pleasure and Narrative Cinema" Inspired by *Duel in the Sun* (King Vidor, 1946)', *Framework*, nos 15/16/17, 1981.

—— *Fetishism and Curiosity* (London: BFI, 1996).

Newman, Kim, 'Three's a Crowd', *Empire*, May 1993.

Oppenheimer, Judy, *Private Demons: The Life of Shirley Jackson* (New York: Ballantine, 1983).

Paglia, Camille, *Sexual Personae: Art and Decadence from Nefertiti to Emily Dickinson* (London: Penguin, 1990).

Palmer, R. Barton, *Hollywood's Dark Cinema: The American Film Noir* (New York: Twayne, 1994).

Perkins, V. F., 'In a Lonely Place', in Ian Cameron (ed.), *The Movie Book of Film Noir*, pp. 222–231.

Petropoulos, Jonathan, *Art as Politics in the Third Reich* (Chapel Hill: University of North Carolina Press, 1996).

Pidduck, Julianne, 'The 1990s Hollywood Femme Fatale (Disfiguring Feminism, Family, Irony, Violence)', *CineAction*, September 1995.

Praz, Mario, *The Romantic Agony* (London: Oxford University Press, 1933; 2nd ed. 1950).

Rabinow, Paul (ed.), *The Foucault Reader* (New York: Pantheon Books, 1994).

Rako, Susan, *The Hormone of Desire* (New York: Harmony Books, 1996).

Renov, Michael, *Hollywood's Wartime Women: Representation and Ideology* (Ann Arbor, MI: UMI Research Press, 1988).

Rentschler, Eric, *The Ministry of Illusion: Nazi Cinema and its Afterlife* (Cambridge, MA: Harvard University Press, 1996).

Rich, B. Ruby, 'Dumb Lugs and Femmes Fatales', *Sight and Sound*, vol. 5 no. 11, November 1995, pp. 6–11.

Rogin, Michael, *Blackface, White Noise: Jewish Immigrants in the Hollywood Melting Pot* (Berkeley: University of California Press, 1996).

Rosen, Marjorie, *Popcorn Venus: Women, Movies and the American Dream* (New York: Avon Books, 1974).

Ruhm, Herbert (ed.), *The Hard-Boiled Detective: Stories from Black Mask Magazine 1920–1951* (London: Coronet Books, 1979).

Russo, Vito, *The Celluloid Closet: Homosexuality in the Movies* (New York: Harper and Row, 1981).

Said, Edward, *Culture and Imperialism* (New York: Vintage Books, 1994).

Schickel, Richard, *Double Indemnity* (London: BFI Film Classics, 1992).

Schrader, Paul, 'Notes on Film Noir', in John Belton (ed.), *Movies and Mass Culture* (London: Athlone Press, 1996).

Shohat, Ella and Robert Stam, *Unthinking Eurocentrism: Multiculturalism and the Media* (London: Routledge, 1994).

Silver, Alain and Elizabeth Ward (eds), *Film Noir: An Encyclopaedic Reference to the American Style*, 3rd ed. (New York: The Overlook Press, 1992).

Silver, Alain and James Ursini, *Film Noir Reader* (New York: Limelight Editions, 1996).

Stacey, Jackie, *Star Gazing: Hollywood Cinema and Female Spectatorship* (London: Routledge, 1994).

Stam, Robert and Louise Spence, 'Colonialism and Representation', *Screen*, vol. 24 no. 2, 1983, pp. 2–20.

Starr, Paul, *The Social Transformation of American Medicine* (New York: Basic Books, 1982).

Stempel, Tom, *Framework – a History of Screenwriting in the American Film* (New York: Continuum, 1988).

Stott, Rebecca, *The Fabrication of the Late Victorian Femme Fatale: The Kiss of Death* (Basingstoke: Macmillan, 1992).

Straayer, Chris, *Deviant Eyes, Deviant Bodies: Sexual Re-Orientations in Film and Video* (New York: Columbia University Press, 1996).

Taylor, Helen, *Scarlett's Women: Gone with the Wind and its Female Fans* (London: Virago, 1989).

Taylor, J.R., *Hollywood – 50 Great Years* (Godalming: Colour Library Books, 1991).

Telotte, J.P., *Voices in the Dark: The Narrative Patterns of Film Noir* (Urbana: University of Illinois Press, 1989).

Thomas, Bob, *King Cohn: The Life and Times of Harry Cohn* (London: Barrie and Rockliff, 1967).

Thomas, D., 'How Hollywood Deals with the Deviant Male', in Ian Cameron (ed.), *The Movie Book of Film Noir*, pp. 59–70.

Thomson, David, *A Biographical Dictionary of the Cinema* (London: Secker & Warburg, 1975; rev. ed., London: Andre Deutsch, 1994).

Tuska, Jon, *Dark Cinema: American Film Noir in Cultural Perspective* (Westport, CT: Greenwood Press, 1984).

Tyler, Parker, *Screening the Sexes: Homosexuality in the Movies* (New York: Holt, Rinehart and Winston, 1972).

Vernet, Marc, 'Film Noir on the Edge of Doom', in Joan Copjec (ed.), *Shades of Noir*, pp. 1–32.

Vincendeau, Ginette, 'Noir is also a French word – The French antecedents of Film Noir', in Ian Cameron (ed.), *The Movie Book of Film Noir*, pp. 49–58.

Walker, J., *Couching Resistance – Women, Film and Psychoanalytic Psychiatry* (Minneapolis: University of Minnesota Press, 1993).

Walker, Michael, 'Film Noir Introduction' in Ian Cameron (ed.), *The Book of Film Noir*, pp. 8–38.

Waller, Willard Walter, *The Veteran Comes Back* (New York: Dryden Press, 1944).

Warner, Marina, *From the Beast to the Blonde* (London: Vintage, 1995).

Weldon, Michael, *The Psychotronic Encyclopedia of Film* (New York: Ballantine, 1988).

Willett, Ralph, 'The nation in crisis', in Philip Davies and Brian Neve (eds), *Cinema, Politics and Society in America*, pp. 76–96.

Williams, Joseph J. S. J., *Whence the 'Black Irish' of Jamaica?* (New York: Dial Press, 1932).

Williams, Linda, 'When the Woman Looks', in Mary Ann Doane, Patricia Mellencamp, and Linda Williams (eds), *Re-Vision* (Frederick, MD: University Publications of America and the American Film Institute, 1984).

—— *Hardcore: Power, Pleasure and the Frenzy of the Visible* (London: Pandora Press, 1990).

Williams, Linda Ruth, 'Erotic Thrillers and Rude Women', *Sight and Sound*, vol. 3 no. 7, July 1993, pp. 12–15.

Wood, Robert E., 'Somebody Has to Die: *Basic Instinct* as White Noir', *PostScript*, vol. 12 no.3, Summer 1993.

Index